The Timing of God's Visitations
Lion and Lamb

Cliff K.K. Lun, Ph.D.

THE TIMING OF GOD'S VISITATIONS
Copyright © 2023 by Cliff K.K. Lun, PhD.

All rights reserved. Neither this publication nor any part of this publication may be reproduced or transmitted in any form or by any means, electronic or mechanical, including photocopying, recording or any information storage and retrieval system, without permission in writing from the author.

Unless otherwise indicated, scripture quotations taken from the (NASB®) New American Standard Bible®, Copyright © 1960, 1971, 1977, 1995, 2020 by The Lockman Foundation. Used by permission. All rights reserved. www.lockman.org • Scripture quotations marked (ESV) are from The ESV® Bible (The Holy Bible, English Standard Version®), copyright © 2001 by Crossway, a publishing ministry of Good News Publishers. Used by permission. All rights reserved. • Scripture quotations marked (NIV) are taken from the Holy Bible, New International Version®, NIV®. Copyright © 1973, 1978, 1984, 2011 by Biblica, Inc.™ Used by permission of Zondervan. All rights reserved worldwide. www.zondervan.com The "NIV" and "New International Version" are trademarks registered in the United States Patent and Trademark Office by Biblica, Inc.™ • Scripture quotations marked (NRSVUE) are taken from the New Revised Standard Version Updated Edition. Copyright © 2021 National Council of Churches of Christ in the United States of America. Used by permission. All rights reserved worldwide. • Scriptures marked (KJV) taken from the Holy Bible, King James Version, which is in the public domain. • Scriptures marked (YLT) taken from the Holy Bible, Young's Literal Translation, which is in the public domain.

Soft coverISBN: 978-1-4866-2410-2
Hard cover ISBN: 978-1-4866-2414-0
eBook ISBN: 978-1-4866-2411-9

Word Alive Press
119 De Baets Street Winnipeg, MB R2J 3R9
www.wordalivepress.ca

Cataloguing in Publication information can be obtained from Library and Archives Canada.

Contents

Preface	vii
Introduction	ix
1: Herod the Tyrant	**1**
1.1 TWENTY-SEVEN YEARS BETWEEN CAPTURES OF JERUSALEM	1
1.2 JUDEAN EARTHQUAKE AND BATTLE OF ACTIUM IN 31 B.C.	13
1.2.1 BATTLE OF PHILIPPI (42 B.C.), TREATIES OF BRUNDISIUM (40 B.C.) AND MISENUM (39 B.C.)	15
1.2.2 JOSEPHUS USES HEBREW CALENDAR FOR DATING	19
1.3 CAESAR AUGUSTUS VISITED SYRIA (20 B.C.)	22
1.4 HEROD'S DEATH BETWEEN A LUNAR ECLIPSE AND A PASSOVER	23
1.5 HEROD'S WILL	26
1.6 HEROD'S SONS ANTEDATED THEIR REIGNS TO 4 B.C.	29
1.7 SCHÜRER'S CONSENSUS FOR HEROD'S REIGN AND DEATH	32
1.8 EVIDENCE FROM SABBATICAL YEARS	34
1.8.1 BIBLICAL SABBATICAL YEARS INSTRUCTION	34
1.8.2 WAR AGAINST ANTIOCHUS EUPATOR IN 150 S.E.	39
1.8.3 MURDER OF SIMON AND HIS FAMILY IN 177 S.E.	41
1.8.4 SECOND TEMPLE DESTRUCTION BY TITUS (70 A.D.)	43
1.8.5 BAR KOKHBA WAR AGAINST HADRIAN IN 132 A.D.	50
1.8.6 ZOAR TOMBSTONES 20, 22, 23, 30	54
1.8.7 SABBATICAL YEAR EARTHQUAKE IN 749 A.D.	59
1.8.8 GAIUS CAESAR CALIGULA'S STATUE (40/41 A.D.)	60
1.9 SUMMARY	62

2: Temple Treasure Plunderers — 67
- 2.1 SABINUS, CAESAR'S PROCURATOR — 67
- 2.2 MAIL BY LAND AND SEA — 68
- 2.3 MEETING OF ARCHELAUS, VARUS, AND SABINUS — 70
- 2.4 SABINUS'S WAR WITH THE JEWS — 71
- 2.5 ARCHELAUS, ANTIPAS, AND PHILIP IN ROME — 73
- 2.6 SUMMARY — 74

3. Avenger Prince Gaius Caesar — 75
- 3.1 BIRTHS OF GAIUS AND LUCIUS CAESAR — 75
- 3.2 ARMENIA SOUGHT INDEPENDENCE — 77
- 3.3 TRIP TO ARABIA — 79
- 3.4 AUGUSTUS, FATHER OF THE COUNTRY IN 2 B.C. — 81
- 3.5 TEMPLE OF MARS ULTOR DEDICATION — 82
- 3.6 JULIA'S EXILE — 85
- 3.7 GAIUS IN ROME IN 1 B.C. — 86
- 3.8 GAIUS'S DISPATCH TO SYRIA IN 1 A.D. — 88
- 3.9 SUMMARY — 95

4. Sulpicius Quirinius's Censuses — 97
- 4.1 QUIRINIUS IN HISTORY (45 B.C.-21 A.D.) — 98
- 4.2 ARCHELAUS'S DEPOSITION IN 6 A.D. — 99
- 4.3 QUIRINIUS'S SECOND CENSUS IN 6 A.D. — 102
- 4.4 QUIRINIUS'S FIRST CENSUS IN 2 B.C. — 102
- 4.5 QUIRINIUS IN ARCHAEOLOGY — 107
- 4.6 SEQUENCE OF EVENTS AROUND JESUS'S BIRTH — 111
- 4.7 SUMMARY — 118

5. Debate Over the Date of Herod's Death — 119

- 5.1 HEROD'S SONS MEETING PRINCE GAIUS CAESAR IN 1 B.C.? — 119
- 5.2 SCHÜRER CONSENSUS SUPPORTERS — 125
- 5.3 BERNEGGER'S VERSION OF JOSEPHUS'S INCLUSIVE RECKONING — 125
  - 5.3.1 ROMAN TAXATION CENSUS IN 6 A.D. — 126
  - 5.3.2 HIGH PRIESTHOOD FROM DAYS OF HEROD TO TEMPLE DESTRUCTION — 127
- 5.4 COULD HEROD HAVE CAPTURED JERUSALEM IN 38 B.C.? — 129

6. First Visitation as Lamb of God — 135

- 6.1 YEAR OF JESUS'S BIRTH — 135
- 6.2 TIME OF YEAR WHEN JESUS WAS BORN — 136
- 6.3 DAY OF JESUS'S BIRTH — 143
- 6.4 ANNUNCIATION AND INCARNATION — 147
- 6.5 PASSOVER LAMB CHOSEN ON NISAN 10 — 148
- 6.6 JESUS, THE LAMB OF GOD — 150
- 6.7 SUMMARY — 154

7. Second Visitation as Lion from Judah — 155

- 7.1 SEVEN SEALS, SEVEN TRUMPETS, AND SEVEN BOWLS — 157
- 7.2 GOSPEL PREACHED IN THE WHOLE WORLD — 162
- 7.3 JESUS, PRINCE OF PEACE — 163

Early Christian Consensus — 167

- APPENDIX A — 167

Flavius Josephus's Hebrew Calendar — 171

- APPENDIX B — 171

Endnotes — 177

Preface

The birth of Jesus Christ in a manger is one of the best-known stories in the world. The era in which Jesus came into the world was a turbulent one. The weak were constantly oppressed by the strong. For example, the Romans collected taxes from all their subjects. Any rebellion was put down with lethal force. They controlled their vassal kings, such as Herod, who ruled over the Jews, with an iron fist. Herod had the power to take anyone's life, and he massacred even infants and toddlers. The concepts of basic human rights and the sanctity of life were nonexistent.

Scholars have recognized for a long time that the common dates for Jesus's birth—December 24/25, 1 B.C. or January 6/7, 3/2 B.C. or March/April or December/January of 5/4 B.C.—are all questionable and likely incorrect. The actual date of Jesus's birth remains a mystery for a number of reasons.

One of the reasons is that a genuine definitive historical record of Jesus's day of birth is non-existent, and seemingly not even in the New Testament. Although large volumes of modern-day literature are dedicated to the life and teachings of Jesus Christ, there is still a lack of convincing evidence and scripture-based exposition on the subject of his birth. Some articles on the topic are overly dogmatic in their speculation and opinion. Some scholars suffer from tunnel vision and utilize only a small portion of the limited available data, ignoring the rest. It seems that their goal is to affirm their views, not acknowledge the actual history.

Ironically, some people don't seem to know the difference between assumption and proven fact.

The Timing of God's Visitations

I was educated as an engineer and specialized in thermal multiphase flows.[a] I performed my postdoctoral research at the Massachusetts Institute of Technology for almost two years in 1986–1988. Since then, I've taught engineering at Dalhousie University—as an assistant professor starting in 1988, as a tenured professor in 1991, and as an associate professor in 1997—and been a lecturer at the University of Toronto for a total of 17 years. I have practiced my engineering problem-solving skills and research for more than 33 years.

I've made tangible and significant contributions to science and engineering in the development of numerical simulations of fluid-solids flows and the kinetic theory of rapid granular flows. My pioneering work in the kinetic theory of fluid-solids flows has been published in peer-refereed journals, featured in a number of textbooks, and adopted in industrial computational fluid dynamics (CFD) software packages.

I endorse this motto: "An honest question deserves an honest answer." If the questions are real, honest, fair, and not hypothetical, then we should seek answers to them.

When was Jesus born? Are we living in the end-times? What kind of a world will it be when Jesus comes again? These are honest questions that deserve answers.

In this book, we attempt to lay out the relevant records from pertinent and reliable sources to provide us with a fair picture of the background and timeline associated with Jesus's birth. By examining these records in detail, we will be able to determine the exact date on which Jesus was born as the Lamb of God in his first visitation. Furthermore, we will explore the events and timing of Jesus's Second Advent when he will return as a Lion from Judah.

---

[a] I graduated with a B.Eng. in Mechanical Engineering in Honours, Mechanical Program and Aeronautical Concentration in 1981, an M.Eng. in 1983, and a Ph.D. with Dean's Honour in 1986 in Civil Engineering and Applied Mechanics from McGill University.

Introduction

The Bible is the most amazing book in the world and by far the best-selling book of all time. According to the United Bible Societies, 80 million Bibles are printed annually in the twenty-first century. The British and Foreign Bible Society has estimated that the total number of printed Bible probably lies between five and seven billion copies.[1] As of 2020, the whole Bible has been translated into 704 languages, and the New Testament has been translated into 1,551 languages.[2] Definitely, the popularity of the Bible is unmatched in the world today.

Paul taught that all scripture in the Bible is inspired by God.[a] Peter corroborated this by saying that the authors of the Bible had been moved by the Holy Spirit to write down what they had been inspired to address.[b]

Luke 19:41–44 records the instance when Jesus was riding a donkey on his way to Jerusalem:

> *When He approached Jerusalem, He saw the city and wept over it, saying, "If you had known on this day, even you, the conditions for peace! But now they have been hidden from your eyes. For the days will come upon you when your enemies will put up a barricade against you, and surround you and hem you in on every side, and they will level you to the ground, and throw down your children within you, and*

---

[a] "All Scripture is inspired by God and beneficial for teaching, for rebuke, for correction, for training in righteousness; so that the man or woman of God may be fully capable, equipped for every good work" (2 Timothy 3:16–17).

[b] "But know this first of all, that no prophecy of Scripture becomes a matter of someone's own interpretation, for no prophecy was ever made by an act of human will, but men moved by the Holy Spirit spoke from God" (2 Peter 1:20–21).

The Timing of God's Visitations

they will not leave in you one stone upon another, because you did not recognize the time of your visitation."

Paul wrote,

But when the fullness of the time came, God sent His Son, born of a woman, born under the Law, so that He might redeem those who were under the Law, that we might receive the adoption as sons and daughters. (Galatians 4:4–5)

Jesus's first visitation on the earth as the Lamb of God took place when the fullness of time had come. During his triumphal entry into Jerusalem, he lamented over the fact that the Jews didn't recognize the time of his visitation. As the Prince of Peace, he could have brought peace to them. However, due to the hardness of their hearts and their indulgence of wealth and power, the majority of the Jewish leadership rejected Jesus as the Messiah sent by God.

Jesus knew the outcome of their future. As he rode the donkey on his way from the Mount of Olives to Jerusalem, he wept over the calamities the Jews would face and suffer while under siege by their enemies, including the Roman legions and auxiliary infantries from other nations.

There is no lack of critics who have questioned the authorship, authenticity, and historical accuracy of the Bible. Some people raise objections out of malicious intent, but others do so out of a genuine desire to know the truth.

The fullness of time which God appointed for Jesus's birth is described in the gospels of Matthew and Luke. For a long time, scholars have criticized the veracity of Matthew and Luke. Critics accuse these two books of offering conflicting accounts of Jesus's birth.[3]

The Bible has withstood all sorts of criticism throughout the ages. Undoubtedly, like much literature from antiquity, the Bible contains passages that might be difficult to interpret and comprehend, yet there are always reasonable explanations for them. A large volume of literature is readily available that deals with difficult questions in the Bible.

When was Jesus born? This question remains unsettled after almost 2,000 years. The answer is obscure for a number of reasons, but the date is important in terms of biblical chronology and world history. Furthermore, it marks a significant and meaningful occasion for Christians to show their appreciation by celebrating Christ's incarnation and love for mankind.

After the visitation of the magi from the East, Joseph was instructed in a dream by an angel to flee with Jesus to Egypt that very night. According to Matthew

2:16, Herod sought to kill the baby Jesus the following day by slaughtering every boy two years old and under in Bethlehem and its vicinity.

Since Jesus was born at least one to two years before the passing of Herod the Great, Herod's death has been the dominant marker for dating Jesus's birth. There are two major schools of thought regarding the date of Jesus's birth and year of Herod's death:

1. The Schürer[a] consensus advocates that Herod died in 4 B.C. and Jesus was born in 6/5 B.C.[4]

2. The early Christian consensus holds that Jesus was born in 3/2 B.C., implying that Herod died in 1 B.C.[b]

A second marker, which has gone largely unexamined, concerns Sabinus,[c] [5] the procurator whom Caesar Augustus commanded to secure Herod's assets after his death, as recorded by Flavius Josephus.[d]

A third marker is the crown prince Gaius Caesar, who presided over the hearing of Herod's will for his sons before Caesar Augustus.[e]

The fourth marker is Quirinius, who took the census in Judea, as recorded in Luke 2:2. Critics have accused Luke of being wrong when he wrote, *"This was the first census taken while Quirinius was governor of Syria"* (Luke 2:2). According to Tertullianus, a Carthaginian theologian who lived from 160–220 A.D., "But there is historical proof that at this very time a census had been taken in Judea by Sentius Saturninus."[f] [6] In the year of Jesus's birth, Saturninus was governor of Syria, not Quirinius. Furthermore, Luke is supposed by some to have erred in implying that Quirinius took the census in 3/2 B.C. or earlier, when in fact he did it in 6 A.D.[7]

Luke declares that *"it seemed fitting to me as well, having investigated everything carefully from the beginning, to write it out for you in an orderly sequence, most excellent Theophilus"* (Luke 1:3).

---

a Emil Schürer lived from 1844–1910.

b See Appendix A.

c Josephus, *Antiquities*, 17.9.3.

d Flavius Josephus was a Jewish historian who lived from 37–100 A.D. See Appendix B.

e Josephus, *Antiquities*, 17.9.5.

f Tertullianus, *Against Marcion*, 4.19.10.

The Timing of God's Visitations

The unique material in the first three chapters of Luke's gospel strongly suggests that he interviewed Mary, mother of Jesus, as part of his investigation into when and how the life and ministry of Jesus began.[8]

Luke said that Jesus was about 30 years old when he began his ministry after his baptism by John the Baptist (Luke 3:23[a]). In the fifteenth year of the reign of Tiberius, John had arrived in the region around the Jordan preaching a baptism of repentance for the forgiveness of sins (Luke 3:1–3).[b]

When Caesar Augustus died in August 19, 14 A.D. in the town of Nola, Livia recalled her son Tiberius to the town so he could claim the Roman Empire from his diseased stepfather.[c] [9]

According to Tacitus,[d] Tiberius entered upon "the ninth year of his reign"[e] in the consular year of C. Asinius and C. Antistius, a year during which the Roman Empire enjoyed complete tranquility. The consular year of Asinius and Antistius is fixed as the year 23 A.D.[f] [10] Thus, the fifteenth year of Tiberius's reign must be 29 A.D. (23 + 6).

In other words, Jesus was baptized in 29 A.D. when he was about 30 years old and began his ministry right after. Thus, according to Luke, Jesus was born in 3/2 B.C.

---

a "When He began His ministry, Jesus Himself was about thirty years old…" (Luke 3:23).

b "Now in the fifteenth year of the reign of Tiberius Caesar, when Pontius Pilate was governor of Judea, and Herod [Antipas] was tetrarch of Galilee and his brother Philip was tetrarch of the region of Ituraea and Trachonitis, and Lysanias was tetrarch of Abilene, in the high priesthood of Annas and Caiaphas, the word of God came to John, the son of Zechariah, in the wilderness. And he came into all the region around the Jordan, preaching a baptism of repentance for the forgiveness of sins" (Luke 3:1–3).

c "Whatever the truth of the affair, Tiberius had hardly set foot in Illyricum, when he was recalled by an urgent letter from his mother; and it is not certainly known whether on reaching the town of Nola, he found Augustus still breathing or lifeless. For house and street were jealously guarded by Livia's ring of pickets, while sanguine notices were issued at intervals, until the measures dictated by the crisis had been taken: then one report announced simultaneously that Augustus had passed away and that Nero [Tiberius] was master of the empire" (Tacitus, *Annals*, 1.5.1).

d Tacitus was a Roman historian and politician who lived from 56–120 A.D.

e "In the consulship of C. Asinius and C. Antistius [A.D. 23], Tiberius entered upon the ninth year of his reign, which up to this time had proved an era of complete tranquillity for the State and a period of prosperity for his own house (for he looked upon the death of Germanicus in the light of a contribution to that prosperity); but suddenly the tide of fortune turned, a time of trouble and confusion supervened, and the Emperor began to evince signs of cruelty in his own disposition or to stimulate the cruelty of others" (Tacitus, *Annals*, 4.1.1).

f Unless specified otherwise, all consular years are taken from the work of Ehrenberg and Jones, *Documents Illustrating the Reigns of Augustus and Tiberius*.

Luke, the physician, lived in Rome with Paul and others for some time (Colossian 4:14, Acts 28:30). Obviously, he knew the Roman culture and calendar well. He investigated and researched everything carefully, as he stated in the first verse of his gospel. In fact, Luke is well-known for his accurate and detailed historical records of names and places.[11]

If Jesus were born in 6/5 B.C., as advocated by the Schürer consensus, he would have been 33 or 34 years old when he was baptized. It would be a bit far from being "careful" for Luke to have said that Jesus was about 30 years old when he should have said that Jesus was about 33 years old instead.

On the other hand, if Jesus had been born in 3/2 B.C., he would have been 30 or 31 years old at his baptism and Luke would have been perfectly right. In fact, most early Christian writers place the birth of Jesus in the 3/2 B.C. period.[a] [12]

Dionysius Exiguus[b] established the modern-day Christian calendar by equating the year 1 A.D. (*anno domini*, meaning "in the year of the Lord") to 754 AUC (*anno urbis conditae*, meaning "in the year of the founded city [of Rome]"). He dated Christ's incarnation to March 25 (Passover) and birth to December 25, 1 B.C. (or 753 AUC).

How exactly Dionysius came to such conclusions and why he deviated from the early Christian consensus is unknown to this day.[13] The common belief is that he wrongly computed and dated those events. The Christian calendar was spread by the use of Dionysius's new table of Easter dates throughout the Roman Empire in his era.[14]

By examining in detail the four markers of Herod the Great, Caesar's procurator Sabinus, the crown prince Gaius Caesar, and Quirinius in Syria, we will be able to determine the most probable year in which Jesus was born.

In Jesus's first visitation, he came into the world as the Passover Lamb of God. Does the Bible mention the year, the season, and the date of Jesus's birth at all?

In his second visitation, Jesus will appear not only as the Lamb but also the Lion, the ruler from Judah. When would be the time of his second visitation? What will happen to the world when Jesus comes again? Where does our present age stand on the timeline of God? How will the world recognize Jesus's Second Advent?

We will explore and find answers to all those questions in this book.

---

a See Appendix A.

b Dionysius Exiguus was a Scythian monk who lived from 475–554 A.D.

Herod the Tyrant

Chapter One

The most dominant figure associated with the date of Jesus's birth is Herod the Great. Flavius Josephus has provided in his books[15] a substantial amount of historical information about the lives of Herod and his family.

1.1 TWENTY-SEVEN YEARS BETWEEN CAPTURES OF JERUSALEM

Herod's father, an Edomite named Antipater, was a Roman-appointed procurator of Judea[a] who designated his eldest son, Phasaelus, to be the governor (commander) of Jerusalem and its vicinity. Antipater also made Herod governor (commander) of Galilee when Herod was very young, 25 years old.[b] Note that Edomites are descendants of Esau, Jacob's brother.

Antigonus, the last Jewish Hasmonean king, with the assistance of the Parthians from modern-day Iran, captured Jerusalem and killed Phasaelus.[c]

---

a "When [Julius] Caesar heard this, he declared Hyrcanus to be the most worthy of the high priesthood, and gave leave to Antipater [Herod's father] to choose what authority he pleased; but he left the determination of such dignity to him that bestowed the dignity upon him; so he was constituted procurator of all Judea" (Josephus, *War*, 1.10.3).

b "And seeing that Hyrcanus was of a slow and slothful temper, he [Antipater] made Phasaelus, his eldest son, governor of Jerusalem, and of the places that were about it, but committed Galilee to Herod, his next son, who was then a very young man, for he was but fifteen years of age" (Josephus, *Antiquities*, 14.9.2). Comment [14] in *Antiquities* notes that instead of 15 years, it should read 25 years, because Herod died at about 70 years old.

c "This was the death of Phasaelus; but the Parthians, although they had failed of the women they chiefly desired, yet did they put the government of Jerusalem into the hands of Antigonus, and took away Hyrcanus, and bound him, and carried him to Parthia" (Josephus, *War*, 1.13.11).

Herod escaped and travelled to Rome, seeking Mark Antony's assistance in avenging his brother's death. The Roman Senate voted in favor of appointing Herod to be the so-called king of the Jews, as recommended by Antony, and they commissioned him to retake Judea from the Parthians.[a]

Herod and his army, with the support of Roman troops and General Sosius, seized Jerusalem. He then sent to Antony not only the defeated ruler Antigonus, but also a hefty sum of money, partly for his promised tribute[16] and partly for ensuring Antigonus's speedy execution.

According to Josephus, Pompey the Great—also known as Gnaeus Pompeius Magnus—took control of Jerusalem exactly 27 Hebrew years prior to Herod doing the same.[b] Pompey captured Jerusalem in 63 B.C. on "the day of the fast":[c]

> Which thing when the Romans understood, on those days which we call Sabbaths they threw nothing at the Jews… the city was taken on the third month, on the day of the fast, upon the hundred and seventy-ninth Olympiad, when Caius Antonius and Marcus Tullius Cicero [63 B.C.] were consuls…[d]

The identity of "the day of the fast" has been debated among scholars for a long time. Some scholars[17] suggest that Josephus took the phrase directly from Greek geographer and historian Strabo (63 B.C.–23 A.D.) regarding Pompey's capture of Jerusalem. Some propose that Strabo mistook the Sabbath as the "fast"

---

a "At the same time, they [Senate] accused Antigonus, and declared him an enemy, not only because of his former opposition to them, but that he had now overlooked the Romans, and taken the government from the Parthians. Upon this the senate was irritated; and Antony informed them further, that it was for their advantage in the Parthian war that Herod should be king. This seemed good to all the senators; and so they made a decree accordingly… And thus did this man receive the kingdom, having obtained it on the hundred and eighty-fourth Olympiad, when Caius Domitius Calvinus was consul the second time, and Caius Asinius Pollio [40 B.C.]" (Josephus, *Antiquities*, 14.14.4–5).

b "This destruction befell the city of Jerusalem when Marcus Agrippa and Caninius Gallus [37 B.C.] were consuls of Rome on the hundred eighty and fifth Olympiad, on the third month, on the solemnity of the fast, as if a periodical revolution of calamities had returned since that which befell the Jews under Pompey; for the Jews were taken by him on the same day, and this was after twenty-seven years' time" (Josephus, *Antiquities*, 14.16.4).

c "Which thing when the Romans understood, on those days which we call Sabbaths they threw nothing at the Jews… the city was taken on the third month, on the day of the fast, upon the hundred and seventy-ninth Olympiad, when Caius Antonius and Marcus Tullius Cicero [63 B.C.] were consuls…" (Josephus, *Antiquities*, 14.4.3).

d Josephus, *Antiquities*, 14.4.3.

Herod the Tyrant

and Josephus either followed suit or tried to correct Strabo's mistake. Others suggest that the 27 years between the anniversary fast days reported by Josephus is simply anecdotal and exaggerated.

Pompey and his associates knew about the Jewish customs. From a tactical point of view, it makes perfect sense that they prepared for a final assault on Jerusalem by filling up a trench,[a] 60 feet deep and 260 feet wide, and constructing crossover ladders on Sabbath days,[b] as described by Strabo, because Jews wouldn't attack on the Sabbath. Filling the trench with earth one day per week would easily have taken 13 weeks, or three months.

Josephus reckoned that the city was taken on the third month, which is likely measured from the beginning of the siege.

Pompey waited for the weakest moment of the Jewish defenders to minimize Roman casualties, just as Strabo indicated in saying that he attacked "after the watching for the day of fasting." A fast is the time when Jews would have been weakest due to hunger. They wouldn't attack on that religious day, only defend.

The ordained major fast on the Day of Atonement (Yom Kippur, according to Leviticus 16:29 and 23:27) is the best candidate.[18] Jews refrain from eating for 24 hours from sunset to sunset on Tishri 10.[c] [19] In other words, Jews would have

---

a "At any rate, when now Judaea was under the rule of tyrants, Alexander was first to declare himself king instead of priest; and both Hyrcanus and Aristobulus were sons of his; and when they were at variance about the empire, Pompey went over and overthrew them and razed their fortifications, and in particular took Jerusalem itself by force; for it was a rocky and well-watered fortress; and though well supplied with water inside, its outside territory was wholly without water; and it had a trench cut in rock, sixty feet in depth and two hundred and sixty feet in breadth; and, from the stone that had been hewn out, the wall of the temple was fenced with towers. Pompey seized the city [Jerusalem], it is said, after watching for the day of fasting, when the Judaeans were abstaining from all work; he filled up the trench and threw ladders across it; moreover, he gave orders to raze all the walls and, so far as he could, destroyed the haunts of robbers and the treasure-holds of the tyrants" (Strabo, *Geography*, 16.2.40).

b "...nor had the Romans succeeded in their endeavors, had not Pompey taken notice of the seventh days, on which the Jews abstain from all sorts of work on a religious account, and raised his bank, but restrained his soldiers from fighting on those days; for the Jews only acted defensively on Sabbath days" (Josephus, *War*, 1.7.3).

c There are two major public fasts that Israelites observe. The major 24-hour fasts are Yom Kippur on Tishri 10 (September/October, ordained) and Temple Destruction on Ab 9 (July/August, unordained). There are four minor unordained communal fasts in which Jews refrain from eating during the 12-hour daylight period—namely, the Fast of Shivah Asar B'Tammuz on Tammuz 17 (June/July), the Fast of Gedaliah on Tishri 3 (September/October), the Fast of Asarah B'Tevet on Tevet 10 (December/January), and the Fast of Esther on Ada 13 (February/March). The most sacred fast is the ordained one of Yom Kippur.

had no food in their stomachs for at least 12 hours, or possibly more, when the Romans struck during the daytime period of Tishri 10. The Romans probably had enjoyed good meals before launching their assault, thus giving them a tactical advantage.

Josephus was once a Jewish general who defended Jotapata, Galilee against Roman legions. He knew their military tactics better than most and had been trained as a priest prior to picking up the sword. When he wrote the phrase "the day of the fast," he knew exactly what he was talking about.

Josephus realized the significance of the date when Pompey captured the temple and entered the Holy of Holies. He dated the event to "the third month, on the day of the fast, in the hundred and seventy-ninth Olympiad, in the consulship of Gaius Antonius and Marcus Tullius Cicero [63 B.C.]."[a] He provided a lot more temporal information than Strabo.

Since Strabo was Greek, he might have mistaken a Sabbath for a fast. However, Josephus couldn't have made such a mistake. The reason is that according to both the Jerusalem Talmud[b 20] and the Babylonian Talmud,[c 21] fasting on a Sabbath was strictly prohibited. As declared in the book of Jubilee, anyone who fasted on the Sabbath could be punishable by death.[d 22]

Based on the above reasons, we conclude that "the day of the fast" could not be a Sabbath in Josephus's rendering. In addition, Josephus could not have simply copied what Strabo wrote without authenticating Pompey's capture of Jerusalem, and then paired it with Herod's capture of Jerusalem on the same anniversary fast day, since both incidents were Jewish historical events of major importance that multitudes of people knew about in his era.

There is strong support for the notion that the day of the fast refers to Tishri 10 from the timeline of Antigonus capturing Jerusalem and his eventual death. Pompey reinstated Hyrcanus to the high priest office in 63 B.C. Afterwards Hyrcanus reigned 24 years, until Antigonus and his supporters fought against the guards led by Herod and Phasaelus in an attempt to take over Jerusalem on

---

a Jospehus, *Antiquities*, 14.4.3.

b "Later commentators state that, since on the Sabbath one may not fast, eating on the Sabbath is a consequence of it being Sabbath and the Sabbath has to be mentioned in reciting Grace" (Guggenheimer, *The Jerusalem Talmud, First Order: Zeraim Tractate Berakhot*, 540).

c "On the day preceding the Sabbath they would not fast, in honor of the Sabbath, and most assuredly not on the Sabbath itself. Why did they not fast on Sunday?" (Rodkinson, *The Babylonian Talmud, Volume VIII*, 82)

d "...whoever fasts or makes war on the Sabbaths: The man who does any of these things on the Sabbath shall die" (Charles, *The Apocrypha and Pseudepigrapha of the Old Testament, Volume II*, 82).

Pentecost (May/June 39 B.C.), as reported by Josephus.ᵃ Antigonus then proposed the Parthian prince Pacorus as a reconciler between them, and Phasaelus fell for it.

Antigonus and Pacorus executed their takeover plots to near perfection, except that Herod and his family escaped to Masada. Phasaelus was captured in Jerusalem and killed by Antigonus. Shortly afterwards, in June/July of 39 B.C., Antigonus took the high priesthood from Hyrcanus and proclaimed himself king of the Jews. Pacorus then sent Hyrcanus to Parthia, in modern-day Iran.

Antigonus reigned three years and three months before he was captured by Herod.ᵇ In other words, Herod and Sosius seized Jerusalem in 36 B.C. (63 - 24 - 3) around September/October. The only major ordained official day of fast around this period would have been the one on Tishri 10, the Day of Atonement.

Furthermore, Josephus's guileless mention of "the day of the fast" without further elaboration implies that it was the most common, well-known activity to both Jews and Gentiles in his era. In Acts 27:9,ᶜ Luke also refers to the ordained fast on the Day of Atonement as simply "the fast."

Besides, Josephus also reports the timeline of Herod's capture of Jerusalem. As the winter was ending (March/April), Herod marched to Jerusalemᵈ and

---

a "Now when that festival which we call Pentecost was at hand, all the places about the temple, and the whole city, was full of a multitude of people that were come out of the country, and which were the greatest part of them armed also, at which time Phasaelus guarded the wall, and Herod, with a few, guarded the royal palace; and when he made an assault upon his enemies, as they were out of their ranks, on the north quarter of the city, he slew a very great number of them, and put them all to flight; and some of them he shut up within the city, and others within the outward rampart. In the mean time, Antigonus desired that Pacorus might be admitted to be a reconciler between them; and Phasaelus was prevailed upon to admit the Parthian into the city with five hundred horse, and to treat him in an hospitable manner, who pretended that he came to quell the tumult, but in reality he came to assist Antigonus..." (Josephus, *War*, 1.13.3).

b "Pompey came upon him, and not only took the city of Jerusalem by force, but put him and his children in bonds, and sent them to Rome. He also restored the high priesthood to Hyrcanus, and made him governor of the nation, but forbade him to wear a diadem. This Hyrcanus ruled, besides his first nine years, twenty-four years more, when Barzapharnes and Pacorus, the generals of the Parthians, passed over Euphrates, and fought with Hyrcanus, and took him alive, and made Antigonus, the son of Aristobulus, king; and when he had reigned three years and three months, Sosius and Herod besieged him, and took him, when Antony had him brought to Antioch, and slain there" (Josephus, *Antiquities*, 20.10.1).

c "When considerable time had passed and the voyage was now dangerous, since even the fast was already over, Paul started admonishing them" (Acts 27:9). The fast refers to the Day of Atonement in September/October, when the Mediterranean Sea was known to become treacherous.

d "Now as winter was going off, Herod marched to Jerusalem, and brought his army to the wall of it" (Josephus, *War*, 1.17.8).

The Timing of God's Visitations

besieged it for five months, eventually taking the city.[a] From this, we know that the timing of Herod's capture of Jerusalem is around August/September, which matches well with the end of Antigonus's reign, as discussed earlier.

Twenty-seven Hebrew years after Pompey's capture of Jerusalem in 63 B.C., Herod took the city on the same anniversary fast day, Tishri 10, the Day of Atonement, which aligns with about September 22/23, 36 B.C.[b] [23] According to Josephus, it was the third year since Herod had been appointed king of the Jews by the Roman Senate.[c] Thus his accession year would have taken place in 39/38 B.C.,[24] as shown in Figure 1.1.

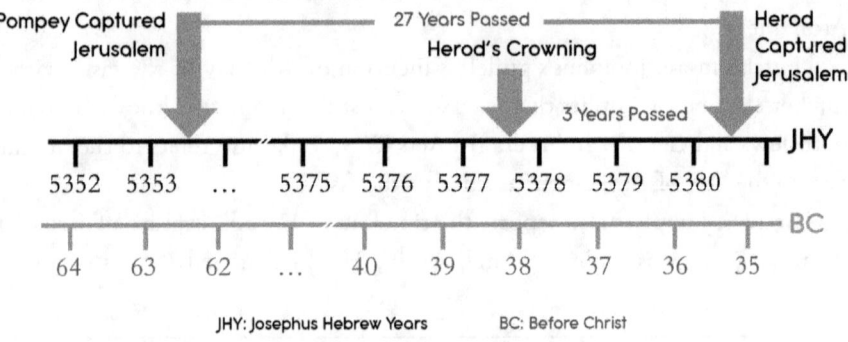

Figure 1.1. Precisely 27 Hebrews years separate the capture of Jerusalem of Pompey and the city's capture by Herod.

Based on Josephus's chronological records, the year of creation occurred in about 5415 B.C.[d] This enables us to define the beginning of his Old Testament timeline, starting with year one at creation and reaching 5415 at 1 B.C. We will call his Old Testament calendar the Josephus Hebrew Years (JHY).

---

a "Indeed, though they had so great an army lying round about them, they bore a siege of five months, till some of Herod's chosen men ventured to get upon the wall, and fell into the city, as did Sosius's centurions after them; and now they first of all seized upon what was about the temple; and upon the pouring in of the army, there was slaughter of vast multitudes everywhere" (Josephus, *War*, 1.18.2).

b September 22/23 corresponds to Tishri 10, which can be computed based on numerical calculations of new moons in 36 B.C. Nisan 1 is the day of the first new moon after the vernal equinox, which can also be determined numerically. Tishri is the seventh month from Nisan.

c "Now as winter was going off, Herod marched to Jerusalem, and brought his army to the wall of it; this was the third year since he had been made king at Rome; so he pitched his camp before the temple, for on that side it might be besieged, and there it was that Pompey took the city" (Josephus, *War*, 1.17.8).

d See Appendix B.

We will utilize Josephus's timeline in conjunction with the Julian calendar to assess several pertinent historical events associated with Herod's reign and death in Judea.

Josephus regarded the Hebrew new year as beginning on the evening of Nisan 1[a] with a new moon. He clearly states at least four times in *Antiquities of the Jews* that Nisan is the first month of the Hebrew year.[b]

For example, he writes, "In the month of Xanthicus, which is by us called Nisan, and is the beginning of our year."[c] For the present discussion, it is extremely important to define and establish the Josephus Hebrew Year from Nisan to Adar, because it lays the foundational point of reference for all chronological data and analyses based on his Jewish histories.

God has decreed that the first day of the Hebrew new year begins on Abib 1 (or Nisan 1) in the Torah (Exodus 12:1–2, 13:4[d]).

---

a For the sake of simplicity, Nisan is used throughout this book to represent the ordained first month of the Jewish year.

b "This calamity happened in the six hundredth year of Noah's government, in the second month, called by the Macedonians Dius, but by the Hebrews Marchesvan: for so did they order their year in Egypt. But Moses appointed that Nisan, which is the same with Xanthicus, should be the first month for their festivals, because he brought them out of Egypt in that month: so that this month began the year as to all the solemnities they observed to the honor of God, although he preserved the original order of the months as to selling and buying, and other ordinary affairs" (Josephus, *Antiquities*, 1.3.3). "But at the beginning of the second year, on the month Xanthicus, as the Macedonians call it, but on the month Nisan, as the Hebrews call it, on the new moon, they consecrated the tabernacle, and all its vessels, which I have already described" (Josephus, *Antiquities*, 3.8.4). "In the month of Xanthicus, which is by us called Nisan, and is the beginning of our year, on the fourteenth day of the lunar month, when the sun is in Aries, (for in this month it was that we were delivered from bondage under the Egyptians,) the law ordained that we should every year slay that sacrifice which I before told you we slew when we came out of Egypt, and which was called the Passover; and so we do celebrate this passover in companies, leaving nothing of what we sacrifice till the day following" (Josephus, *Antiquities*, 3.10.5). "And as the feast of unleavened bread was at hand, in the first month, which, according to the Macedonians, is called Xanthicus, but according to us Nisan, all the people ran together out of the villages to the city, and celebrated the festival, having purified themselves, with their wives and children, according to the law of their country; and they offered the sacrifice which was called the Passover, on the fourteenth day of the same month, and feasted seven days, and spared for no cost, but offered whole burnt-offerings to God, and performed sacrifices of thanksgiving, because God had led them again to the land of their fathers, and to the laws thereto belonging, and had rendered the mind of the king of Persia favorable to them" (Josephus, *Antiquities*, 11.4.8).

c Ibid.

d "Now the Lord said to Moses and Aaron in the land of Egypt, 'This month shall be the beginning of months for you; it is to be the first month of the year to you'... 'On this day in the month of Abib, you are about to go out from here'" (Exodus 12:1–2, 13:4).

Nehemiah 8:1–18 records that in the first day of the seventh month, Ezra and the Levites read and explained the law to the Jews who had returned to Judea after about 70 years of their first exile to Babylon. When they learned that Moses had commanded them to live in temporary shelters during the festival of Tabernacle, they gladly complied and celebrated it.

The Tabernacle festival thereafter took place on Tishri 15 of the "seventh month," just as God had ordained in the Torah. In other words, Nisan was still regarded as the first month of the Jewish calendar in the post-exile period of 586 B.C. to 135 A.D.

The authors of 1 and 2 Maccabees, written around 100 B.C., indicate that Nisan was considered to be the beginning of the Jewish year.[25] For example, 1 Maccabees 10:21 records, *"So Jonathan put on the sacred vestments in the seventh month of the one hundred sixtieth year, at the Festival of Booths, and he recruited troops and equipped them with arms in abundance"* (NRSVUE).

The Feast of Booths takes place in Tishri, the seventh month from Nisan, which was still regarded as the first month of the Hebrew year. Other pertinent dates also appear in 1 Maccabees. An example can be found in 2 Maccabees 15:35–36:

> *Judas hung Nicanor's head from the citadel, a clear and conspicuous sign to everyone of the help of the Lord. And they all decreed by public vote never to let this day go unobserved but to celebrate the thirteenth day of the twelfth month—which is called Adar in the Aramaic language—the day before Mordecai's day.* (NRSVUE)

Judas defeated the army of Nicanor in the war on the thirteenth day of the "twelfth [last] month" of the year, Adar, which is reckoned from the first month Nisan.

A passage in the Babylonian Talmud, compiled around 200–500 A.D., states,

On the first of Nisan is the New Year for kings and feasts…[26]

> The year of Gentile kings being counted from Tishri, and of Jewish kings from Nisan, in the present time we count the years from Tishri; were we then to say that our Era is connected with the Exodus it is surely Nisan that we ought to count. Does this not prove that our reckoning is based on the reign of the Greek kings [and not on the Exodus]? That indeed proves it.[27]

The Babylonian Talmud bears witness to the fact that Jews, during the 200–500 A.D. period, changed the first month of the Hebrew year from Nisan to Tishri to follow the calendar of the Greek kings.

Ben Zion Wacholder points out that the Hebrew years during the periods of the Jewish revolts of 66–70 and 132–135 A.D. still began with the month of Nisan.[a] [28]

In general, it is safe to say that Tishri 1 has been designated as Rosh Hashanah,[b] [29] "head of the year," since sometime after 135 A.D., which marks the end of the Bar Kokhba war and a watershed moment in Jewish calendar computations.

Nisan 1 falls between March and April, whereas Tishri lands between September and October in the Julian calendar year. Josephus didn't consider the Feast of Trumpets (Tishri 1) as the first day of a new year and recounted nothing special about it except that some extra sacrifices were offered at the temple.[c]

Josephus didn't once mention Tishri as marking the start of the reigning year for any Jewish king, ethnarch, or tetrarch, and neither did the Old and New Testaments of the Bible.

According to the Babylonian Talmud, a collection of Jewish traditions which was compiled around 500 A.D.,[30] Nisan 1 marks the new year for festivals and the ascension of kings,[d] and Tishri 1 marks the new year for ordinary years, sabbatical years, and jubilee years, including the planting of trees and herbs.[31]

---

a "Thus the Shemitah year differed basically from the civil and religious calendar which in preexilic as well as in postexilic times commenced on the first day of Nisan. Even during the Judaean revolts of 66–70 and 132–135 when the era of 'the Redemption of Israel' was proclaimed, the year began in the spring. But such was the influence of the institution of Shemitah that it played a major role in the gradual shifting of the Near Year from Nisan to Tishri, which has been formalized into our Rosh Hashanah" (Wacholder, "The Calendar of Sabbatical Cycles during the Second Temple and the Early Rabbinic Period," 155).

b "It [Rosh Hashanah] is a latter term, found for the first time in the Mishnad (first through third centuries C.E.)" (Cohen, *1,001 Questions and Answers on Rosh Hashanah and Yom Kippur*, 3).

c "But on the seventh month, which the Macedonians call Hyperberetaeus [Tishri], they make an addition to those already mentioned, and sacrifice a bull, a ram, and seven lambs, and a kid of the goats, for sins" (Josephus, *Antiquities*, 3.10.2).

d "MISHNA I.: There are four New Year days, viz.: The first of Nissan is New Year for (the ascension of) Kings and for (the regular rotation of) festivals; the first of Elul is New Year for the cattle-tithe, but according to R. Eliezer and R. Simeon, it is on the first of Tishri. The first of Tishri is New Year's day, for ordinary years, and for sabbatic years and jubilees; and also for the planting of trees and for herbs. On the first day of Shebhat is the New Year for trees, according to the school of Shammai; but the school of Hillel says it is on the fifteenth of the same month" (Rodkinson, *Babylonian Talmud*, 908).

The Timing of God's Visitations

The relatively new teachings, opinions, and interpretations of the Torah (Old Testament laws) in different versions of the Talmud form essentially the major traditions in Judaism from the first century B.C. to the modern day.

Josephus says,

> Moses appointed that Nisan, which is the same with Xanthicus, should be the first month for their festivals, because he brought them out of Egypt in that month: so that this month began the year as to all the solemnities they observed to the honor of God, although he preserved the original order of the months as to selling and buying, and other ordinary affairs.[a]

Steinmann and Young retranslated the last part of Josephus's statement to read:

> ...buying and selling and the other financial administration [or tax administration] he [Moses] preserved the earlier arrangement.[b]

Yet Josephus doesn't mention anywhere that a sabbatical year should begin on Tishri 1, and any such belief is unfounded. Josephus said nothing of the sort.

Rather, he tallied the number of years that passed between the capture of Jerusalem by Pompey and later by Herod, coming to 27 actual Hebrew years (5380 − 5353 = 27), as shown in Figure 1.1.

If one were to use the Julian calendar, it would also be 27 years (63 − 36 = 27).

If Herod had seized Jerusalem in 37 B.C. instead of 36 B.C., as the Schürer consensus insists,[32] then 26 years would have passed between the two captures. Schürer justified this discrepancy by writing,

> But we know that Josephus elsewhere counts a year too much, according to our reckoning. Thus, he counts from the conquest of Jerusalem by Pompey to that by Herod twenty-seven years, whereas the true number is twenty-six (B.C. 63–B.C. 37).[33]

Schürer argued that Josephus used inclusive reckoning, which means that he included both the first and last year of Herod's reign in his tally to reach a total of 27 (63 − 37 + 1 = 27). He believed that Herod took Jerusalem in July 37

---

[a] Josephus, *Antiquities*, 1.3.3.

[b] Stienmann and Young, "Elapsed Times for Herod the Great in Josephus," 314.

B.C.,³⁴ because Josephus records that Herod took Jerusalem in the consular year of Marcus Agrippa and Caninius Gallus, which corresponds to 37 B.C. instead of 36 B.C. This is one of the major hurdles left to us by Josephus.

Nonetheless, we can be sure of one fact. Since the interval between the captures of Jerusalem by Pompey and Herod is precisely 27 Hebrew years, the use of inclusive reckoning would be unnecessary and meaningless with respect to the Hebrew calendar. It is the transposition of the 27 Hebrew years into Roman consular years that creates the problem.

Josephus was a meticulously precise historian who handled chronological dating of events with great care. He wrote *War* and *Antiquities of the Jews* around 75–93 A.D. in Rome, where he had a tremendous amount of data at his disposal. He was a friend of the emperors Vespasian, Titus, and Domitian and was given their family name, Flavius.ᵃ He likely had access to the Senate decrees for granting rulership to client kings and tetrarchs, such as Herod and his sons. All these records were stored in the Tabularium in Rome. Josephus directly quoted a number of official letters and decrees in his books.

One probable reason for Josephus's choice to report Herod's capture of Jerusalem as taking place during the consular year of Marcus Agrippa and Caninius Gallus in 37 B.C. instead of 36 B.C. is that he decided to follow the norm of Roman inclusive reckoning³⁵ for the span of time between the two events. Perhaps his Roman reviewers—possibly Caesar Domitian, among others—suggested that he do so at the last minute before publication.

The year of Pompey's capture of Jerusalem is well-known by the Romans and fixed in the consular year of Caius Antonius and Marcus Cicero (63 B.C.), according to records such as tablet inscriptions. If Josephus were to have reported that Herod's capture of Jerusalem occurred in 36 B.C., the consular year of Gellius Publicola and Coccelius Nerva, his Roman readers might have mistaken the duration between the captures of Jerusalem by Pompey and Herod to be 28 years (63 − 36 +1 = 28) instead of the actual 27 years. In order to avoid such a misunderstanding, Josephus had no choice but to put down the consular year of Agrippa and Gallus (37 B.C.) in *Antiquities*. He could have added a qualifying statement of some sort regarding the consular year equivalence based on inclusive reckoning, but he didn't.

Since Herod had been made king of the Jews three years earlier by the Roman Senate, Josephus had to use the consular year of Domitius Calvinus and Asinius Pollio in 40 B.C. for Herod's ascension,ᵇ instead of the consular year of Marcius

---

a See Appendix B.
b Josephus, *Antiquities*, 14.14.5.

The Timing of God's Visitations

Censorinus and Calvisius Sabinus in 39 B.C. This case is special and should not be taken as the norm in order to conclude that Josephus used inclusive reckoning throughout his chronological records.[a]

There is ample evidence that Josephus used non-inclusive reckoning in his other chronological data.[36]

For example, he stated that the government of the Hasmoneans ceased after 126 years.[b] Table 1.1 shows the chronology of the Hasmonean dynasty starting from Judas Maccabeus and ending with Antigonus. If Josephus had used inclusive reckoning, then an extra year would have been added to each ruler in the list. The total would include 10 extra years. Clearly, this is not the case based on the records of 1 Maccabees and *Antiquities*. Thus, Josephus used inclusive reckoning here.

Table 1.1. Chronology of the Hasmonean dynasty.

Hasmonean	Governing		Reign	Source
	S.E.*	B.C.	Year	
Judas Maccabeus	150	162/161	12.5	1 Maccabees 6:20 Antiquities 12.11.2
Jonathan	162	149/148	7	Antiquities 20.10.1
Simon	169	142/141	8	1 Maccabees 13:41 Antiquities 20.10.1
John Hyrcanus	177	134/133	31	1 Maccabees 16:14 Antiquities 13.10.7
Aristobolus	209	103/102	1	Antiquities 20.10.1
Alexander	210	102/101	27	Antiquities 20.10.1

---

a Another piece of evidence demonstrating that Josephus deliberately converted the actual years from non-inclusive reckoning in *War* to Roman inclusive reckoning in *Antiquities* can be found in Section 4.2 of this book regarding Archelaus's deposition in B.C. 6.

b "And thus did the government of the Asamoneans cease, a hundred twenty and six years after it was first set up" (Josephus, *Antiquities*, 14.16.4).

Alexandra	237	75/74	9	Antiquities 20.10.1
Aristobolus	246	66/65	3.25	Antiquities 20.10.1
Hyrcanus	249	63/62	24	Antiquities 20.10.1
Antigonus	273	39/38	3.25	Antiquities 20.10.1
End	276	36/35	-	-
		Total	**126**	

Note: *S.E. (Seleucid Era)

1.2 JUDEAN EARTHQUAKE AND BATTLE OF ACTIUM IN 31 B.C.

Josephus provided a second marker for dating Herod's accession as king of the Jews. He wrote,

> …for in the seventh year of his reign, when the war about Actium was at the height, at the beginning of the spring, the earth was shaken, and destroyed an immense number of cattle, with thirty thousand men; but the army received no harm, because it lay in the open air.[a]

The famous Battle of Actium began sometime in March and ended on September 2, 31 B.C. with Octavius (Caesar Augustus) coming out the victor against Mark Antony and Cleopatra.[37]

The vernal equinox, which marks the beginning of spring in modern times, falls mostly between March 20–21.[38] Adar 29/Nisan 1, which arrives around the time of the vernal equinox, was often regarded as the beginning of spring in ancient Hebrew times. Nisan and Ada are the first and the last month in the Hebrew calendar, respectively.

On about Adar 29, 5384 JHY (corresponding to about March 25, 31 B.C.), in the seventh year of Herod's reign, an earthquake shook Judea, causing enormous damage and many casualties.

Again, Herod's regnal year is always reckoned based on the Hebrew calendar from Nisan 1 to Adar 29. From this, one can easily compute that Herod was

---

a Josephus, *War*, 1.19.3.

The Timing of God's Visitations

appointed king of the Jews in JHY 5377 (5384 – 7), which overlaps with the years 39/38 B.C., as shown in Figure 1.2.

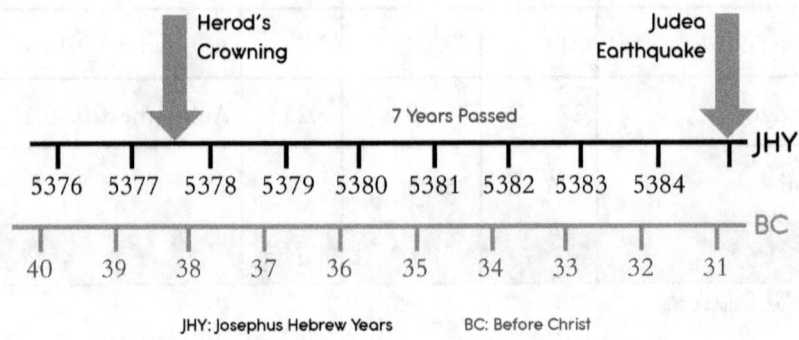

Figure 1.2. Seven Hebrews years separate Herod's accession and the Judean earthquake.

The Greek historian Appian of Alexandria, who lived from 95–165 A.D., recorded that right after the appointment of Herod and others as client kings, Antony,

> desiring to enrich as well as to exercise the soldiers, who were to go with him into winter quarters, he sent some of them against the Partheni... He spent the winter at Athens with Octavia [Octavius's sister] just as he had spent the previous one at Alexandria with Cleopatra... He took his meals in the Greek fashion, passed his leisure time with Octavia, with whom he was much in love, being by nature excessively fond of women.[a]

The accession of Herod would have occurred shortly before the approaching winter in December. In other words, the Romans made Herod a client king not in 38 B.C., but around October 39 B.C.

Even though Josephus does not state exactly when Herod arrived in Rome, it is very clear that he fled Jerusalem after Pentecost in May/June. After settling his family at Masada, Herod went first to Arabia, then Egypt and Rome.[b] According to Appian, Herod was appointed vassal king by the Senate shortly before winter in 39 B.C. Thus, his investiture would have taken place around October.

---

a Appian, *Roman History IV*, 5.8.75–76.
b Josephus, *War* 2.13.1–2.14.4; and *Antiquities* 14.13.3–14.14.3.

1.2.1 BATTLE OF PHILIPPI (42 B.C.), TREATIES OF BRUNDISIUM (40 B.C.) AND MISENUM (39 B.C.)

About three years earlier from 39 B.C., Octavius and Antony had divided the Roman Empire between them after their decisive victory over the two masterminds behind Julius Caesar's assassination, Marcus Brutus and Cassius Longinus, in the final battle at Philippi, Greece on October 23, 42 B.C.[39]

Octavius then went back to Rome while Antony travelled east through Galatia, Cilicia, and Syria in 41 B.C. Many Jews came from various cities to Antony at Bithynia and accused Phasaelus and Herod of controlling the Jewish government by their military forces and treating the high priest and ethnarch Hyrcanus as a puppet figure. Herod had given Antony a large sum of money, such that Antony wouldn't even hear the accusation.[a]

Cleopatra went looking for Antony and met him in Cilicia, where she made him fall in love with her.[b]

A hundred Jews then came to Antony in Daphne, near Antioch Cilicia, to once again accuse Phasaelus and Herod. This time, Antony heard arguments from both sides. He then asked the ethnarch Hyrcanus which party was the fittest to govern, and Hyrcanus replied that Herod and his party were. Thus, Antony appointed Phasaelus and Herod to serve as tetrarchs of Judea and Galilee to assist Hyrcanus, despite strong protests from the Jews. He took 15 of them into custody and drove away the rest.[c]

---

a "But when Caesar and Antony had slain Cassius near Philippi, and Caesar was gone to Italy, and Antony to Asia, amongst the rest of the cities which sent ambassadors to Antony unto Bithynia, the great men of the Jews came also, and accused Phasaelus and Herod, that they kept the government by force, and that Hyrcanus had no more than an honorable name. Herod appeared ready to answer this accusation; and having made Antony his friend by the large sums of money which he gave him, he brought him to such a temper as not to hear the others speak against him; and thus did they part at this time" (Josephus, *War*, 1.12.4).

b "When after this Antony came into Syria, Cleopatra met him in Cilicia, and brought him to fall in love with her" (Josephus, *Antiquities*, 14.13.1).

c "However, after this, there came a hundred of the principal men among the Jews to Daphne by Antioch to Antony, who was already in love with Cleopatra to the degree of slavery; these Jews put those men that were the most potent, both in dignity and eloquence, foremost, and accused the brethren [Phasaelus and Herod]... When Antony had heard both sides, he asked Hyrcanus which party was the fittest to govern, who replied that Herod and his party were the fittest. Antony was glad of that answer, for he had been formerly treated in an hospitable and obliging manner by his father Antipater, when he marched into Judea with Gabinius; so he constituted the brethren tetrarchs, and committed to them the government of Judea. But when the ambassadors had indignation at this procedure, Antony took fifteen of them, and put them into custody, whom he was also going to kill presently, and the rest he drove away with disgrace" (Josephus, *War*, 1.12.5–6).

The Timing of God's Visitations

Antony marched south to Tyre, where he was met by a thousand Jews from Jerusalem. Antony sent out his troops to slay and wound them. He also killed the ones he had taken prisoner.[a]

After this, Antony sailed from Tyre to Egypt to indulge himself with Cleopatra. He left Plancus to govern the province of Asia, and Saxa in Syria.[b] [40]

This took place in 41 B.C., likely close to December. Roman troops regularly took breaks during the winter.

Shortly after Antony left Tyre in 41 B.C., a group of Parthians led by Labienus (the defected Roman general) and Pacorus (the son of the Parthian king Orodes) from Iran took Syria and Cilicia from the Romans. Labienus captured Saxa and put him to death.[c]

After Pacorus secured the rest of Syria, Antigonus promised him women and gold as rewards for capturing Judea. So they invaded Judea around the time of the Feast of Shavuot (Pentecost) on about May 29, 39 B.C., two years after Anthony's visit to Tyre in 41 B.C., as noted by Josephus.[d] Antigonus seized Jerusalem and

---

a "...a still greater tumult arose at Jerusalem; so they sent again a thousand ambassadors to Tyre, where Antony now abode, as he was marching to Jerusalem; upon these men who made a clamor he sent out the governor of Tyre, and ordered him to punish all that he could catch of them, and to settle those in the administration whom he had made tetrarchs... Antony sent out armed men, and slew a great many, and wounded more of them; of whom those that were slain were buried by Hyrcanus... he slew those whom he had in bonds also" (Josephus, *War*, 1.12.6–7).

b "And finally he left Plancus in the province of Asia and Saxa in Syria and departed for Egypt" (Dio, *Roman History*, 48.24.3).

c "Now when Labienus overtook the fugitives, he slew most of them, and then, when Saxa made his escape to Antioch, he captured Apamea, which no longer resisted, since the inhabitants believed that Saxa was dead; and subsequently he brought Antioch also to terms, now that Saxa had abandoned it, and finally, after pursuing the fugitive into Cilicia, he seized Saxa himself and put him to death" (Dio, *Roman History*, 48.25.4).

d "Now two years afterward, when Barzapharnes, a governor among the Parthians, and Pacorus, the king's son, had possessed themselves of Syria, and when Lysanias had already succeeded upon the death of his father Ptolemy, the son of Menneus, in the government [of Chalcis], he prevailed with the governor, by a promise of a thousand talents, and five hundred women, to bring back Antigonus to his kingdom, and to turn Hyrcanus out of it... Now when that festival which we call Pentecost was at hand, all the places about the temple, and the whole city, was full of a multitude of people that were come out of the country, and which were the greatest part of them armed also, at which time Phasaelus guarded the wall, and Herod, with a few, guarded the royal palace... As for the Parthians in Jerusalem, they betook themselves to plundering, and fell upon the houses of those that were fled, and upon the king's palace, and spared nothing but Hyrcanus's money, which was not above three hundred talents" (Josephus, *War* 1.13.1–9). "...Pacorus secured all the rest of Syria. He then invaded Palestine and deposed Hyrcanus, who was at the moment in charge of affairs there, having been appointed by the Romans, and in his stead set up his brother Aristobulus [Antigonus] as a ruler because of the enmity existing between them" (Dio, *Roman History*, 48.26.2).

killed Phasaelus; Herod and his family escaped to Masada, a mountaintop fortress near the Dead Sea.[a]

Herod decided to seek Antony's help to avenge Phasaelus's death, so he travelled through Arabia to Egypt, but Antony had left Egypt about a year earlier.

Antony had sailed first to Tyre, where he found out that most of Syria had already been taken by the Parthians.[b] So he gave up Tyre and sailed to Greece to meet his mother and wife. Here, he took Octavius as his enemy and made an alliance with Sextus Pompey.[c] Antony then engaged Octavius in open war in Brundisium. Both sides took heavy losses since they were evenly matched.

Suddenly, Antony's wife Fulvia died of sickness in Sicyon. Her death served as an excuse for ending all previous conflict and both parties laid down their arms. Antony and Octavius divided the empire anew, with Octavius taking the West and Antony taking all territory east of the Ionian Sea; Africa was held by Lepidus and Sicily by Sextus.[d] This agreement is known as the treaty of Brundisium, which took place in September of 40 B.C.

---

a "...So he [Herod] encouraged his mother, and took all the care of her the time would allow, and proceeded on the way he proposed to go with the utmost haste, and that was to the fortress of Masada... Antigonus sent physicians to cure it, and, by ordering them to infuse poison into the wound, killed him [Phasaelus]" (Josephus, *Antiquities*, 14.13.8–10).

b "So when at last he was forced to bestir himself, he sailed to Tyre with the intention of aiding it, but on seeing that the rest of Syria had already been occupied before his coming, he left the inhabitants to their fate, on the pretext that he had to wage war against Sextus [Pompey]; and yet he excused his dilatoriness with regard to the latter by alleging his business with the Parthians. And thus on account of Sextus, as he pretended, he gave no assistance to his allies, and none to Italy on account of his allies, but coasted along the mainland as far as Asia and crossed to Greece. There, after meeting his mother and wife, he made Caesar his enemy and made an alliance with Sextus. After this he went over to Italy, got possession of Sipontum, and proceeded to besiege Brundisium, which had refused to come to terms with him" (Dio, *Roman History*, 48.27.2–5).

c Sextus was the son of Pompey the Great, who was assassinated in Egypt after losing the Battle of Pharsalus in August 48 B.C. to Julius Caesar in Greece.

d "While he was thus engaged, Caesar, who had already arrived from Gaul, had collected his forces and had sent Publius Servilius Rullus to Brundisium and Agrippa against Sipontum. Agrippa took the city by storm, but Servilius was suddenly attacked by Antony, who destroyed many of his men and won many over. The two leaders thus broke out into open war... While the leaders themselves and those who were to assist them in the war were in a state of suspense, Fulvia died in Sicyon, where she had been staying... nevertheless, when this news was announced, both sides laid down their arms and effected a reconciliation... By the arrangement then made Caesar received Sardinia, Dalmatia, Spain, and Gaul, and Antony all the districts that belonged to the Romans across the Ionian Sea, both in Europe and Asia; as for the provinces in Africa, they were of course still held by Lepidus, and Sicily by Sextus" (Dio, *Roman History*, 48.28.1–4).

The Timing of God's Visitations

Afterward Antony went back to Rome to marry Octavius's sister, Octavia, whose husband Caius Marcellus had died recently. She was pregnant at the time.[a] [41]

Following the treaty, Sextus Pompey caused critical food shortages in Italy by using his fleet for piracy and to blockade the high seas. In the summer of 39 B.C., Octavius and Antony reached a peace treaty with Sextus at Misenum, which is known as Miseno, Italy today. This halted the civil war between them.[b] [42] Both Octavius and Antony went back to Rome afterwards.

Shortly after the Misenum settlement, Antony sent Ventidius Bassus into Syria to oppose the further advancement of the Parthians, while he himself took the priesthood in Rome.[c] Ventidius would have left for Syria around August/September in 39 B.C.

After missing Antony in Egypt but learning that he had returned to Italy, Herod set sail into a storm from Alexandria, Egypt in July/August of 39 B.C. and ended up casting loads from the ship to stay afloat. He arrived at Rhodes with difficulty, fitted up a larger ship, and continued sailing to Rome.[d]

Herod likely reached Rome in October of 39 B.C., just prior to Antony's nomination of his foreign acquaintances for vassal kingships. After interviewing Herod, Antony decided to recommend him together with others to the Senate to serve as client kings on the condition that they pay tribute to him.[e] Antony knew very well that he needed all the wealth he could collect in order to finance his wars both within and without the Roman Empire.

Herod stayed in Rome for only seven days[f] and sailed back to Asia. He landed on Ptolemais, which is today in Lebanon, and started gathering an army

---

a "...had espoused to Antony, Caesar's sister, Octavia, now that her husband was dead, though she was pregnant" (Dio, *Roman History*, 48.31.3). "...Octavia was a sister of Caesar, older than he, though not by the same mother... Her husband, Caius Marcellus, had died a short time before, and she was a widow... Accordingly, when both men were agreed, they went up to Rome and celebrated Octavia's marriage" (Plutarch, *Life of Antony*, 31.1–3).

b Plutarch, *Life of Antony*, 32.1–2; and Dio, *Roman History*, 48.34.1–48.36.

c "After this settlement, Antony sent Ventidius on ahead into Asia to oppose the further progress of the Parthians, while he himself, as a favour to Caesar, was appointed to the priesthood of the elder Caesar" (Plutarch, *Life of Antony*, 33.1).

d Josephus, *Antiquities*, 14.14.2–3.

e "The Senate having voted to ratify all that he had done or should do, Antony again despatched his lieutenants in all directions and arranged everything else as he wished. He set up kings here and there as he pleased, on condition of their paying a prescribed tribute: in Pontus, Darius, the son of Pharnaces and grandson of Mithridates: in Idumea and Samaria, Herod: in Pisidia, Amyntas; in a part of Cilicia, Polemon, and others in other countries" (Appian, *Roman History IV*, 5.72–75).

f Josephus, *Antiquities*, 14.14.5.

and marching towards Galilee. Generals Silo and Ventidius came to assist him, as ordered by Antony.ᵃ Obviously, Ventidius was already in the area before Herod arrived. This demonstrates that Herod's investiture as king of the Jews by Rome must have happened after the treaty of Misenum in 39 B.C. and not before. According to Schürer, the Senate appointed Herod to be a vassal king in 40 B.C., which directly contradicts this solid evidence.

Ventidius was awarded a triumph in Rome in 38 B.C. for his defeat of the Parthians in Syria. His triumph was inscribed in the tablet of triumph at Rome and was reported by Plutarch and Pliny the Elder.[43] Ventidius's army slew the Parthian prince Pacorus during the conflicts.ᵇ This happened during the summer of 38 B.C., a year after the treaty of Misenum.

The combined records of Josephus, Dio, Appian, Fasti Triumphales, Plutarch, and Pliny the Elder corroborate the fact that Herod received his kingship over Judea in the fall of 39 B.C. (or 5377 JHY) from the Roman Senate. Filmer was the first to propose a chronology for Herod that is coherent with the historical records outlined above.[44]

1.2.2 JOSEPHUS USES HEBREW CALENDAR FOR DATING

Josephus did not regard the Julian calendar as being the same as the traditional Hebrew one. He never quoted the Roman Republic's AUC calendar in his books.

Table 1.2 summarizes the number of times Josephus employed the Macedonia, Hebrew, Olympiad, Roman AUC, and consular calendars in his chronological dating. He dated events 40 times using various Syro-Macedonian months in *War*, and 27 times in *Antiquities*. Furthermore, 18 times in *Antiquities* he added Hebrew months alongside the Macedonian ones to show their correspondence. He basically treated the Syro-Macedonian timeline as being the same as the Hebrew one, except for the names of the months.

Josephus didn't use any Roman months in his own written text, except in direct quotes of Roman letters, decrees, or declarations. In total, he quoted different Roman months nine times. He mentioned Roman consular years seven times and the Olympiad 11 times.

---

a "By this time Herod had sailed out of Italy to Ptolemais, and had gotten together no small army, both of strangers and of his own countrymen, and marched through Galilee against Antigonus. Silo also, and Ventidius, came and assisted him, being persuaded by Dellius, who was sent by Antony to assist in bringing back Herod" (Josephus, *Antiquities*, 14.15.1).

b Josephus, *War*, 1.16.6.

The Timing of God's Visitations

Interestingly, Josephus reported that Vitellius was defeated and killed after the battle he fought in Rome against Antonius Primus on the third day of the Macedonian month Apelleus.[a]

In December of 69 A.D., shortly after the death of Vitellius, news came from Rome to Alexandria congratulating Vespasian, father of Titus and Domitian, for his advancement as the new emperor. Josephus was resolutely insistent on using the Macedonian month Appelleus instead of Julian month October or November in dating this significant Roman historical event.

Table 1.2. Survey of various calendars used by Josephus in chronological dating.

Calendar	War	Antiquities
Syro-Macedonia	40	27
Hebrew	0	18
Olympiad	1	10
Roman Consular	0	7
Roman AUC	0	0
Roman Months	0	9

The Julian calendar is based on the old Egyptian solar calendar, which was then improved by the Alexandrian astronomer Sosigenes, who lengthened the year from 365 to 365.25 days, using a leap year cycle that added one day every four years. Julius Caesar adopted it to replace the seriously problematic Roman AUC lunar calendar in 45 B.C.[45] From then onward, the Julian calendar and Roman AUC calendar are essentially one and the same.

Josephus lived in Rome from around 75 to 100 A.D. He could have used the Roman AUC calendar, but clearly he preferred using Roman consular years to date the small number of major events he deemed important. He dated no more than seven events using Roman consular years in *Antiquities*.

---

a Josephus, *War*, 4.11.4–5.

Herod the Tyrant

Josephus was born and raised in a prominent Jewish priesthood-related family and knew the Hebrew laws and calendar well. He had the right to be a priest,[a] since his mother was a descendant of the priesthood Hasmonean family.[b] The simplest way for him to treat the matter of chronological dating of Jewish histories would have been to continue using the Hebrew (same as Syro-Macedonian) calendar as a base, quoting the equivalences in other calendars, such as the Athenian and Roman consulships whenever they were applicable to his Greek and Roman audience in *Antiquities*. This would have been the smart thing to do, and perhaps the only viable option.

As discussed earlier, the year of Herod's accession, consistent with Josephus's record of having taken place seven years from the Judean earthquake or the battle of Actium (in 31 B.C.), was 5377 JHY, or 39 B.C., as shown in Figure 1.2. However, if one does the math using Julian years (39 − 31 = 8), the result is not seven but eight years between Herod's accession and the earthquake. Why?

This discrepancy is essentially caused by two effects. Firstly, it was caused by the natural stagger of each Hebrew year against the Julian year. Secondly, Josephus's record of seven years was actually a truncated value of about 7.4 years, as shown in Figure 1.2. Since he was using a year as the basic unit, the extra 0.4 year (about five months) obviously got left out of his statement.

Since Nisan 1 shifts between March and April, the Hebrew year is offset from the Julian one by three to four months. Precisely, it was because of this offset that the dates of the two events—Herod's accession and the Judean earthquake—fell on 39 and 31 B.C. respectively. As a result, if one uses these two Julian values to calculate the number of years between the events, the answer is eight years. This illustrates the fact that seven years in the Hebrew lunisolar calendar does not always equate to seven years in the Julian solar calendar, due to the rounding and offset effects.

Further details regarding the offset effect between calendars can be found in the fundamental principles of chronology presented by Edwin Thiele.[46]

In referencing the Hebrew years from Josephus's work, one must exercise caution and specify the years in the unit of the intended timeline—in this case, the Josephus Hebrew Year (JHY). This is akin to specifying inches in imperial units or centimeters in metric. Without accounting for the difference, confusion and error become inevitable.

---

a "Joseph [Josephus], the son of Matthias, by birth a Hebrew, a priest also…" (Josephus, *War*, Preface 1)

b See Appendix B.

The Timing of God's Visitations

Many scholars take the number of years given by Josephus and treat them as Julian years, or vice versa. In some cases, such treatments are valid, but in others they are not, since Josephus's Hebrew calendar and the Julian calendar are based on different timelines.

In fact, some scholars make the faulty assumption that Josephus was using the Julian calendar in all his chronological reckonings, but in reality he was using a Hebrew one.

1.3 CAESAR AUGUSTUS VISITED SYRIA (20 B.C.)

According to Dio, Augustus travelled to Syria in the spring of the year when Marcus Apuleius and Publius Silius were consuls.[a] The consular year was 20 B.C.

Josephus mentioned that Herod had already reigned 17 years when Caesar came to Syria.[b] In other words, Caesar arrived in Syria during Herod's eighteenth regnal year.

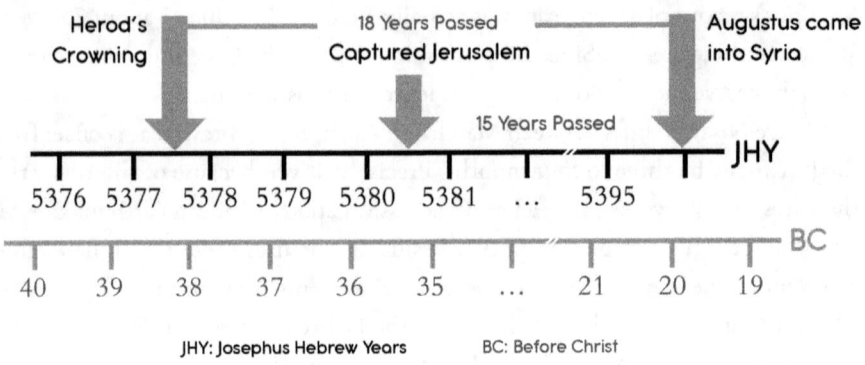

Figure 1.3. In Herod's eighteenth regnal year, Augustus came into Syria in the spring of 20 B.C.

The timing of Caesar's arrival in spring must have landed near the end of Adar in 5395 JHY and before the commencement of Herod's nineteenth regnal year in

---

a "Augustus, now, after transacting what business he had in Greece, sailed to Samos, where he passed the winter; and in the spring of the year when Marcus Apuleius and Publius Silius were consuls [20 B.C.], he went on into Asia, and settled everything there and in Bithynia" (Dio, *Roman History*, 54.7.4).

b "Now when Herod had already reigned seventeen years, Caesar came into Syria; at which time the greatest part of the inhabitants of Gadara clamored against Herod, as one that was heavy in his injunctions, and tyrannical" (Josephus, *Antiquities*, 15.10.3).

Nisan 1 (around March 23 for the vernal equinox), as shown in Figure 1.3. Counting back 18 years from 5395 JHY results in 5377 JHY, which corresponds to 39 B.C. and concurs with the year of Herod's investiture as king of the Jews in Rome.

1.4 HEROD'S DEATH BETWEEN A LUNAR ECLIPSE AND A PASSOVER

Herod was well-known for his brutality towards the Jews, and even his own family. Herod murdered the deposed high priest Hyrcanus and his young grandson Aristobulus in order to secure his kingship over the Jews.[a]

Hyrcanus was the grandfather of Mariamne (Herod's wife) and Aristobulus, and they were the last of the immediate descendants of the Hasmonean clan. They were murdered not long after Herod captured Jerusalem in 36 B.C.

Around 5 B.C., Herod executed two of his sons, Alexander and Aristobulus, for their alleged parricide plot, not knowing that they had been framed by their eldest half-brother, Antipater, who had been named after Herod's own father. Antipater had secretly pursued his succession to the throne by eliminating all obstacles.[b]

Back in 29 B.C., Herod had killed the two brothers' mother, Mariamne the Hasmonean, in a rage, suspecting her of attempting to poison him.[47] After Mariamne's death, Herod's mental and physical health deteriorated. At one time, he fell seriously ill after an outbreak of pestilential disease; nonetheless, he seemed to recover from it.[48]

In order to gain popularity among the Jews, Herod funded the reconstruction of the second temple and the enlargement of the Temple Mount's base, starting in 21/20 B.C.[c] The temple had been built under the leadership of Zerubbabel about 500 years earlier, and now it needed repairs.

Herod enlarged and raised the foundation of the temple to a new height right on top of the foundations laid by Solomon and Zerubbabel. Obviously, the temple was reconstructed after the laying of the main foundation, and perhaps in parallel

---

a "But Mariamne's hatred to him was not inferior to his love to her. She had indeed but too just a cause of indignation from what he had done, while her boldness proceeded from his affection to her; so she openly reproached him with what he had done to her grandfather Hyrcanus, and to her brother Aristobulus; for he had not spared this Aristobulus, though he were but a child" (Josephus, *War*, 1.22.2).

b Josephus, *Antiquities*, 16.7.2–16.11.7.

c "And now Herod, in the eighteenth year of his reign, and after the acts already mentioned, undertook a very great work, that is, to build of himself the temple of God, and make it larger in compass, and to raise it to a most magnificent altitude, as esteeming it to be the most glorious of all his actions" (Josephus, *Antiquities*, 15.11.1).

The Timing of God's Visitations

with the building of several aboveground bridges and stairways and underground corridors leading to the temple court above. Establishing the foundation alone would have taken a number of years.

Jews mentioned to Jesus that it had taken 46 years to build the temple. However, they provided no point of reference for the timing.[a] The 46-year period likely refers to the time taken to erect the elaborate foundation and temple through Jesus's time. It may or may not have included the time taken in design and planning. The rest of the temple complex wasn't completed until 63/64 A.D.[b]

The funding for Herod's construction projects came from various forms of taxation in his kingdom, which encompassed Judea, Samaria, Idumea, Galilee, Perea, Trachonitis, Gaulanitis, Auranitis, and Batanea.[c]

The year of Herod's death was undoubtedly well-known to the Jews in the first century, since they hated him so much. According to Josephus, Herod burnt two popular rabbis and some young people alive. He also put other dissidents to the sword for dismantling a golden eagle he had hung on the temple gate. A lunar eclipse appeared that evening. This event took place before a Passover[d] and it's the only time Josephus recorded a lunar eclipse in his books.

Furthermore, Herod rounded up all the principal men of the Jewish nation and kept them in a hippodrome near Jericho prior to his death. These Jews were to be executed right after he died to ensure a nationwide mourning instead of celebration. His order was not carried out.

Both years given for Herod's death, 4 and 1 B.C., are substantiated by some evidence, but neither are without major difficulties.[49] The two pertinent lunar events visible in Israel were the partial eclipse on March 13, 4 B.C. and the full eclipse on January 10, 1 B.C.[50] Based on these two dates, Jesus could have been born either in 6/5 or 3/2 B.C.

Back in the 1890s A.D., scholars had already recognized that there wasn't quite enough time between the lunar eclipse on March 13, 4 B.C. and Passover on April 11, 4 B.C. to allow for all the events related to Herod's final days and burial, as recorded in Josephus's work.[51]

Andrew Steinmann tallied the days that elapsed between the lunar eclipse shortly before Herod's death and the following Passover.[52] He assumed the

---

a "The Jews then said, 'It took forty-six years to build this temple, and yet You will raise it up in three days?'" (John 2:20)

b Josephus, *Antiquities*, 20.9.7.

c Josephus, *Antiquities*, 17.11.4.

d Josephus, *Antiquities*, 17.6.4–17.9.3.

minimum amount of time for each event and arrived at a total of 41 days. Steinmann and Young revised the previous numbers between Herod's death and Passover using a new set of extreme minimums, as shown in Table 1.3.[53]

Table 1.3. Tally of events in Herod's final days between the lunar eclipse and Passover.[a]

1 B.C.	Days Elapsed	Event	4 B.C.
January 10	-	Lunar eclipse	March 13
11	1	1. Herod seeks treatments from physicians and tries them all.	14
14	3	2. Herod travels from Jericho to Callirrhoe.	17
15	1	3. Herod receives treatment at Callirrhoe.	18
18	3	4. Herod returns to Jericho.	21
24	6	5. Herod summons all Jewish elders to Jericho.	27
25	1	6. Herod receives words from Augustus permitting him to make the final sentence of Antipater.	28
30	5	7. Herod dies five days later from executing Antipater.	April 2

a Josephus, *Antiquities*, 17.6.5 – 17.9.3.

February 2	3	8. Funeral arrangements and preparation, gathering of jewels and wealth from Jerusalem to Jericho for Herod's burial.	5
5	3	9. Funeral procession and burial.	8
-	-	Passover April 11, 4 B.C. →	-
12	7	10. Seven days of mourning.	15
13	1	11. Feast in Herod's honor.	16
14	1	12. Archelaus initial governance, removal of Joazar as high priest on the Jews' demand.	17
15	1	13. Archelaus sends armies and they slay 3,000 Jews; Passover cancelled.	18
-	-	←Passover April 7, 1 B.C.	-
	36	**TOTAL**	

Based on the extreme minimum span of time for each event, a total of 36 days is absolutely required for all the events to have occurred between the lunar eclipse and the Passover. If Herod died in 4 B.C., the 29 days between March 13 and April 11 are clearly insufficient.

If Herod died around January 27, 1 B.C., then all the related events, including Herod's death and funeral, fit comfortably within the 88-day period that fall between the total lunar eclipse on January 10, 1 B.C. and the Passover on April 7, 1 B.C. We shall come back to this topic.

1.5 HEROD'S WILL

Antipater had tried to stay in Rome as long as he could, and when he returned to Jerusalem he walked right into Herod's announcement of his trial for having

Herod the Tyrant

plotted parricide. He had received Augustus's approval to take Herod's throne and was afraid of Herod discovering how he'd framed his two half-brothers. At the same time, he was exceedingly impatient to see his father dead.[a]

The trial began the next day. According to Josephus, Herod testified before Quinctilius Varus, governor of Syria, against his son for plotting to assassinate him. Herod said,

> Indeed what kindness did I do to them that could equal what I have done to Antipater to whom I have in a manner, yielded up my royal authority while I am alive, and who I have openly named for the successor to my dominions in my testament…[b]

Antipater responded by saying,

> And indeed what was there that could possibly provoke me against you? Could the hope of being a king do it? I was a king already… whom as you yourself said, you brought into the palace; who you did prefer before so many of your sons; whom you made a king in your own lifetime, and, by the vast magnitude of the other advantages you bestowed on me, you made me an object of envy.[c]

Antipater was co-reigning with his father—not officially, but unofficially like a king. In fact, all public affairs of the kingdom depended on Antipater.[d] According to Josephus, "He governed the nation jointly with his father, being indeed no other than a king already."[e] Herod had made known to all that he was the only one to be esteemed as king and lord of all. The reason is that all client kings had to be approved by Caesar in order to be legitimate. Caesar gave Herod the power to appoint any of his sons for his successor as he pleases, but the final decision still lay with Caesar.[f]

With all the witnesses and evidence presented at the trial, Varus found Antipater guilty as charged and reported to Caesar Augustus about his judgment.

---

a Josephus, *Antiquities*, 17.1.1.
b Josephus, *War*, 1.32.2–3
c Ibid.
d Josephus, *Antiquities*, 17.2.4.
e Ibid., 17.1.1.
f Ibid., 16.4.5–6.

The Timing of God's Visitations

Meanwhile, Antipater was jailed in Herod's palace where he awaited the final verdict from Rome.

In the meantime, Herod the Great divided his kingdom among his three other sons. In his last will, he gave Archelaus the Judean kingdom—which was reduced to Judea, Samaria, and Idumea—appointed Antipas as tetrarch in Galilee and Perea, and placed Philip II as tetrarch in Gaulanitis, Panea, Trachonitis, and Batanea. He designated part of his wealth to various individuals, such as his sister Salome, Augustus, and his queen Julia (Livia Drusilla).[a]

> When he had done these things, he died, the fifth day after he had caused Antipater to be slain; having reigned, since he had procured Antigonus to be slain, *thirty-four* years; but since he had been declared king by the Romans, *thirty-seven*.[b]

Herod was made king by the Romans in the fall of 39 B.C., and he reigned for 37 years. Thus his death should have occurred in JHY 5414 (5377 + 37), which overlapped with 2/1 B.C. as shown in Figure 1.4.

Similarly, after sending Antigonus for execution in the fall of 36 B.C., Herod ruled in Jerusalem for 34 years. Therefore, his death should also have occurred in JHY 5414 (5380 + 34).

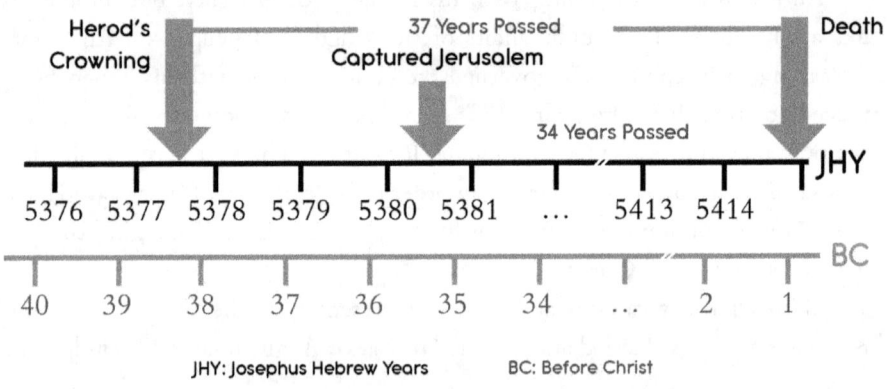

Figure 1.4. Time intervals between Herod's accession, capture of Jerusalem, and death.

---

a Ibid., 17.8.1.

b Josephus, *War*, 1.33.8. Emphasis added.

Based on computations related to the orbit of the moon,[54] a total lunar eclipse would have been visible in Israel on January 10, 1 B.C. The Passover that year took place on April 7, 1 B.C. Herod must have died sometime between these two dates.

Macrobius, a philosopher who lived from 395–423 A.D., documented some of Caesar Augustus's famous sayings in *Saturnalia*. He wrote,

> When he [Augustus] heard that Herod king of the Jews had ordered boys in Syria under the age of two years to be put to death and that the king's son was among those killed, he said, "I'd rather be Herod's pig than Herod's son."[55]

Of course, there is a chance that Macrobius made up this story, since we don't know the original source of his information. Yet we should give him the benefit of the doubt.

Judea had always been under the jurisdiction of the governor of Syria, and Romans viewed it as part of Syria. Macrobius's statement supports the narrative in Matthew 2:16–18 regarding Herod's killing of boys two years old and under in Bethlehem and agrees that it took place within the same period when Antipater was executed by his father.

1.6 HEROD'S SONS ANTEDATED THEIR REIGNS TO 4 B.C.

The year 4 B.C. is probably the best temporal marker for Antipater being granted by Caesar Augustus the title of king of the Jews.

When Antipater returned to Jerusalem from Rome, likely in the fall of 2 B.C., he went into the palace wearing purple.[a] Wearing purple was the sign of a king, but he had no idea that he had just walked into a setup.

Although Antipater was convicted of parricide the next day, it didn't change the fact that Herod the Great had already officially "resigned" in 4 B.C. Herod's will, also serving as his resignation letter, along with other relevant official documents, would have been saved in the Tabularium in Rome the day Augustus granted Antipater client kingship in Judea.

Herod's remaining sons—Archelaus, Antipas, and Philip—had every intention of antedating their accession year to 4 B.C., because Antipater was a disgrace to the family and his rulership was terminated from day one in Jerusalem.

---

a Josephus, *Antiquities*, 17.5.2.

To the people in the Judean kingdom, Antipater was never officially a king. Herod's family would have been glad to erase all records of Antipater's kingship if they could. Herod then had to rename his heirs in a new testament.

Throughout history, it has been common for retired kings to live a few more years after relaying their thrones to their heirs. Too many scholars assume that all royal retirees died at the same time as their heirs' accessions. Herod is a good example.

After Antipater's downfall, his brothers—Archelaus, Antipas, and Philip—replaced him and claimed before Caesar their shares of the inheritance as divvied by Herod. They might have even requested Augustus's permission to antedate their accession year to 4 B.C. to erase the mistake made by their father in picking the evil Antipater to be king.

Furthermore, Archelaus was accused by his cousin Antipater of long exercising royal authority,[a] plausibly in aiding Herod to govern during his half-brother Antipater's absence.

There existed no reason in the Roman court to object to the brothers' request. Most of Herod's immediate family, including his sister Salome, appeared before Caesar Augustus in Rome in mid-1 B.C. Crown prince Gaius Caesar was seated in the hearing as well.[b] Augustus probably wasn't surprised to see Herod's family, since not too long ago he had permitted Herod to sentence Antipater as he wished. When Augustus authorized Herod's sentence of Antipater, he had nullified Herod's previous testament. Caesar should therefore have been agreeable to endorse Herod's new testament, granting his heirs their assigned portions.

The dating of the investitures of Herod's three sons is as follows:

---

a "Then stood up Salome's son, Antipater (who of all Archelaus's antagonists was the shrewdest pleader), and accused him in the following speech: That Archelaus did in words contend for the kingdom, but that in deeds he had long exercised royal authority, and so did but insult Caesar in desiring to be now heard on that account, since he had not staid for his determination about the succession, and since he had suborned certain persons, after Herod's death, to move for putting the diadem upon his head; since he had set himself down in the throne, and given answers as a king, and altered the disposition of the army, and granted to some higher dignities; that he had also complied in all things with the people in the requests they had made to him as to their king, and had also dismissed those that had been put into bonds by his father for most important reasons... When Antipater had spoken largely to this purpose, and had produced a great number of Archelaus's kindred as witnesses, to prove every part of the accusation, he ended his discourse" (Josephus, *War*, 2.2.5–6).

b Josephus, *War* 2.2.4; *Anitquities* 17.9.5.

Herod the Tyrant

1. According to Dio, Archelaus was deposed as ethnarch[a] of Judea in the consulship of Aemilius Lepidus and Lucius Arruntius (6 A.D.).[b] In *War* 2.7.3,[c] Josephus records that Archelaus was banished to Vienne (in France) in his ninth regnal Hebrew year. Thus, Archelaus's investiture to ethnarch of Judea is dated to 4 B.C.

2. Antipas lost his tetrarchy in the second year of Caesar Caligula (38/39 A.D.) and reigned according to the evidence of dated coins for 43 years.[56] Thus, Antipas's investiture as tetrarch of Galilee and Perea is also dated to 4 B.C.

3. Philip's case is a bit more complicated due to serious transcription errors in various editions of Josephus's books. Some editions of Josephus's *Antiquities* prior to 1544 A.D. record that Philip died in the "twenty-second year of the reign of Tiberius after he had been tetrarch of Trachonitis and Gaulanitis, and of the nation of Bataneans also, thirty-seven years."[d] Some editions after 1544 A.D. read that he died in the twentieth year of the reign of Tiberius.[57] Some older versions state that Philip had been tetrarch for 32 years, and some say 36 years.[58] No definitive investiture year for Philip can be determined owing to these transcription errors. However, it is safe to say that Philip's accession year is antedated likely to 4 B.C., the same as his brothers, because they all stood in front of Caesar Augustus in Rome at the same time in 1 B.C.

Most likely, Augustus granted Herod's heirs the right to antedate their accession year to 4 B.C. It would have been easy for him to do this as a goodwill gesture, to encourage the demoralized and infighting family. With just a few words, he could have gained their undivided loyalty. Caesar would have had nothing to lose and everything to gain. After all, he was a prudent and shrewd leader who knew how to play the political game. Furthermore, it would have solved the problem of having

---

a An ethnarch is the ethnic national leader, equivalent to being a governor.

b "After this, in the consulship of Aemilius Lepidus and Lucius Arruntius [6 A.D.]... Herod of Palestine, who was accused by his brothers of some wrongdoing or other, was banished beyond the Alps and a portion of the domain was confiscated to the state" (Dio, *Roman History*, 55.25.1, 55.27.6).

c "Whereupon they both of them sent ambassadors against him to Caesar; and in the ninth year of his government he was banished to Vienne, a city of Gaul, and his effects were put into Caesar's treasury" (Josephus, *War*, 2.7.3).

d Josephus, *Antiquities*, 18.4.6.

no client king in Judea for the period 4/1 B.C., since Herod had officially retired in 4 B.C., at least on paper in the official Roman record.

So far, no regnal year one coin has ever been found for Herod's three sons, despite the fact that hundreds of their dated coins have surfaced.[59] The earliest known dated coin of Antipas shows a regnal year of four, whereas Philip's indicates year five.[60]

Why are there no earlier coins for the sons of Herod? The most probable answer is that they antedated their investitures, somewhat similar to what their father did. Since Augustus had approved this in the summer of 1 B.C., the earliest set of coins attributed to Herod's sons would have been year four (corresponding to 1 A.D.), which is exactly what has been found thus far.

1.7 SCHÜRER'S CONSENSUS FOR HEROD'S REIGN AND DEATH

If Herod died between the partial lunar eclipse on March 13, 4 B.C. and Nisan 1 in 4 B.C., and if he was appointed king of the Jews by the Roman Senate in late 40 B.C. according to Schürer, then the actual number of Hebrew years between the two events would be only 35, as shown in Figure 1.5 (5411 − 5376 = 35, or 36 years by inclusive reckoning).

Similarly, if Herod had captured Jerusalem in 37 B.C., then the actual number of Hebrew years from 5379 to his death in 5411 would have been 32 (or 33 years by inclusive reckoning). Both sets of numbers (35/32 by non-inclusive reckoning and 36/33 by inclusive reckoning) fall short of Josephus's values of 37 and 34 years. The Schürer consensus is off by at least one year in both accounts.

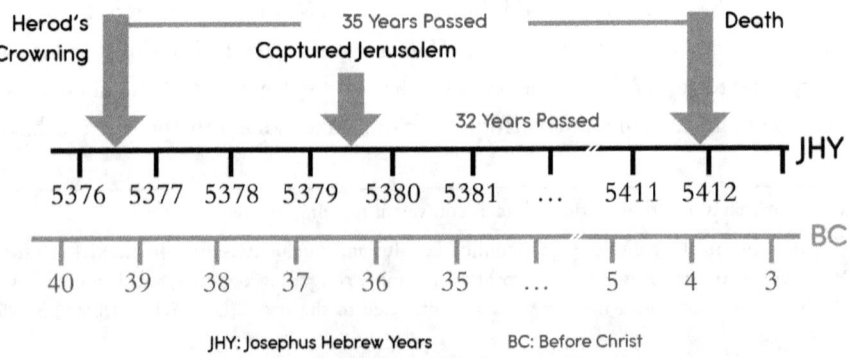

Figure 1.5. Time intervals between Herod's accession, capture of Jerusalem, and death before Nisan 1, 4 B.C.

Schürer states that

> his [Herod's] reign beginning with July B.C. 37… The thirty-fourth year of Herod would begin on the 1st Nisan of the year B.C. 4, and Herod must in that case have died between 1st and 14th Nisan, since his death occurred before the Passover.[61]

According to Schürer, Herod began his reign in 37 B.C. and after 34 years he died after Nisan 1 in 4 B.C. (37 − 34 + 1, by inclusive reckoning). Schürer's rendering reduces the time for Herod's death and funeral to less than 14 days. This is simply not enough time when compared to the extreme minimum of 16 days needed to accommodate all the events of Herod's death and funeral, as listed in Table 1.3. This conflict raises serious doubt about the validity of Schürer's hypothesis of 37 B.C. being the year during which Herod captured Jerusalem.

Furthermore, Schürer's advocacy of Herod's reign starting in 37 B.C. contradicts Josephus's record. Josephus writes, "Antony also made a feast for Herod on the first day of his reign."[a] This feast took place either on the same day of his coronation or the next day. Josephus regarded Herod's rulership as having started in Rome, not after the death of Antigonus in Judea.

In addition, the first set of minted coins by Herod after seizing Jerusalem was dated year three.[62] Undoubtedly, Herod considered his accession year for kingship and reign as having begun legally and officially when he was made a client king by the Roman Senate in 5377 JHY, or 39 B.C., and his first year of reign is 38 B.C. The third year of his reign would have been 36 B.C., when he took Jerusalem. However, if Herod became a client king in 40 B.C. as advocated by Schürer, the year he captured Jerusalem in 37 B.C. should have been his fourth year based on inclusive reckoning. This obviously does not match the numismatic evidence.

As pointed out by Filmer, according to Dio, General Sosius purposely accomplished nothing with his legions in 37 B.C. when Antony was travelling back and forth between Italy and Syria.[b] Schürer's assumption of Sosius and Herod taking Jerusalem that year directly contradicts Dio's statement.

---

a Josephus, *War*, 1.14.4.

b "This was the course of events in the consulship of Claudius and Norbanus [38 B.C.]; during the following year [37 B.C.] the Romans accomplished nothing worthy of note in Syria. For Antony spent the entire year in reaching Italy and returning again to the province; and Sosius, because anything he did would be advancing Antony's interests rather than his own, and he therefore dreaded his jealousy and anger, spent the time in devising means, not for achieving some success and incurring his enmity, but for pleasing him without engaging in any activity. The Parthian state, in fact, with no outside interference underwent a severe revolution from the following cause" (Dio, *Roman History*, 49.23.1).

The Timing of God's Visitations

1.8 EVIDENCE FROM SABBATICAL YEARS

According to Josephus, the sabbatical year was still going on after Herod took full control of Jerusalem.[a] Since sabbatical years repeat every seven years, if one can pinpoint one sabbatical year, the rest can be established.

In the following, we will examine a number of pertinent historical records to confirm the sabbatical year during which Herod seized Jerusalem.

1.8.1 BIBLICAL SABBATICAL YEARS INSTRUCTION

A sabbatical year is the last year of a seven-year cycle, and the year of jubilee is the fiftieth year after seven sabbatical-year cycles. In Leviticus 25:1–12,[b] God instructs the Israelites to keep the sabbatical year and the year of jubilee. These years, like any other Old Testament years, begin on Nisan 1 (Exodus 12:2). Nowhere in the entire Bible is it mentioned that Tishri 1 serves as the beginning of the Hebrew year in a civil or ecclesiastical sense.

---

a "At this time Herod, now he had got Jerusalem under his power, carried off all the royal ornaments, and spoiled the wealthy men of what they had gotten; and when, by these means, he had heaped together a great quantity of silver and gold, he gave it all to Antony, and his friends that were about him. He also slew forty-five of the principal men of Antigonus's party, and set guards at the gates of the city, that nothing might be carried out together with their dead bodies. They also searched the dead, and whatsoever was found, either of silver or gold, or other treasure, it was carried to the king; nor was there any end of the miseries he brought upon them; and this distress was in part occasioned by the covetousness of the prince regent, who was still in want of more, and in part by the Sabbatic year, which was still going on, and forced the country to lie still uncultivated, since we are forbidden to sow our land in that year" (Josephus, *Antiquities*, 15.1.2).

b "The Lord then spoke to Moses on Mount Sinai, saying, 'Speak to the sons of Israel and say to them, "When you come into the land which I am going to give you, then the land shall have a Sabbath to the Lord. For six years you shall sow your field, and for six years you shall prune your vineyard and gather in its produce, but during the seventh year the land shall have a Sabbath rest, a Sabbath to the Lord; you shall not sow your field nor prune your vineyard. You shall not reap your harvest's aftergrowth, and you shall not gather your grapes of untrimmed vines; the land shall have a sabbatical year. All of you shall have the Sabbath produce of the land as food; for yourself, your male and female slaves, and your hired worker and your foreign resident, those who live as strangers among you. Even your cattle and the animals that are in your land shall have all its produce to eat. You are also to count off seven Sabbaths of years for yourself, seven times seven years, so that you have the time of the seven Sabbaths of years, that is, forty-nine years. You shall then sound a ram's horn abroad on the tenth day of the seventh month; on the Day of Atonement you shall sound a horn all through your land. So you shall consecrate the fiftieth year and proclaim a release throughout the land to all its inhabitants. It shall be a jubilee for you, and each of you shall return to his own property, and each of you shall return to his family. You shall have the fiftieth year as a jubilee; you shall not sow, nor harvest its aftergrowth, nor gather grapes from its untrimmed vines. For it is a jubilee; it shall be holy to you. You shall eat its produce from the field"'" (Leviticus 25:1–12).

Herod the Tyrant

Moses instructed the Israelites to celebrate the year-end harvest of seeds and produce in the feast of ingathering (Booths, Tabernacle, or Sukkot) on Tishri 15 at the turn of the year (near the autumnal equinox) in each of the six non-sabbatical years (Exodus 34:22).[a] After the fall harvest, they would sow new seeds and prune the fruit trees for the following year, except for the sixth year prior to the sabbatical one.

Figure 1.6 illustrates the BN (Biblical-Nisan) sabbatical year scheme.[b] After the fall harvest in year six, no sowing of seeds and pruning of fruit trees are allowed. The land rests for a full year until the fall of the seventh year, when sowing and pruning resume once again. A new crop of barley will arrive around Nisan 1 of year eight.

For labelling purpose, the seventh year is called the sabbatical year and is reckoned from Nisan, although technically the resting of the land has already begun in Tishri of year six after the fall harvest.

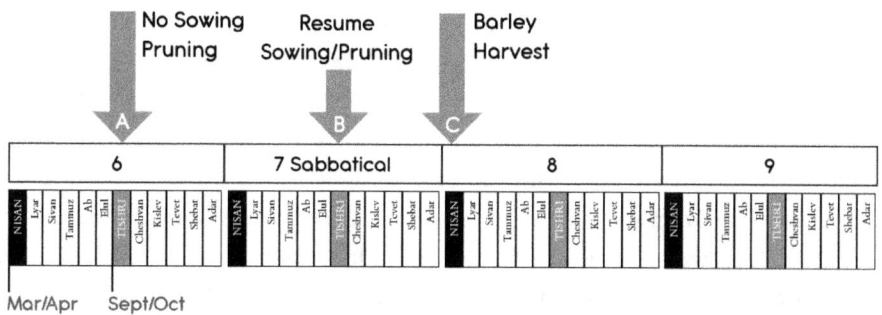

Figure 1.6. Scheme BN: biblical sabbatical year from Nisan 1 (March/April) to Adar 29. After the fall harvest in year six, no sowing and pruning is allowed (A). Sowing and pruning resumes in Tishri of year seven (B). A new crop of barley arrives in Nisan of the eighth year (C).

---

a "Celebrate the Festival of Weeks with the firstfruits of the wheat harvest, and the Festival of Ingathering at the turn of the year" (Exodus 34:22, NIV). Note that other translations incorrectly use the phrase "at the end of the year." This should be translated as "at the turn of the year," as in the New International Version, in the sense of reaching the turnaround point at the autumnal equinox in its circuit.

b There are two schemes. The first is Biblical-Nisan (BN) and the second, which we will discuss later in the chapter, is Talmudic-Tishri (TT).

> Then Moses commanded them, saying, "At the end of every seven years, at the time of the year of the release of debts, at the Feast of Booths, when all Israel comes to appear before the Lord your God at the place which He will choose, you shall read this Law before all Israel so that they hear it." (Deuteronomy 31:10–11)

Some scholars infer erroneously from Deuteronomy 31:10–11 that the end of every sabbatical year occurs at the Feast of Booths, and that Moses taught using a Tishri to Elul sabbatical year. Such an interpretation is basically out of context and wrong.

The phrase "at the end of every seven years" should be rendered as "at the end of every sabbatical-year cycle," not "at the end of the seventh sabbatical year." The plural form of the Hebrew word שָׁנִים (sanim), used here for "years," indicates that it refers to the seven-year cycle.

Furthermore, the phrase "at the time of the year of the release of debts, at the Feast of Booths" is not the same as what some scholars propose: "at the end of the year of the release of debt, at the Feast of Booths." People are changing this passage to reflect what they think the meaning should be, but the Bible gives dire warnings for people who do such a thing (Deuteronomy 4:2, Proverbs 30:5–6, Revelation 22:18).

In the sabbatical year for remission of debts at the Feast of Booths, the law will be read to all the Jews who gather in Jerusalem. This passage says nothing about defining or implying a sabbatical year that lasts from Tishri 1 to Elul 29.

There's a second reason why Moses didn't teach using a Tishri-to-Elul sabbatical year in this verse—namely, the names Tishri and Elul did not exist in the Hebrew language at the time. The Jewish month of Abib/Aviv is the only one named by Moses (Exodus 13:4, Deuteronomy 16:1). All the other months are referred numerically as the second month, the third month, and so on (e.g., Genesis 8:4, Leviticus 23:27). Feast of Booths which takes place on Tishri 15 the middle of the month is unfit to be designated as the beginning of a sabbatical year.

After the Jewish settlement in Canaan, three more month names appeared in the Old Testament: Ziv (1 King 6:1, 6:37; the second month), Ethanim (1 King 8:2; the seventh month), and Bul (1 King 6:38; the eighth month). These names were likely borrowed from the Canaanites. Once the Jews had returned from their first exile, they adopted the 12 Babylonian months[a] and dropped these Canaanite ones.[63]

---

a Nisan (30 days), Lyar (29), Sivan (30), Tammuz (29), Ab (30), Elul (29), Tishri (30), Cheshvan (29/30), Kislev (29/30), Tevet (29), Shebat (30), Adar I Leap (30), and Adar II (29).

According to Deuteronomy 15:1–18, all debts are cancelled for fellow Jews, and all Hebrew slaves are set free, in the sabbatical year which is called *Shemitah* in Hebrew, meaning "to release."

Evidence for Nisan being the first month of a sabbatical year is found in Leviticus 25:9. The Hebrew word (יוֹבֵל; *yobel*), jubilee, literally means "ram's horn."[64]

You shall then sound a ram's horn abroad on the tenth day of the seventh month; on the Day of Atonement you shall sound a horn all through your land. So you shall consecrate the fiftieth year and proclaim a release throughout the land to all its inhabitants. It shall be a jubilee for you, and each of you shall return to his own property, and each of you shall return to his family. (Leviticus 25:9–10)

The Day of Atonement (Yom Kippur) on Tishri 10 takes place in the "seventh month" reckoned from Nisan, which is ordained the first month of the year (Exodus 12:2). As shown in Figure 1.7, blowing the ram's horn on the Day of Atonement in the last year of the seventh sabbatical cycle (the forty-ninth year) signals the official release of all Jewish and Gentile slaves, and all land to its original owners. At the same time, it consecrates the upcoming year of jubilee and makes it holy. Jews are not to sow or reap produce from the land in the year of jubilee. They are not to prune trees or harvest fruit. They simply take what they need to eat from the field, like in any other sabbatical year.

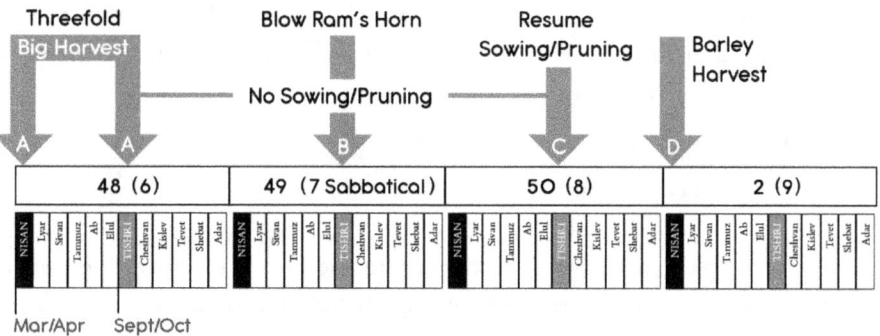

Figure 1.7. Scheme BN: biblical sabbatical year and year of jubilee. After the promised threefold crops are harvested in year six, no sowing and pruning is allowed (A). The blowing of ram's horns to announce liberty for all in the upcoming year of jubilee (year 50) (B). Sowing and pruning is resumed in the fall of the eighth year (C). The arrival of a new crop of barley on Nisan of the ninth year (D).

The Timing of God's Visitations

When the year of jubilee comes right after seven sabbatical-year cycles, the farmers will miss reaping two consecutive crops, as shown in Figure 1.7. God knows what the Israelites are thinking, though, and anticipates their query:[a] *"What shall we eat in the seventh year, if we may not sow or gather in our crop?"* (Leviticus 25:20, ESV)

God's solution is that he will bless them in the sixth year, so that the land will produce a crop sufficient for three years. When Jews sow again in the fall of the eighth year (the year of jubilee being regarded as the first year of a new sabbatical cycle), they will be eating some of the old crops until the ninth year (being the second year of the new sabbatical cycle) when the new crop of barley arrives, as illustrated in Figure 1.7.

The designations of both the time of sowing and the labelling of the sabbatical year and the year of jubilee are provided in Leviticus 25:18–22.[b]

1. Jews can sow in Tishri (September/October) of the year of jubilee (the eighth year). In other words, if it is not the seventh sabbatical cycle with a year of jubilee appended, one can sow in Tishri of the seventh year after the land has rested for a full year since Tishri of year six.

2. After sowing in Tishri of the year of jubilee (year eight), Jews wait to reap the new crop in the ninth year. The first crop must be the traditional barley, which will be harvested and presented at the temple for the wave sheaf offering. The wave sheaf offering will be performed at the altar by the priests during the Festival of Firstfruits (Leviticus 23:9–14) on the Sunday right after Passover. Passover takes place on Nisan 14 (Exodus 12:6), which means that year nine must start on Nisan.

3. For labelling purpose, the seventh year is referred as the sabbatical year, which of course must also begin on Nisan.

As Wacholder points out,[65] according to the Jewish Mishnad, the year of jubilee was abolished after the exile of the northern Jewish kingdom in Samaria

---

a "Therefore you shall do my statutes and keep my rules and perform them, and then you will dwell in the land securely. The land will yield its fruit, and you will eat your fill and dwell in it securely. And if you say, 'What shall we eat in the seventh year, if we may not sow or gather in our crop?' I will command my blessing on you in the sixth year, so that it will produce a crop sufficient for three years. When you sow in the eighth year, you will be eating some of the old crop; you shall eat the old until the ninth year, when its crop arrives" (Leviticus 25:18–22, ESV).

b Ibid.

in 722 B.C., since Jews believe that Leviticus 25:10 prescribes the institution only when all the inhabitants of Israel live in the Holy Land.

According to 2 Chronicles 36:20–21,[a] we know that both the northern kingdom of Israel and the southern kingdom of Judah did not observe the sabbatical year, never mind the year of jubilee, for at least 490 years prior to the destruction of the first temple in about 587 B.C.

In addition to their disobedience of the sabbatical year law, the two nations were guilty of idolatry, child sacrifice, religious prostitution, and the oppression of the weak and lowly. In other words, from approximately 1077 B.C. to the return of the Jews from the first exile in about 517 B.C., no sabbatical-year cycle was kept on Jewish soil.

After the release of captives from Babylon by King Cyrus in about 538 B.C., Jews started constructing a second temple under the leadership of the Judean governor Zerubbabel, a descendant of King David. God used Ezra, Nehemiah, and prophets Haggai and Zechariah to bring about a spiritual reform in the Jewish land. All Jews pledged to obey God's Law (Nehemiah 10:28–29), including observing the weekly Sabbath (Nehemiah 13:15–22). Likely, the practice of keeping sabbatical-year cycles resumed from then onward.

Historical evidence of the Jews observing sabbatical-year cycles in the post-exilic era can be found in Josephus's books for the period of 332 B.C. to 100 A.D.[b], as well as in 1 Maccabees for the period of 175 to 130 B.C.

1.8.2 WAR AGAINST ANTIOCHUS EUPATOR IN 150 S.E.

We read in 1 Maccabees 6,

Meanwhile the garrison in the citadel kept hemming Israel in around the sanctuary... Judas therefore resolved to destroy them and assembled all the people

---

a "He [Nebuchadnezzar] carried into exile to Babylon the remnant, who escaped from the sword, and they became servants to him and his successors until the kingdom of Persia came to power. The land enjoyed its sabbath rests; all the time of its desolation it rested, until the seventy years were completed in fulfillment of the word of the Lord spoken by Jeremiah" (2 Chronicles 36:20–21, NIV).

b "Alexander [lived 356 – 323 B.C.]... he went up into the temple, he offered sacrifice to God, according to the high priest's direction, and magnificently treated both the high priest and the priests. And when the Book of Daniel was showed him wherein Daniel declared that one of the Greeks should destroy the empire of the Persians, he supposed that himself was the person intended. And as he was then glad, he dismissed the multitude for the present; but the next day he called them to him, and bid them ask what favors they pleased of him; whereupon the high priest desired that they might enjoy the laws of their forefathers, and might pay no tribute on the seventh year [Sabbatical year]. He granted all they desired" (Josephus, *Antiquities*, 11.8.5).

to besiege them. They gathered together and besieged the citadel in the one hundred fiftieth year [150 S.E.], and he built siege towers and engines of war. But some of the garrison escaped from the siege, and... went to the king [Antiochus Eupator] and said, "How long will you fail to do justice and to avenge our kindred? ... unless you quickly prevent them, they will do still greater things, and you will not be able to stop them...

Then Judas marched away from the citadel and encamped at Beth-zechariah, opposite the camp of the king... They [the king's soldiers] offered the elephants the juice of grapes and mulberries, to arouse them for battle...

He [Antiochus] made peace with the people of Beth-zur, and they evacuated the town because they had no provisions there to withstand a siege, since it was a sabbatical year for the land. So the king took Beth-zur and stationed a guard there to hold it. Then he encamped before the sanctuary for many days. He set up siege towers, engines of war, devices to throw fire and stones, machines to shoot arrows, and catapults. The Jews also made engines of war to match theirs and fought for many days. But they had no food in storage, because it was the seventh year; those who had found safety in Judea from the nations had consumed the last of the stores. Only a few men were left in the sanctuary; the rest scattered to their own homes, for the famine proved too much for them. (1 Maccabees 6:18–22, 27, 32, 34, 49–54, NRSVUE)

This passage describes the war between Judas Maccabeus and the Seleucid king Antiochus Eupator in 150 S.E. (162/161 B.C. or 5254 JHY, as shown in Figure 1.8)[a] during a sabbatical year. The war likely took place in late summer (August), because Antiochus's soldiers used the juice of grapes (which ripen in August/September) and mulberries (which ripen in July/August) to arouse the elephants for battle.

Based on 1 Maccabees 6:20, the sabbatical year corresponding to the year in which Herod seized Jerusalem can be computed readily as 5380 JHY (5254 + 18 x 7) or B.C. 36/35. Filmer was the first to point this out.[66]

---

[a] Rome adopted the Julian calendar by adding 90 days in 708 AUC (46 B.C.) to ensure that 709 AUC (45 B.C.) would align with the solar seasons. In other words, the Julian years prior to 46 B.C. don't exist. They are provided in the present study as straight extensions in the Julian calendar mainly for computational and reference purposes. These earlier Julian years will suffice for our discussion. In contrast, the Hebrew calendar is relatively more accurate than the Roman AUC one since its years are based not only on lunar phases but also solar seasons.

Herod the Tyrant

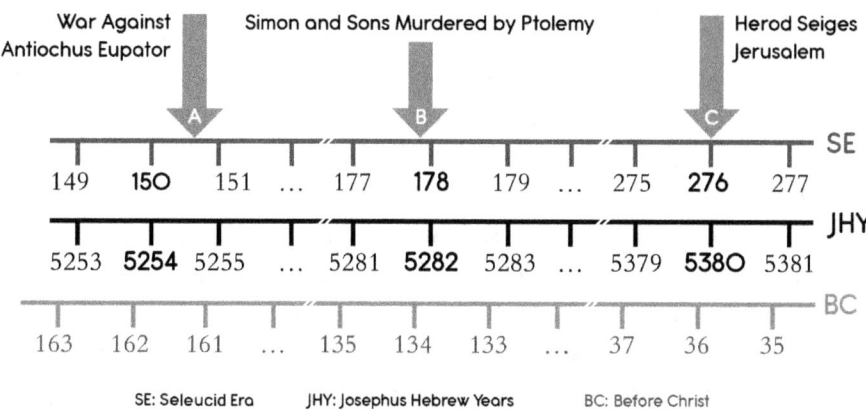

Figure 1.8. The sabbatical years associated with the Jewish war against Antiochus Eupator in 150 S.E. (A), the murder of Simon Hasmonean and his two sons by Ptolemy before the sabbatical year commencement in 178 S.E. (B), and the beginning of Herod's siege of Jerusalem (C).

1.8.3 MURDER OF SIMON AND HIS FAMILY IN 177 S.E.

The murder of Simon Hasmonean and his two sons by his son-in-law Ptolemy in 1 Maccabees 16:14–22 provides a second marker for the sabbatical year:

> Now Simon was visiting the towns of the country and attending to their needs, and he went down to Jericho with his sons Mattathias and Judas, in the one hundred seventy-seventh year [177 S.E.], in the eleventh month, which is the month of Shebat [January/February]. The son of Abubus received them treacherously in the little stronghold called Dok, which he had built; he gave them a great banquet, and hid men there. When Simon and his sons were drunk, Ptolemy and his men rose up, took their weapons, rushed in against Simon in the banquet hall and killed him and his two sons, as well as some of his servants.
>
> ...he [Ptolemy] sent other troops to take possession of Jerusalem and the temple hill. But someone ran ahead and reported to John [Hyrcanus] at Gazara that his father and brothers had perished, and that "he has sent men to kill you also." When he heard this, he was greatly shocked; he seized the men who came to destroy him and killed them. (1 Maccabees 16:14–17, 20–22, NRSVUE)

Josephus also records this murder:

> So Ptolemy retired to one of the fortresses that was above Jericho, which was called Dagon. But Hyrcanus having taken the high priesthood that had been his father's before... and when he [Hyrcanus] made his attacks upon the place... Ptolemy brought them [Hyrcanus's mother and brothers] upon the wall, and tormented them in the sight of all, and threatened that he would throw them down headlong, unless Hyrcanus would leave off the siege... And as the siege was drawn out into length by this means, that year on which the Jews used to rest came on; for the Jews observe this rest every seventh year, as they do every seventh day; so that Ptolemy being for this cause released from the war, he slew the brethren of Hyrcanus, and his mother; and when he had so done, he fled to Zeno, who was called Cotylas, who was then the tyrant of the city Philadelphia.[a]

John Hyrcanus's two brothers and their father Simon were murdered in the month of Shevat/Shebat in 177 S.E., which corresponds to January/February of 134 B.C. By the time Hyrcanus killed the assassins in Gezer, succeeded the priesthood, and gathered the Jews to lay siege to Jericho where Ptolemy took Hyrcanus's mother and other brothers hostage, the sabbatical year 178 S.E. or 5282 JHY would have commenced in Nisan 1 (March/April 134 B.C.), as shown in Figure 1.8.

Obviously, Jews have fought wars in sabbatical years before, like the one mentioned earlier in 1 Maccabees 6:18–60 (150 S.E.).

John kept up the siege for some time. However, due to the shortage of food and the fact that he couldn't bear to see the suffering of his mother and brothers in the hands of his enemies, he let Ptolemy go, perhaps after negotiating for the release of his family. Contrary to his wish, however, Ptolemy killed the hostage before fleeing to the city Philadelphia, which is located in modern-day Turkey.

Based on the fact that John's siege of Jericho took place in a sabbatical year, the subsequent year of 5380 JHY (5282 + 14 x 7), or 36/35 B.C.,[67] when Herod captured Jerusalem, was also a sabbatical year.

Benedict Zuckermann and Donald Blosser have proposed different Julian years in dating the above two Hasmonean dynasty events.[68] They established the chronology of sabbatical years based on the consular year cited by Josephus for Herod's capture of Jerusalem in 37 B.C. and worked their way back.[69] As a result,

---

a Josephus, *Antiquities*, 13.8.1.

they dated the events of 1 Maccabees 6:20 (150 S.E.) as corresponding to 163/162 B.C. instead of 162/161 B.C., and similarly they dated the events of 1 Maccabees 16:14–21 (177 S.E.) as corresponding to 135/134 B.C. instead of 134/133 B.C.

As Filmer pointed out, Zuckermann's argument is circular and therefore invalid.[70] To be fair, this applies to both sides of the argument. More independent evidence is needed to establish the most probable chronology of sabbatical years.

1.8.4 SECOND TEMPLE DESTRUCTION BY TITUS (70 A.D.)

Josephus has tallied the events leading to the final destruction of the second temple by Titus in 70 A.D. These events are summarized in Table 1.4. Note that Hebrew days are reckoned from sundown to sundown.

Table 1.4. Chronology of the second temple destruction in 70 A.D. by Titus.

Date 70 A.D.	Event	Source
Nisan 14 (April 12/13)	Romans pitch their camp around Jerusalem.	*War* 5.13.7
Tammuz 1 (June 27/28)	Jews attempt without success to burn down the banks built by Romans for assaulting the outer walls.	*War* 6.1.3
Tammuz 3 (June 29/30)	Romans assault the inner wall without success after the outer wall fell near the tower of Antonia.	*War* 6.1.6
Tammuz 5 (July 1/2)	Romans gain possession of the inner wall and tower of Antonia.	*War* 6.1.7
Tammuz 17 (July 13/14)	The daily sacrifice ceases. Jews defend the temple mount.	*War* 6.2.1
Tammuz 24 (July 20/21)	The temple and northwest cloisters are set on fire but later quenched.	*War* 6.2.9

Tammuz 27 (July 23/24)	Jews set a fire trap and kill many Romans at the western cloister.	*War* 6.3.1
Ab 8 (August 2/3)	Titus orders his troops to bring in the battering rams on the completed banks against the western edifice of the inner temple. He also orders the temple gates to be set on fire.	*War* 6.4.1
Ab 9 (August 3/4)	Jews gather their whole force together to attack the Romans guarding the outer court of the temple at the east gate.	*War* 6.4.4
Ab 10 (August 4/5)	The temple is burnt down.	*War* 6.4.5

According to Jeremiah, the captain of King Nebuchadnezzar's bodyguard, Nebuzaradan, came to Jerusalem on the tenth day of the fifth month (Ab, July/August) and burnt down the first temple, the palace, and all the important buildings. The army broke down the walls around Jerusalem.[a]

Josephus records,

> But as for that house [temple], God had, for certain, long ago doomed it to the fire; and now that fatal day was come, according to the revolution of ages; it was the tenth day of the month Lous [Ab], upon which it was formerly burnt by the king of Babylon.[b]

Josephus believed that it was by divine decree that both the first and second temples were burnt and destroyed on the same anniversary day, Ab 10. Both Jeremiah and Josephus were eyewitnesses to the destruction of the first and second Jerusalem temples, respectively. It is unbelievable that they could have made a mistake as to the date.

---

a "On the tenth day of the fifth month, in the nineteenth year of Nebuchadnezzar king of Babylon, Nebuzaradan commander of the imperial guard, who served the king of Babylon, came to Jerusalem. He set fire to the temple of the Lord, the royal palace and all the houses of Jerusalem. Every important building he burned down. The whole Babylonian army, under the commander of the imperial guard, broke down all the walls around Jerusalem" (Jeremiah 52:12–14, NIV).

b Josephus, *War*, 6.4.5.

Scholars pointed out long ago that the Mishnah (200 A.D.) identifies the anniversary day to be Ab 9 instead of Ab 10. The passage in the Mishnah reads,

> Five things befell our fathers on the 17th of Tammuz and five on the 9th of Ab. On the 17th of Tammuz the Tables [of the Ten Commandments] were broken, and the Daily Whole-offering ceased, and the City was breached, and Apostomus burnt the [Scrolls of the] Law, and an idol was set up in the Sanctuary. On the 9th of Ab it was decreed against our fathers that they should not enter into the Land [of Israel] and the Temple was destroyed the first and the second time, and Beth-Tor was captured and the City was ploughed up. When Ab comes in, gladness must be diminished.[71]

Similar to the Mishnah, the Jewish religious chronology in Seder Olam compiled around 200 A.D. identifies the anniversary day as Ab 9:

> R. Yose says: A day of rewards attracts rewards and a day of guilt attracts guilt. You find it said that the destruction of the first Temple was at the end of Sabbath, at the end of a Sabbatical year, when the priests of the family of Yehoiariv was officiating, on the Ninth of Ab, and the same happened the second time. Both times the Levites were standing on their podium and sang. Which song did they sing? (Psalm 94:23) "He repaid them for their evil deeds..." The city wall was breached on the Ninth of the Fourth month the first time and on the Seventeenth the second time.[72]

Rabbi Yose states that the day of the first temple destruction happened at the end of a sabbatical year. He said that the same happened to the second temple, which was destroyed on the ninth of Ab, also at the end of a sabbatical year.

Yose's statement that the first temple was destroyed at the end of a sabbatical year remains doubtful. The reason is that Jews were not keeping sabbatical years during the 490 years prior to the destruction of the first temple and exile of Jews to Babylon, according to 2 Chronicles 36:21[a] and Jeremiah

---

a "The land enjoyed its sabbath rests; all the time of its desolation it rested, until the seventy years were completed in fulfillment of the word of the Lord spoken by Jeremiah" (2 Chronicles 36:21, NIV).

25:11–12.[a] So on what basis did Yose assign a sabbatical year to the year of the first temple's destruction when the Jews were observing none?[73] Yose's source of information is unknown, nor is his method of calculation.

For the same reason, other similar statements regarding the year of destruction of the first temple, such as the one found in the Babylonian Talmud,[74] should be taken with caution:

> Whence do we know that the second Temple was also destroyed on the 9th of Ab? We have learned in a Boraitha: "A happy event is credited to the day on which another happy event happened, while a calamity is ascribed to the day when another calamity occurred; and it was said that when the first Temple was destroyed it was on the eve preceding the 9th of Ab, which was also the night at the close of the Sabbath and also the close of the sabbatical year." The watch at the time was that of Jehoyoreb, and the Levites were chanting in their proper places, at that moment reciting the passage [Psalms 94:23]: "And he will bring back upon them their own injustice, and in their own wickedness will he destroy them."

The Babylonian Talmud says that the first temple was destroyed on the eve preceding Ab 9, at the close of the Sabbath and also the close of the sabbatical year. The explanation it gives for the discrepancy between Ab 9 and Ab 10 is that the fire actually started in the evening of the eighth and the first temple was completely burnt down on the tenth.

The destruction of the second temple in 70 A.D., at the end of a sabbatical year on Ab 10 (August 5), according to Seder Olam, is more reliable than the one for the first temple, simply because the event occurred at a time much closer to the era of the rabbis who wrote the manuscripts, around 100–200 A.D., and many of the survivors and their children would have still been around.

Steinmann and Young point out that Rabbi Yose's mentor, Rabbi Akiba, was a young man of about 20 when the second temple was destroyed, thus it is unlikely that Rabbi Yose was mistaken on the matter of the sabbatical year.[75]

Scholars such as Caspari,[76] Steinmann, and Young expound on the accuracy of the translation of Seder Olam from Hebrew to English. The pertinent paragraph

---

a "This whole country will become a desolate wasteland, and these nations will serve the king of Babylon seventy years. 'But when the seventy years are fulfilled, I will punish the king of Babylon and his nation, the land of the Babylonians, for their guilt,' declares the Lord, 'and will make it desolate forever'" (Jeremiah 25:11–12, NIV).

states that "the destruction of the first Temple was at the end of Sabbath, at the end of a sabbatical year." They conclude that this sentence should not be interpreted to mean that "the destruction of the first temple occurred in the year after the sabbatical year." The latter statement is what Zuckermann and Schürer advocate.

According to the rabbinic tallying, the sabbatical year started on Tishri 1 (September/October 69 A.D.) and ended on Elul 29 (August/September 70 A.D.). Ab is the month preceding Elul. Even though the day of the second temple's destruction on Ab 10 was actually about 49 days (20 + 29) before the end of the Talmudic sabbatical year, it would still be fair to say, in a broad sense, that the event happened "at the end of the sabbatical year."

Figure 1.9A illustrates the Scheme BN (Biblical Nisan) approach to the sabbatical year, from Nisan 1 to Adar 29 in 70 A.D., whereas Figure 1.9B displays the Scheme TT (Talmudic Tishri) approach to the sabbatical year, from Tishri 1 to Elul 29.

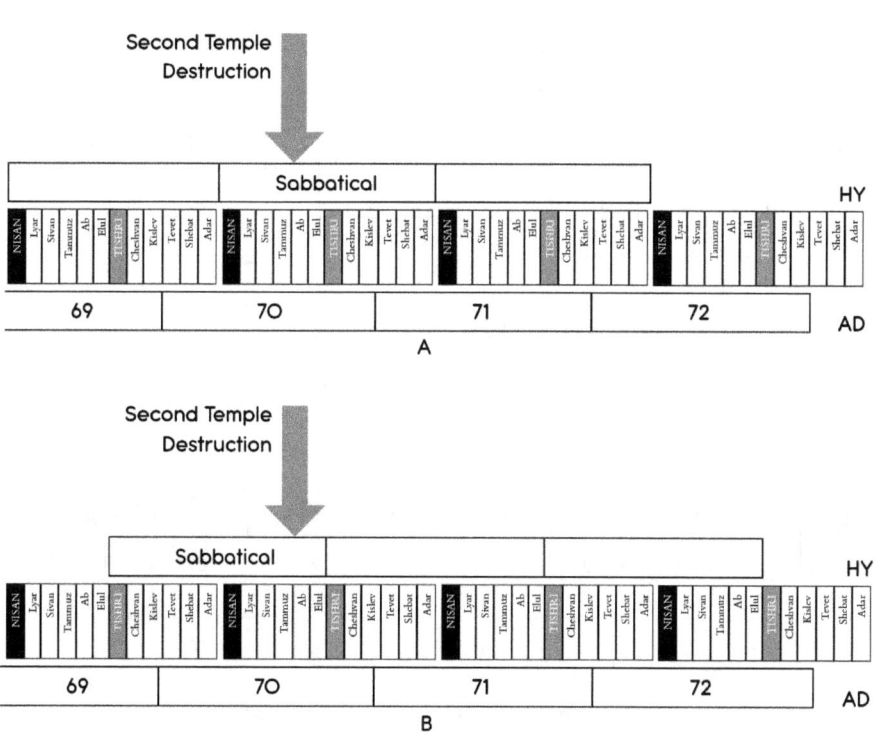

Figure 1.9. Scheme BN: the biblical sabbatical year from Nisan 1 to Adar 29 in 70 A.D. (A). Scheme TT: the Talmudic sabbatical year from Tishri 1 to Elul 29 (B).

The Timing of God's Visitations

No matter which sabbatical scheme one might invoke, Scheme BN differs from the Scheme TT by only six months. As far as the year of the second temple's destruction is concerned, a good portion (about eight to nine months) of the Julian year of 70 A.D. lies within the sabbatical year. The number of years between 36 B.C. and 70 A.D. is 105, with 15 seven-year cycles. This demonstrates that indeed 36 B.C. would also be part of a sabbatical year.

After Herod captured Jerusalem on Tishri 10, the Day of Atonement, in 36 A.D., the sabbatical year was still going on, according to Josephus.[a][77] This statement fully supports the premise that Josephus utilizes Scheme BN, from Nisan 1 to Adar 29, as shown in Figure 1.10A, and not Scheme TT, as shown in Figure 1.10B, which dictates that the sabbatical year would have already ended on Elul 29, 10 days before Herod's capture of Jerusalem, contradicting Josephus's record.

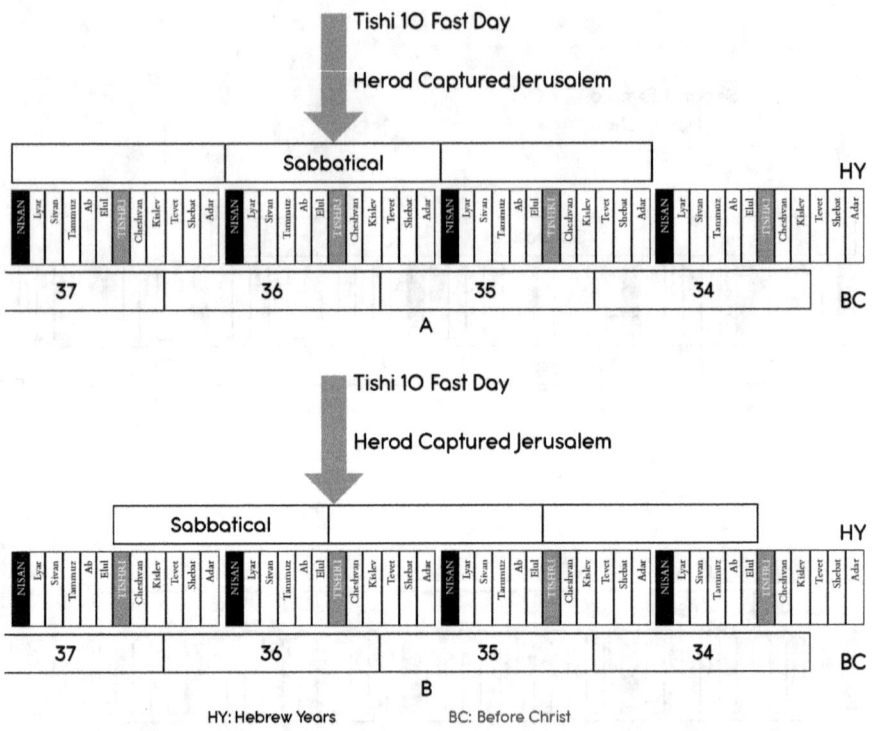

Figure 1.10. Scheme BN: the biblical sabbatical year from Nisan 1 to Adar 29 in 36/35 B.C. (A). Scheme TT: the Talmudic sabbatical year from Tishri 1 to Elul 29 in 37/36 B.C. (B).

---

a Josephus, *Antiquities*, 15.1.2.

Herod the Tyrant

A second Talmudic option, referred as Scheme TT-1 (minus 1 year), places the sabbatical year between 36 and 35 B.C., starting in Tishri, as shown in Figure 1.11A. However, this will cause the sabbatical year in 70/71 A.D. to start about 49 days after the destruction of the second temple, as illustrated in Figure 1.11B. This contradicts the records in Seder Olam and Babylonian Talmud for the second temple's destruction at the end of the sabbatical year. As a result, Scheme TT-1 should be dismissed.

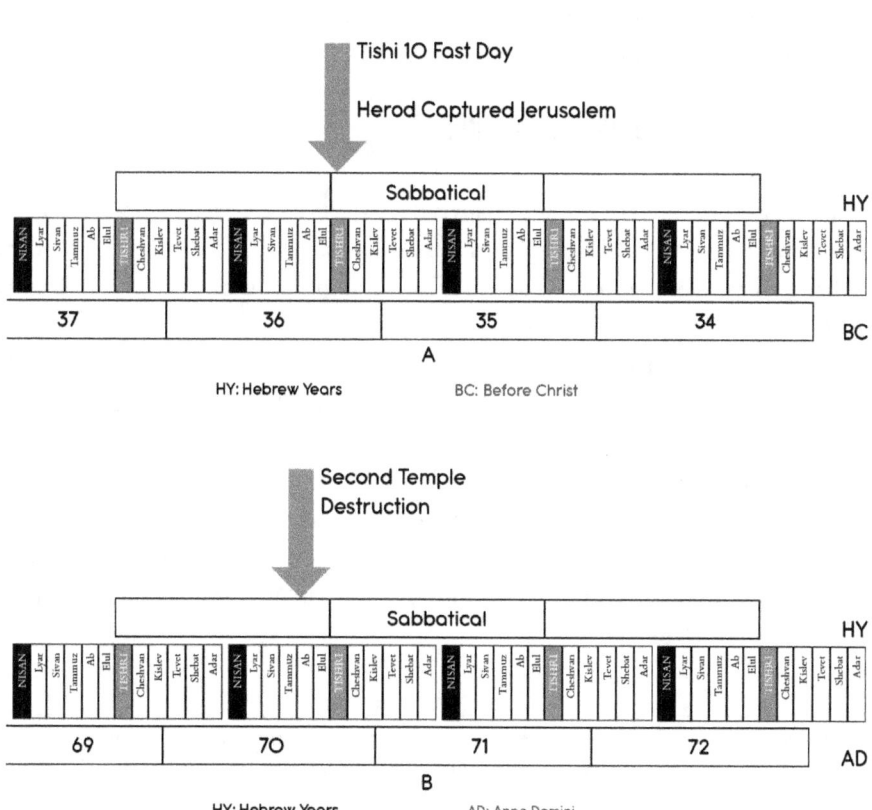

Figure 1.11. Scheme TT-1: the Talmudic sabbatical year from Tishri 1 to Elul 29 in 36/35 B.C. (A). Scheme TT-1: the subsequent Talmudic sabbatical year from Tishri 1 to Elul 29 in 70/71 A.D. (B).

In summary, the above evaluations illustrate that the Talmudic sabbatical year from Tishri to Elul in both Schemes TT and TT-1 conflict with either the timing of the second temple's destruction (Figure 1.10B) or the timing of Herod's

The Timing of God's Visitations

capture of Jerusalem (Figure 1.11B), irrespective of whether the regular Hebrew year starts from Nisan or Tishri.

In contrast, all historical records fall naturally in their places within Scheme BN, which runs from Nisan to Adar.

During the Jewish war against the Romans from 66 to 70 A.D., Jews minted silver and bronze coins with the inscriptions from "year one" to "year four" alongside paleo-Hebrew slogans meaning "Jerusalem the Holy," "freedom of Zion," "redemption of Zion," or "deliverance of Zion."[78] These inscriptions are useful in identifying the periods of archeological finds. We shall refer to them in the following discussion.

1.8.5 BAR KOKHBA WAR AGAINST HADRIAN IN 132 A.D.

Jack Finegan summarized various papyri discoveries in the Wadi Murabba'at caves in the Judean desert.[79] These papyri pertain to the second Jewish revolt led by Shimeon Ben Kosba (Simon Bar Kokhba, meaning "son of star"), who fought against the Roman emperor Hadrian.

Hadrian was born in Rome on January 24, 76 A.D.[80] and died on July 10, 138 A.D.[a] He acceded to the throne on August 11, 117 A.D.[b] and reigned 20 years and 11 months.

According to Dio, the Jews revolted after Hadrian decided to build a colonial city, Aelia Capitolina, over the ruins of Jerusalem and a new temple to Jupiter at the Jewish temple site.[c] Hadrian made this decision during a visit to Judea in A.D. 130. A series of Hadrian's travel coins associated with his visit in Judea were struck prior to the Bar Kokhba War.[81]

---

a "Hadrian was born in Rome on the ninth day before the Kalends of February in the seventh consulship of Vespasian and the fifth of Titus [76 A.D.]" (Magie, *Historia Augusta*, 1.1.3). "He had lived sixty-two years, five months and nineteen days, and had been emperor twenty years and eleven months" (Dio, *Roman History* 69.23.1).

b "On the third day before the Ides of August he received the news of Trajan's death, and this day he appointed as the anniversary of his accession" (Magie, *Historia Augusta*, 1.4.7).

c "At Jerusalem he founded a city in place of the one which had been razed to the ground, naming it Aelia Capitolina, and on the site of the temple of the god he raised a new temple to Jupiter. This brought on a war of no slight importance nor of brief duration, for the Jews deemed it intolerable that foreign races should be settled in their city and foreign religious rites planted there. So long, indeed, as Hadrian was close by in Egypt and again in Syria, they remained quiet, save in so far as they purposely made of poor quality such weapons as they were called upon to furnish, in order that the Romans might reject them and they themselves might thus have the use of them; but when he went farther away, they openly revolted" (Dio, *Roman History*, 69.12.2–3).

Herod the Tyrant

The Jews did not immediately respond militarily to Hadrian's offensive and derogatory decision, but they continued to build up their weaponries, food, and defenses while Hadrian was close by in Egypt and Syria. According to Jerome, a historian and theologian from 347–420 A.D., Hadrian went away to Rome and then Athens in his regnal year 15 (131 A.D.).[a] The following year, 132 A.D., the Jews revolted in either the spring or summer. Jerome used Roman inclusive reckoning to determine Hadrian's regnal years.

In *Commentary on Daniel*, Jerome stated that this Jewish war lasted three years and six months.[b] [82] However, he seemingly contradicted himself in *Chronicle of Hadrian*, in which the Jewish war supposedly lasted only two years between regnal years 16 (132 A.D.) and 18 (134 A.D.).

A papyrus deed known as "Mur 30" was found in a Judean desert cave, and it specifies a date: Tishri 21 of the fourth year of the "redemption of Israel," which corresponds to 136/137 A.D.[83] This period aligns with the second revolt, due to the fact that the slogan during the first revolt from 66 to 70 A.D. was "redemption of Zion" rather than "redemption of Israel."[84] This papyrus demonstrates that Bar Kokhba's revolt might have lasted as long as four years, but definitely not two.

Furthermore, the Caesarean historian Eusebius (260–339 A.D.) wrote,

> The war reached its height in the eighteenth year (134 A.D.) of the reign of Hadrian in Beththera, which was a strong citadel not very far from Jerusalem; the siege lasted a long time before the rebels were driven to final destruction by famine and thirst and the instigator of their madness paid the penalty he deserved.[85]

---

a "15 [regnal year, 131 A.D.] The temple of Rome and Venus built by Hadrian... When Hadrian is spending the winter at Athens, he visits Eleusis. 16 [132 A.D.] Hadrian, when he had constructed many notable buildings in Athens held games and erected a library of wondrous construction. The Jews turned to arms and laid waste Palestine, while Tynius Rufus was in control of the province. Hadrian sent an army to him for the purpose of putting down the rebels... 18 [134 A.D.] The Jewish War, which took place in Palestine, came to an end with the complete suppression of the Jews" (Jerome, *Chronicle*, 282–283).

b "And the [other] three years and six months are accounted for in Hadrian's reign, when Jerusalem was completely destroyed and the Jewish nation was massacred in large groups at a time, with the result that they were even expelled from the borders of Judaea" (Jerome, *Commentary on Daniel*, 109).

Eusebius agrees with Dio on how the war ended. The final tactics used by General Julius Severus to defeat Bar Kokhbar was to shut the Jews up and starve them slowly.[a] Consequently, the revolt likely ended in 135/136 A.D.

A Jewish papyrus contract made between Yehudah and Simon Bar Kokhba in Shevat 20 of the second year of redemption of Israel has been found, among several other documents. Wacholder translated the contract, referred to as "Mur 24E," which mentions the sabbatical cycle in the following way:

> On the twentieth of Shevat of year two of the Redemption of Israel by Shimeon ben Kosba, the Prince of Israel, in the camp which is located in Herodium, Yehudah ben Raba said to Hillel ben Grys: I of my free will have rented from you today the land which is my rental in Ir Nahash which I hold as a tenant from Shimeon, the Prince of Israel, this land I have rented from you from today until the end of the eve of Shemitah [release, sabbatical year], which are years full, fiscal years, five, of tenancy; that I will deliver to you in Herodium: wheat, of good and pure quality, three kors and a lethekh, of which a tenth part of the tithe of these you will deliver to the silo of the treasury. And I am obligated in regard of this matter thusly, Yehudah ben Raba, in person, Shimon ben Kosba, by dictation.[86]

During the three and a half years of war with the Romans, from 132 to 135 A.D., the Bar Kokhba government minted several series of silver and bronze coins. These coins were struck with carefully worded slogans.[87] The previous Hasmonean and Herodian governments had been forbidden by Rome from minting silver coins. Obviously, the silver coins struck during the two Jewish wars against the Romans (66–70 A.D. and 132–135 A.D.) were used to make a political statement of Jewish independence.[88]

The silver and bronze coins of the Bar Kokhba revolt were inscribed with paleo-Hebrew slogans such as "year one of the redemption of Israel," "year two of the freedom [or redemption] of Israel [or Jerusalem]",[89] and "for the freedom of Jerusalem" in year three.[90]

---

a "First of these was Julius Severus, who was dispatched from Britain, where he was governor, against the Jews. Severus did not venture to attack his opponents in the open at any one point, in view of their numbers and their desperation, but by intercepting small groups, thanks to the number of his soldiers and his under-officers, and by depriving them of food and shutting them up, he was able, rather slowly, to be sure, but with comparatively little danger, to crush, exhaust and exterminate them. Very few of them in fact survived" (Dio, *Roman History*, 69.13.2–3).

Herod the Tyrant

Wacholder dates the beginning of the Bar Kokhba rebellion and the first year of the redemption at 132/133 A.D. (or 5547 JHY). On the other hand, Zuckermann and Blosser date "year one of redemption of Israel" at 131/132 A.D.[91] (or 5546 JHY).

The followers of Bar Kokhba regarded him as the star promised in Numbers 24:17.[a] According to Wacholder, reputable Rabbi Akiba supported Bar Kokhba and called him "King, Messiah" during the war.[92] Bar Kokhba would likely have closely followed the Old Testament instructions and non-inclusive reckoning of Hebrew calendar years. The year of the revolt on 5547 JHY (132/133 B.C.) would have been his accession year. The Roman armies were regrouping after heavy losses at this time and awaiting reinforcement and instructions from Hadrian, who was away.[93]

Bar Kokhba's first regnal year would have been 5548 JHY (133/134 B.C.), a biblical sabbatical year, a year of release and liberation for Israel starting on Nisan. So as far as Bar Kokhba's first regnal year is concerned, it was a year of freedom with peace and joy in the land, which fits the meaning of Shemitah: the release from all kinds of bondages in a biblical sabbatical year.

Unfortunately, it was a short-lived time of peace before a violent storm, for Hadrian soon recalled General Julius Severus from Britain to handle the Jewish crisis in Judea.

The "Mur 24E" contract was signed on Shebat/Shevat 20 of year two of the redemption of Israel, corresponding to January/February of 135 A.D. (or 5549 JHY), as shown in Figure 1.12. The subsequent year 5550 would have been the first of the five consecutive cultivating years. The contract terminated on the eve of a new sabbatical year, Adar 29, 5554 JHY.

From 5548 JHY (133/134 A.D.) to 5380 JHY (36/35 B.C.), there are 168 years with 24 sabbatical-year cycles. In other words, this supports the premise that 5380 JHY (36/35 B.C.) indeed was a sabbatical year when Herod captured Jerusalem.

---

a "I see him, but not now; I look at him, but not near; a star shall appear from Jacob, a scepter shall rise from Israel, and shall smash the forehead of Moab, and overcome all the sons of Sheth" (Numbers 24:17).

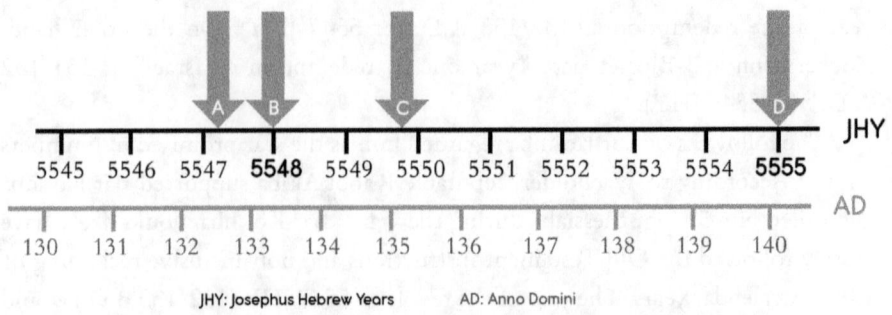

Figure 1.12. The revolt led by Bar Kokhba (A). Year one of the biblical sabbatical year on Nisan 1 (B). The "Mur 24E" land rental contract was signed on Shevat 20 (January/February), "year two of the redemption of Israel" (C). The rental contract was to be terminated on the eve of the following sabbatical year (D).

1.8.6 ZOAR TOMBSTONES 20, 22, 23, 30

A number of Jewish tombstones with epitaphs were found in an ancient cemetery near Zoar, on the southeastern side of the Dead Sea shore, which today is Ghor es-Safi in Jordan.[94] Only a small number of the tombstones have survived theft and antiquity trading.

Table 1.5 presents four epitaphs that were either painted or inscribed on tombstones, including authentic, original, and unmended dates of death in terms of the sabbatical-year cycle. They all reference the year of the second temple's destruction (70 A.D.) as the datum, because the temple was destroyed in a sabbatical year (see Figure 1.9). These tombstones attest to the fact that there exists no discontinuity with respect to the sequence of sabbatical year counts since 70 A.D., and even after the Bar Kokhba revolt in 135 A.D.

For example, as inscribed on Tombstone 20, Jacob died on Shebat 10, 346 years from the destruction of the second temple. This was the third year in the sabbatical cycle. In other words, the sabbatical year is number 343, corresponding to 413/414 B.C. in the Julian calendar. The last completed sabbatical cycle is number 49 [(346 - 3)/7] from 70 A.D. The sabbatical cycle in which Jacob died was number 50. The month of Shebat falls in January/February.

Herod the Tyrant

The authentic, unmended, and independent dates on the Zoar tombstones confirm that 36 B.C. and 70 A.D. were indeed among the sabbatical years. But one important question remains: what scheme of sabbatical year and regular Hebrew year was utilized by the Jews who fabricated these tombstones?

Table 1.5. Unmended dates of death of original Jewish epitaphs from Zoar: Tombstones 20, 22, 23,[95] and 30.[96]

Tombstone	20	22	23	30
Epitaph Inscription	May rest the soul of Jacob the son of Shem'o who died on the second day, the 10th day of the month Shebat, in the 3rd year of the sabbatical cycle, the year three hundred and 46 (of the) years after the destruction of the Temple. May he wake up to the voice of the announcer of peace	May rest the soul of Rabbi Simon Birabi, who died (on) the fourth day, the third day of the month Adar in the seventh year of the Shemita which is the year three hundred and eighty and five years after the destruction of the Temple May he rest (as) a sage in peace May he wake up to the voice of the announcer of peace	May r[es]t the soul of Yehuda the priest he son of Ab[...]ma who died (on) the third day of the month Kislev, in the fifth year of the sabbatical cycle which is the year three hundred and 90 years after the destruction of the Temple. May he hold the altar and wake up to the voice of the announcer of peace. Peace, peace, peace.	This is the tombstone of Hannah daughter of Ha[nie?]l the priest, who died on the Sabbath, the first festival day of Passover, on the fifteenth day of the month of Nisan, in the fifth year of the sabbatical cycle, which is the year three hundred and sixty nine years after the destruction of the Temple. Peace. May her soul rest. Peace.
Decease Date	Shebat 10	Adar 3	Kislev 3	Nisan 15

55

The Timing of God's Visitations

Year of sabbatical cycle	3rd	7th	5th	5th
Year after Temple Destruction	346	385	390	369
Last sabbatical year	343 (413/414 A.D.)	385 (455/456 A.D.)	385 (455/456 A.D.)	364 (434/435 A.D.)
No. of full sabbatical cycle from 70 A.D.	49	55	55	52
sabbatical cycle No. for year of death	50	55	56	53

Figure 1.13 presents the Scheme BN approach, in which both the regular Hebrew year and sabbatical year start from Nisan. The Hebrew year 343 from 70 A.D. corresponds to 413/414 A.D., and Jacob's date of death fits well with Scheme BN.

However, due to the alteration of the Jewish calendar by the rabbis after 135 A.D., Scheme BN might have no longer been used in the fourth century A.D. Thus, we will examine other sabbatical year schemes in the Jewish calendar for the post-135 A.D. era.

There exists one obvious Talmudic sabbatical year scheme which doesn't work with the date of death inscribed on Tombstone 20, as shown in Figure 1.14. We call this Scheme TT-RN, in which the sabbatical year begins in Tishri but the regular year starts in Nisan.

Herod the Tyrant

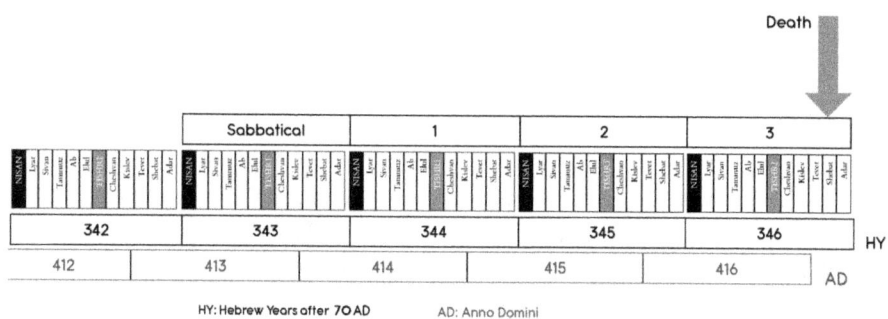

Figure 1.13. Scheme BN: Tombstone 20 with Jacob's date of death on Shebat 10, 346 years after the destruction of second temple, in the third year of the sabbatical cycle.

If the sabbatical year began in Tishri of 342 HY and the regular year started in Nisan of 343 HY, then Jacob's date of death on Shebat 10 of 346 HY would have fallen in year four, not year three, of the sabbatical cycle.

In fact, the same thing can be said about Tombstone 23, with Yehuda's date of death being recorded as Kislev 3[a] of 390 HY. This would lie outside year five of the sabbatical cycle.

Thus, we may conclude that Scheme TT-RN fails as an option to have been in use by the Jews at Zoar in the period of the fourth century A.D.

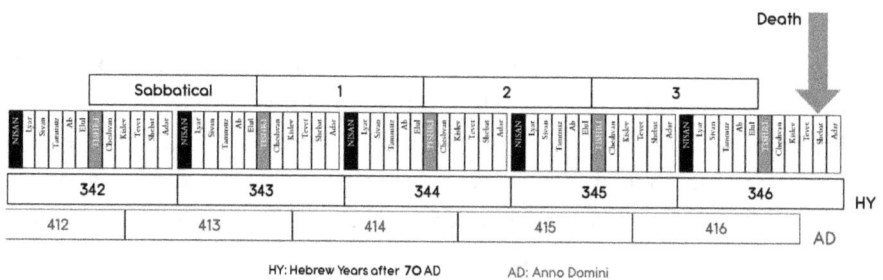

Figure 1.14. Scheme TT-RN: Tombstone 20 with Jacob's date of death on Shebat 10, 346 years after the destruction of second temple, lying outside the third year of the sabbatical cycle.

---

a Kislev occurs in November/December.

The Timing of God's Visitations

If the sabbatical year began on Tishri in the middle of year 343, as shown in Figure 1.15, then the date of Jacob's death would occur inside the third year of the sabbatical cycle. We call this Scheme TT-1-RN.

However, as pointed out in the discussion of Figure 1.11B, Scheme TT-1 (which is the same as Scheme TT-1–RN) would result in a sabbatical year in 70/71 A.D., starting about 49 days after the destruction of the second temple, not at the end of it as rendered by Seder Olam and the Babylonian Talmud.

Thus, both Schemes TT-1 and TT-1–RN should also be dismissed.

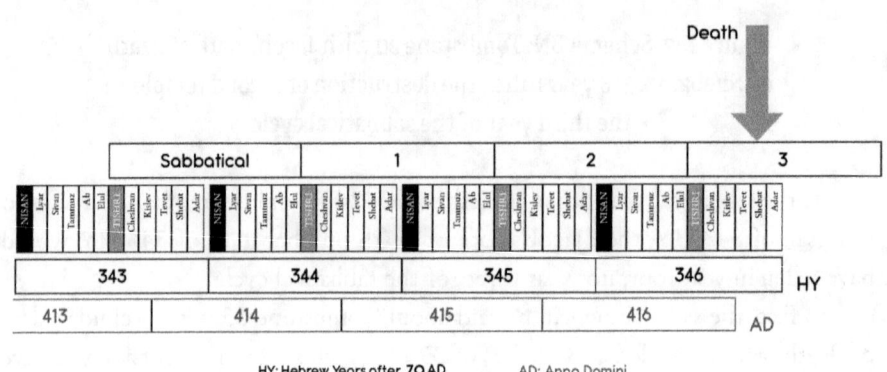

HY: Hebrew Years after 70 AD   AD: Anno Domini

Figure 1.15. Scheme TT-1-RN: Tombstone 20 with Jacob's date of death on Shebat 10, 346 years after the destruction of second temple, in the third year of the sabbatical cycle.

The last option, as advocated by rabbis in the Talmudic era (200–500 A.D.), is the scheme in which both the sabbatical year and the civil Hebrew year begin with Tishri, as shown in Figure 1.16. We call this Scheme TT-CT (Civil Tishri).

This scheme is adequate for reckoning in the new Jewish calendar. However, such relabeling causes the disappearance of six Hebrew months somewhere between 135 A.D. and 500 A.D.

The Jews shifted the Hebrew calendar backward in time from Nisan to Tishri to ensure covering the day of the second temple's destruction on Ab 10 (August 5) in the sabbatical year of 70 A.D., as shown in Figure 1.9B. This is substantiated by the fact that all of the Zoar tombstones attributed their datum for the sabbatical year count to 70 A.D. A consequence of such a backward shift of six months from Nisan to Tishri results in contradicting Josephus's statement that a sabbatical year was still ongoing after Herod capturing Jerusalem on the day of the fast on Tishri 10, the Day of Atonement, as illustrated in Figure 1.10B. The sabbatical year would have ended before Herod's capture.[a]

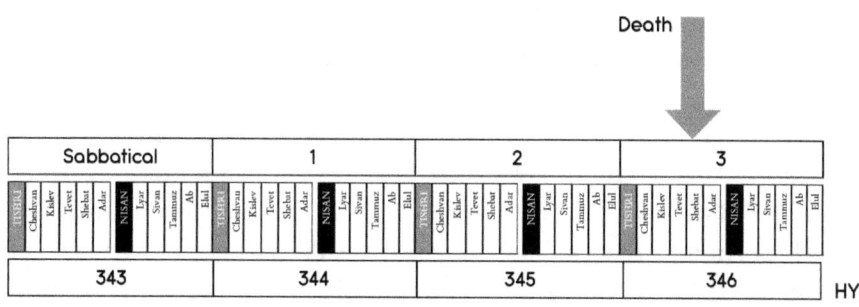

Figure 1.16. Scheme TT-CT: Tombstone 20 with Jacob's date of death on Shebat 10, 346 years after the destruction of second temple, in the third year of the sabbatical cycle.

The sabbatical years marked on these four Zoar tombstones occurred more than 200 years after the Bar Kokhba revolt. In the span from 410 to 460 A.D., the official head of the year, Rosh Hashana, for both the regular Hebrew year and the sabbatical year, had evidently been moved from Nisan to Tishri by the rabbis.

Ever since, Jews have regarded Nisan as marking the beginning of an annual religious cycle of festivals, as is observed in modern times. This concurs with the passage in the Babylonian Talmud (200–500 A.D.), which says,

> In the present time we count the years from Tishri; were we then to say that our Era is connected with the Exodus it is surely Nisan that we ought to count. Does this not prove that our reckoning is based on the reign of the Greek kings [and not on the Exodus]? That indeed proves it.[97]

1.8.7 SABBATICAL YEAR EARTHQUAKE IN 749 A.D.

Margalioth found a reference to a major earthquake that occurred in a sabbatical year around Shevat 23, in the year 679 after the destruction of the second temple.[98]

---

a See Figure 1.10B.

The date was recorded in a book of prayer stored in the Ben Ezra Synagogue's geniza in Cairo regarding a fast for the land of Israel. Many cities fell during the earthquake and suffered extensive casualties.

The Hebrew month Shevat corresponds to the Julian month January/February, and the duration of 679 years is fully divisible by seven (679 / 7 = 97), meaning that year 70 A.D. of the temple's destruction was also a sabbatical year. Consequently, this substantiates the premise that the sabbatical year in which Herod captured Jerusalem was indeed 36 B.C., as discussed earlier.

Shevat 23 in 749 A.D. (649 + 70) corresponds to about January 18, 749 A.D. in the Julian calendar. This date corroborates the one used in a liturgical poem called "Seventh Earthquake" or "Earthquake of the Seventh," referring to a fast on Shevat 23 for lamenting the disaster in Tiberias due to an earthquake in a sabbatical year.[99]

Tsafrir and Foerster provide further archaeological and numismatic evidence that support the 749 A.D. date of the earthquake taking place during a sabbatical year.[100]

1.8.8 GAIUS CAESAR CALIGULA'S STATUE (40/41 A.D.)

It has been known for quite some time that a temporal conflict exists between the historical timing of the episode of Gaius Caesar Caligula's demand to erect his statue in the Jerusalem temple and the Zuckermann-Blosser scheme, with Tishri 38/37 being a sabbatical year.[101] Even though Schürer acknowledged the presence of such a firm contradiction with his hypothesis, he still chose to adopt Zuckermann-Blosser's list of sabbatical years, and they took 37 B.C. to be the sabbatical year in which Herod captured Jerusalem.

Caligula was born on August 31, 12 A.D. and succeeded Tiberius as emperor.[a] [102] His ascension day was March 16, 37 A.D. He reigned for three years, ten months, and eight days[b] and was stabbed to death on January 24, 41 A.D.[c]

Near the end of Caligula's reign, he commissioned Petronius to be the governor of Syria, and he ordered Petronius in writing to erect a statue of

---

a "Caius [Caligula] Caesar was born on the day before the calends [31st August] of September, at the time his father and Caius Fonteius Capito were consuls [12 B.C.]" (Suetonius, *Caligula*, 8).

b "He lived twenty-nine years, and reigned three years, ten months, and eight days" (Suetonius, *Caligula*, 59).

c "On the ninth of the calends of February [24th January]… As he lay on the ground, crying out that he was still alive, the rest dispatched him with thirty wounds" (Suetonius, *Caligula*, 58).

him inside the second temple at Jerusalem and use force if the Jews resisted. He believed he was a god who deserved to be worshiped by all his subjects, including the Jews.

Josephus and Philo of Alexandria record a good deal of detail about Caligula's statue saga.[a] [103]

Petronius led two Roman legions and a great number of auxiliaries into the port city of Ptolemais, in modern-day Lebanon, where they were met with a multitude of Jews who had come to petition Caligula's demand. The meeting possibly occurred around fall (September/October) of 40 A.D.

Afterwards, Petronius and company went to Tiberias, where thousands of peaceful Jews threw their faces down and stretched out their necks to show their determination to be slain rather than see their temple site desecrated. The Jews did this together for 40 days. Meanwhile, it was the fall season and they were required to till the land and sow seeds for the next year's crop.[b]

Petronius took pity on the Jews and decided to write to Caligula, updating him on the progress, informing him of the dire determination of the Jews, and appealing for him to reconsider. According to Philo, Petronius even used stalling tactics, such as ordering Caligula's oversized statue to be fabricated by the finest craftsmen in Sidon, however long it took.

Petronius dismissed all the Jews to catch up with their tilling and sowing in the fall of 40 A.D. Thus, 40/41 A.D. could not have been a sabbatical year.

In Rome, Caligula fumed over Petronius's letter. According to Josephus, Caligula replied as follows:

> Seeing thou esteemest the presents made thee by the Jews to be of greater value than my commands, and art grown insolent enough to be subservient to their pleasure, I charge thee to become thy own judge, and to consider what thou art to do, now thou art under my displeasure; for I will make thee an example to the present and to all future ages, that they may not dare to contradict the commands of their emperor.[c]

---

a Josephus, *War*, 2.10.1–5; *Antiquities*, 18.8.1–9.

b "So they threw themselves down upon their faces, and stretched out their throats, and said they were ready to be slain; and this they did for forty days together, and in the mean time left off the tilling of their ground, and that while the season of the year required them to sow it" (Josephus, *Antiquities*, 18.8.3).

c Josephus, *Antiquities*, 18.8.8.

Philo adds that at the end of the letter, Caligula told Petronius to prioritize the speedy dedication of the statue before everything else.[a]

Caligula's letter amounts to a death sentence to Petronius if he didn't carry out the order. However, Petronius didn't receive this letter while Caligula still lived. The ship carrying the letter was detained at sea for three months due to a storm,[b] while the news of Caligula's death reached Petronius first. Caligula was stabbed to death by his Praetorian guards, Cassius Chaerea, Cornelius Sabinus, and others on January 24, 41 A.D.[104]

The saga of Caligula's statue as a historic testimony that 40/41 A.D. (or 5455 JHY) was not a sabbatical year, and therefore neither was 38/37 B.C. (or 5378 JHY). Both numbers differ by 77 years, which amounts to 11 cycles of seven years. This authentic historical evidence essentially disproves the hypothesis of the Zuckermann-Blosser-Schürer consensus, which states that 38/37 B.C. was the sabbatical year after which Herod captured Jerusalem.

1.9 SUMMARY

In summary, based on the information provided by Josephus, Luke, Dio, Appian, Plutarch, Jerome, Eusebius, Jewish Seder Olam, Mishnah, Talmuds, 1 Maccabees, the Jewish land leasing contract "Mur 24E" between Yehudah and Bar Kokhba within a sabbatical cycle, the Zoar tombstone epitaphs, and a Jewish book of prayer regarding a fast in January 18, 749 A.D. regarding an earthquake in a sabbatical year in Judea, we conclude that Herod was appointed king of the Jews by the Roman Senate around October 39 B.C., that he captured Jerusalem in September of 36 B.C., and that he died around January 27 of 1 B.C.

The interval between the captures of Jerusalem by Pompey and Herod is precisely 27 Hebrew years. In *Antiquities,* Josephus put down the consular year of Agrippa and Gallus (37 B.C.) for Herold's capture of Jerusalem, thus suiting his Roman audiences, who commonly used the Roman convention of inclusive reckoning. Subsequently, he had to report the consular year of Domitius Calvinus and Asinius Pollio (40 B.C.) for Herod's accession three years earlier, instead of Marcius Censorinus and Calvisius Sabinus in 39 B.C.

Caesar Augustus approved Antipater's succession to Herod's throne in late 4 B.C. After Antipater was convicted for his parricide plot in the fall of 2 B.C., Herod divided his kingdom among his three remaining sons. Aside from demoting

---

a Philo, *Legatio Ad Gaium,* 260.

b Josephus, *War,* 2.10.5.

Archelaus from a client king to an ethnarch, Caesar endorsed Herod's revised testament, replacing the previous flawed one. Most likely he granted Herod's sons the right to officially antedate their accession year to 4 B.C., remedying Herod's mistake of choosing Antipater in the first place and filling the void in 4/1 B.C. in the Roman official record of Judean governance.

The Schürer consensus holds that Herod died between March 13 and April 11 in 4 B.C. However, the 29 days that occurred during this period are clearly insufficient for all the events mentioned by Josephus to have taken place. If Herod died around January 27, 1 B.C., then all the events, including Herod's death and funeral, fit comfortably within the 88-day period that elapses between January 10 and April 7 in 1 B.C.

Table 1.6 lists the major contradictions between the Schürer consensus and the historical records. The basis of the Schürer consensus is a faulty one indeed.

Table 1.6. Summary of contradictions between the Schürer consensus and historical records.

Schürer Consensus	Contradiction	Source
1. Josephus uses inclusive reckoning for dating events in his books.	Josephus uses non-inclusive reckoning for the reign of the Hasmonean dynasty for a total of 126 actual years.	Josephus, *Antiquities*, 12.11.2, 20.10.1.
	Josephus tallies 28 high priests from the days of Herod to the destruction of the second temple in a total of 107 actual years using non-inclusive reckoning.	Josephus, *Antiquities*, 20.10.1.
2. The Roman Senate appoints Herod to be the king of the Jews in the consular year of D. Calvinus and A. Pollio in the fall of 40 B.C.	Herod's investiture cannot happen before 39 B.C., because Herod and others were granted client kingships by the Roman Senate after the treaty of Misenum in the summer/fall of 39 B.C. and shortly before the arrival of winter.	Plutarch, *LA*, 31.3–32.4; Dio, *RH*, 48.36.1–48.40.6; Appian, *RH* IV, 5.72–75.

3. Josephus uses the consular year of M. Agrippa and C. Gallus in 37 B.C. to mark the year when Herod and Sosius captured Jerusalem.	Dio states that Sosius and his armies did nothing in 37 B.C.	Dio, *RH*, 49.23.1.
4. Herod's reign starts at his capture of Jerusalem in 37 B.C.	Josephus regards Herod's reign as starting right after his appointment in Rome.	Josephus, *War*, 1.14.4.
	Herod considers his ascension of kingship to have officially started when he was appointed a client king by the Roman Senate, because his first set of coins is dated "year three," commemorating his capture of Jerusalem. The coins aren't dated "year four," as required by the Schürer consensus.	Filmer.[105]
5. Herod dies sometime between Nisan 1–14 in 4 B.C.	The mere 14 or fewer days are insufficient to accommodate all the events that happened between Herod's death and burial as documented by Josephus. The extreme minimum period would be 16 days.	Josephus, *Antiquities*, 17.8.1–17.9.3.
6. Herod's sons reckon the start of their reigns from the death of Herod in 4 B.C.	So far, no regnal year one coin has been found for Herod's heirs—namely Archelaus, Antipater, and Philip. In spite of hundreds of their coins having been discovered, the earliest dated coins are year four from Antipater, and year five from Philip.	Steinmann and Young.[106]

7. Zuckermann's sabbatical year calendar dates the year of Herod's conquest of Jerusalem in the sabbatical year of 38t/37t B.C.*	The Seder Olam, Mishnad, Talmuds, Zoar tombstones, and fast for earthquake on Shevat 23 in 749 A.D. testify that 70/71 A.D. and consequently 36/35 B.C. are sabbatical years, and definitely not 38t/37t B.C.	Mishnad Taanith 4.6; Seder Olam;[107] the Babylonian Talmud;[108] Tombstones;[109] Margalioth.[110]
	Caligula demands that his statue be erected in the Jerusalem temple in 40 A.D. The Jews sow seeds in Tishri/Cheshvan of 40 A.D., which means that 40/41 A.D. and consequently 38/37 B.C. were not sabbatical years; neither was 38t/37t B.C.	Josephus, *War* 2.10.1–5; *Antiquities*, 18.8.1–9; Philo, *LAG*, 260.

*38t/37t B.C. represents the Hebrew year from Tishri in 38 B.C. to Tishri in 37 B.C.

Note the following abbreviations: LA (*Life of Antony*), NH (*Natural History*), RH (*Roman History*), and LAG (*Legatio ad Gaium*).

Temple Treasure Plunderers

Chapter Two

2.1 SABINUS, CAESAR'S PROCURATOR

Chronologically, Josephus introduced Quinctilius Varus into his Jewish history when Varus succeeded Saturninus as governor of Syria and presided over Antipater's hearing in Jerusalem. After the death of Herod the Great, and before the departure of Herod's sons to Rome, Varus and Archelaus intercepted Sabinus, procurator of Syria,[a] at Caesarea and advised him not to go to Jerusalem to secure Herod's assets in that troublesome time. Sabinus agreed to stand down and wait in Caesarea.[b]

Josephus used two other titles for Sabinus: Caesar's Steward for Syrian Affairs[c] and Caesar's Procurator.[d] In other words, Sabinus was a special envoy charged directly by Caesar to administer his financial interests in Syria; he wasn't subject to the authority of Varus, legate of Syria, even though he ranked lower than Varus.

According to Josephus, Sabinus repudiated his agreement subsequent to Archelaus sailing to Rome and Varus leaving Jerusalem. During Sabinus's efforts to secure Herod's assets in Jerusalem, his troops infuriated the Jews who were there for the festival of Pentecost. The Jews fought the Roman soldiers, who set fire to the cloisters and plundered the temple treasury. This happened shortly

---

a Josephus, *War*, 2.2.2.

b Josephus, *Antiquities*, 17.9.3.

c Ibid., 17.9.3.

d Ibid., 17.10.1.

before Pentecost.[a]

Such an instance serves as an additional means of gauging the suitability of the two proposed years for Herod's death, namely 4 and 1 B.C.

2.2 MAIL BY LAND AND SEA

Postal deliveries by horsemen on land were more reliable than by ship, because the weather at sea could be unpredictable. If a ship sank, the message likely wouldn't reach its destination. Furthermore, depending on the season and boarding location, the sea voyage may have taken longer than land transport due to treacherous weather and unfavorable wind conditions.[111]

In some cases, urgent messages would be sent both by land and sea, seeking the safest and quickest arrival. The news of Herod's death was likely sent to Rome by land only, since it wouldn't have been in Herod's sons' best interest to let Caesar know as soon as possible, because Caesar would probably have then sent an envoy to secure the assets of the deceased as a routine procedure. The news was likely sent to Rome by regular mail overland. As long as it could arrive safely, that was all that mattered.

Caesar Augustus created a state-run Roman courier service, the Cursus Publicus, to transport items such as official letters, military hardware, and tax revenue through his vast network of Roman roads.[112] According to Suetonius, Augustus abandoned early in his reign the nonstop courier system in which tired horses and messengers were switched out with new ones at each relay station. Instead he favored the slower post-chaises system of using a single messenger to complete the entire journey.[113] This had the advantage of enabling the recipient to question the messenger for additional information, if required.[b] For urgent

---

a "But on the approach of Pentecost, which is a festival of ours, so called from the days of our forefathers, a great many ten thousands of men got together; nor did they come only to celebrate the festival, but out of their indignation at the madness of Sabinus, and at the injuries he offered them… And this sort of fight lasted a great while, till at last the Romans, who were greatly distressed by what was done, set fire to the cloisters so privately, that those that were gotten upon them did not perceive it… But as to those that retired behind the same way by which they ascended, and thereby escaped, they were all killed by the Romans… The Romans also rushed through the fire, where it gave them room so to do, and seized on that treasure where the sacred money was deposited; a great part of which was stolen by the soldiers, and Sabinus got openly four hundred talents" (Josephus, *Antiquities*, 17.10.2).

b "To enable what was going on in each of the provinces to be reported and known more speedily and promptly, he at first stationed young men at short intervals along the military roads, and afterwards post-chaises. The latter has seemed the more convenient arrangement, since the same men who bring the dispatches from any place can, if occasion demands, be questioned as well"

messages, the mail-bearers would switch tired horses with fresh ones at every relay station.

The average speed in delivering mail by post-chaises messengers was about 50 Roman miles per day, which is equivalent to about 45 English miles per day, since one Roman mile corresponds to about 0.9 of an English mile.[114] The fastest speed, reserved for delivering very urgent messages, could have been 60 Roman miles per day, or 54 English miles per day.[115] The distance between Rome and Jerusalem is about 2,500 English miles on land. Thus, it would have taken an average of 56 days for regular mail, or a speedy 46 days for express mail, to be delivered from Jerusalem to Rome, and vice versa.

The imperial port near Rome, Portus Ostia, was about 1,325 nautical miles from Caesarea, passing through the Strait of Messina. Under the most favorable wind conditions, a Roman ship could sail from Rome eastward at six knots.[116] In general, the ancient sailing ships under a good wind condition could travel at a speed between 4.5 and six knots.[117] However, for a relative long voyage over 10 days for a distance of 1,325 nautical miles, the average sailing speed of an average vessel under average wind condition should have been in the order of about four knots.

Sabinus and his troops would have required a minimum of 18 days for the trip from Rome to Caesarea, including one day for briefing and receiving Augustus's order, one day for assembling the soldiers and servants, one day for trip preparation for everyone involved, one day for travelling from Rome to Portus Ostia and boarding the ships, and 14 days for sailing at four knots to reach Caesarea—for a total of 18 days.

The compiled sailing data from ancient records in Mediterranean Sea by Lionel Casson shows that a southeast downwind sailing from Rome to Caesarea would take 10 to 15 days.[118] The average of these values is about 13 days. In other words, instead of 18 days based on average wind and ship sailing at four knots, Sabinus could have instead reached Caesarea from Rome in 17 (13 + 4) days.

According to Casson, vessels sailing through passage from Caesarea to Rome facing northwest upwind would take 55 to 72 days, which matches or is longer than the regular mail delivery overland of about 56 days.[119]

If Herod had died on Shebat 2 during a festival noted in the Jewish Megillat

---

(Suetonius, *The Lives of the Twelve Caesars*, 2.49).

The Timing of God's Visitations

Taanit,[a] [120] then his death would have occurred on about January 27, 1 B.C., 17 days after the lunar eclipse on January 10. The news of Herod's death was likely sent to Rome the next day. A minimum of 73 (56 + 17) days would have been necessary for Sabinus to mobilize his troops into Caesarea after Herod's death.[b] In other words, the date on which Sabinus could have appeared in Caesarea was April 10, 1 B.C.

2.3 MEETING OF ARCHELAUS, VARUS, AND SABINUS

Archelaus was still in Jerusalem managing the aftermath of slaughtering 3,000 Jews just before Passover on April 7, 1 B.C. After learning the news that Sabinus had landed in Caesarea on April 10, 1 B.C., and following the advice of his councilor Ptolemy, Archelaus sent a request for Varus's assistance. Varus had been stationed at his Syrian headquarters in Antioch, Syria.[c]

It would have taken a minimum of 12 days for Varus and his troops to appear in Caesarea. Antioch was about 350 English miles from Caesarea. An express delivery messenger would have required at least six days to reach Antioch, and about six days or more to return to Caesarea with Varus and his four cavalries; his three legions of foot soldiers would have arrived about a week later. Thus, a possible date for Varus and Archelaus meeting Sabinus is April 22, 1 B.C. During the meeting, Sabinus agreed to stand down and abide in Caesarea.[121]

After the departure of Archelaus to Rome, Varus went first to Jerusalem to punish the captured insurgent Jews who had revolted just prior to Passover. He also advised Philip to go to Rome to claim his rightful share of the inheritance

---

a Herod's death on January 26/27 may be inferred from Shebat 2 of an unnamed festival with no explanation in the Jewish Megillat Taanit (Scroll of Fasting). Many scholars ascribe it to commemorating the death of Herod. Note that Jewish days are reckoned from sundown to sundown.

b One could argue that Sabinus, assuming that he had been stationed in Syria, had been preauthorized by Augustus to secure any client king's assets once they passed away, because a portion of the tax revenue in the local treasury would belong to Rome. It's important to note that Sabinus was Caesar's Steward for Syrian Affairs, not Judean affairs. He had no jurisdiction in Judea unless authorized by Caesar. In the case of Archelaus's exile in 6 A.D., Augustus charged Quirinius directly to secure Archelaus's assets promptly. Thus, it is fair to assume that Sabinus would have needed to receive Augustus's direct order before taking any action.

c "This was foreseen by Varus, who accordingly, after Archelaus was sailed, went up to Jerusalem to restrain the promoters of the sedition, since it was manifest that the nation would not be at rest; so he left one of those legions which he brought with him out of Syria in the city, and went himself to Antioch" (Josephus, *War*, 2.3.1). Note: the fact that Varus brought almost all his armies with him from Syria to Jerusalem indicates that he was at his command center in Antioch when Archelaus's request arrived.

before Caesar.ª Varus would have spent at least three weeks ensuring relative calm in Jerusalem before returning to Antioch, likely around May 18, 1 B.C. He left one legion in Jerusalem to restrain any further Jewish upheaval.ᵇ

2.4 SABINUS'S WAR WITH THE JEWS

While Varus was probably well on his way to Antioch, Sabinus ignored the former counsel of Varus and Archelaus and went into Jerusalem with his troops to secure Herod's palace. Sabinus and his troops probably took about two to three days to reach Jerusalem from Caesarea. He commanded the one legion left by Varus, in addition to his servants and soldiers, to search zealously for Herod's money. Uproars and fighting broke out, resulting in the Jews clashing with Sabinus's armies on the day before the Feast of Pentecost on May 29, 1 B.C. Roman soldiers burnt the porticoes of the temple and plundered the temple treasury.[122]

Afterward, Sabinus and his armies were isolated and surrounded by many angry Jews who had come for the festival. He urgently sent messengers to beseech Varus's support. Varus was afraid of losing his one legion in Jerusalem and hurriedly returned to Jerusalem to seize control of the situation. Sabinus fled with his troops in the chaos and avoided facing Varus. To end the unrest, Varus crucified 2,000 Jews in a show of force.ᶜ

Table 2.1 presents the chronology of the events described by Josephus based on a computation of the minimum number of days that would have needed to elapse to allow for the events associated with Herod's death to occur, leading up to Sabinus meeting with Archelaus and Varus and his subsequent war with the Jews in Jerusalem.

If Herod had died on March 30, 4 B. C., his son Archelaus and family would have sailed for Rome soon after Passover on April 11, way before Sabinus could have arrived at Caesarea from Rome. In other words, the meeting between Sabinus, Archelaus, and Varus could not have happened, because Sabinus would have required about 73 days from the date of Herod's death to reach Caesarea. His arrival date would have been around June 11, 4 B.C., 61 days after Passover (April

---

a Josephus, *Antiquities*, 17.11.1.

b Ibid., 17.10.1.

c "…for as to Sabinus, he durst not come into Varus's sight, but was gone out of the city before this, to the sea-side. But Varus sent a part of his army into the country, against those that had been the authors of this commotion, and as they caught great numbers of them, those that appeared to have been the least concerned in these tumults he put into custody, but such as were the most guilty he crucified; these were in number about two thousand" (Josephus, *War*, 2.5.2).

The Timing of God's Visitations

11, 4 B.C.) and seven days after Pentecost (June 3, 4 B.C).

Table 2.1. Chronology of events from Herod's death leading up to Sabinus's war with Jews just before Pentecost.

1 B.C.	Days Elapsed	Events	4 B.C.
January 10	-	Lunar eclipse.	March 13
January 27	17	1. Herod's death, inferred from the date Shebat 2 of a festival in the Jewish Megillat Taanit.[123]	March 30
-	-	Passover on April 11, 4 B.C. →	-
March 24	56	2. News of Herod's death, sent via regular mail, reaches Augustus in Rome.	May 25
-	-	Pentecost on June 3, 4 B.C.→	-
-	-	←Passover in April 7, 1 B.C.	-
April 10	17	3. Sabinus arrives in Caesarea after sailing from Portus Ostia near Rome.	June 11
April 22	12	4. Archelaus is sent to assist Varus, and 12 days later Varus arrives Caesarea to meet Archelaus and Sabinus. Sabinus agrees to stand down.	June 23
April 23	1	5. Archelaus and company set sail for Rome.	June 24
April 27	4	6. Varus and his cavalries arrive at Jerusalem.	June 28

		7. Varus advises Philip to go to Rome as well. He returns to Antioch after spending likely three weeks in Jerusalem. He leaves one legion to guard Jerusalem.	
May 18	21		July 19
May 26	8	8. Sabinus arrives at Jerusalem from Caesarea after learning that Varus had left for a while.	July 27
May 28	2	9. Sabinus commands all Roman soldiers to search for Herod's money.	July 29
May 29	1	10. Sabinus's soldiers fight the Jews and plunder the temple treasure.	July 30
-	-	←Pentecost on May 30, 1 B.C.	-
	139	**TOTAL**	

2.5 ARCHELAUS, ANTIPAS, AND PHILIP IN ROME

Augustus had his grandson, crown prince Gaius, preside with him over the hearing of Herod's last testament, submitted by Archelaus and his brothers.[124] In that year, Augustus had given Gaius the proconsulship of Syria and planned to send him to reclaim Armenia from the Parthians. This would serve as Gaius's training in governmental affairs in preparation for succeeding to the throne.

In his letters to Caesar, Sabinus would have reported what he had encountered in Jerusalem. He likely put all the blame on Archelaus and accused him for the failure of his mission.[a] Varus also reported to Caesar in letters, and he plausibly supported his friend Archelaus.[b]

In his report to Caesar, Varus probably provided details on the cause of the Jewish revolt on May 30, 1 B.C., which came so close to the earlier one near

---

a "…Sabinus also by letters accused Archelaus to Caesar" (Josephus, *Antiquities*, 17.9.4).

b "…But when Caesar had read these papers, and Varus's and Sabinus's letters, with the accounts of the money, and what were the annual incomes of the Kingdom, and understood that Antipas had also sent letters, to lay claim to the Kingdom; he summoned his friends together, to know their opinions" (Josephus, *Antiquities*, 17.9.5).

Passover April 7, 1 B.C., and explained why he had crucified 2,000 Jews and sent several Jewish commanders to Caesar for final judgment.[125] He undoubtedly confirmed Sabinus's presence in Caesarea and Jerusalem and communicated his mischief to Caesar.

If Caesar had any question about the riots in Jerusalem, he could have interrogated the Jewish commanders, who were eyewitnesses to the events. This indeed was a smart move by Varus, who knew that Caesar's primary concern was the regional stability of Roman governance.

As long as Archelaus was loyal to Caesar, he was fit to be the ruler in Judea. Augustus appointed Archelaus to be ethnarch of the reduced Judean kingdom. He promised Archelaus that he would grant him a client king, just like his father's, if he governed his country virtuously.[126] He appointed Antipas and Philip tetrarchs of the regions Herod had designated to them.

2.6 SUMMARY

In summary, all these events fit well within the 139 days that passed from Herod's execution of the rabbis and young Jews on January 10, 1 B.C. to Sabinus's war with the Jews on the day before Pentecost (May 29, 1 B.C).

In contrast, if Herod had died in 4 B.C., there would have been only 81 days between the lunar eclipse on March 13 and the day before Pentecost on June 2. Sabinus and his troops would have missed their alleged war with the Jews on the day before Pentecost by 58 days, contrary to Josephus's historical record.

One may argue that the news of Herod's death was sent to Rome by express overland mail, which would have taken a shorter time of about 46 days instead of 56 days. However, even by hastening Sabinus's departure from Rome to Caesarea by 10 days, he would still have missed his alleged war in Jerusalem on the day before Pentecost by about 48 days (58 – 10).

Avenger Prince Gaius Caesar

Chapter Three

According to Luke 2:2, Quirinius took the census in Judea when Jesus was born in 3/2 B.C. Around 1 B.C., Augustus selected Quirinius as one of the advisors to assist crown prince Gaius Caesar, imperial proconsul of Syria, to handle the revolt of Armenia and the negotiation with the Parthians.

Herod's sons appeared in Rome before Augustus to hear his decision about their father's will. Gaius Caesar presided over that hearing as well.[a] Critics of the early Christian consensus claim that Gaius was not in Rome in 1 B.C. to meet Herod's sons, and thus Herod could not have died in 1 B.C.; instead they say that Gaius was available in 4 B.C.

It is worthwhile to undertake an in-depth examination of Gaius's life to evaluate the possibility of him having been available to meet Herod's sons in those times.

3.1 BIRTHS OF GAIUS AND LUCIUS CAESAR

Gaius Caesar was the firstborn son of Julia,[b] Augustus's only daughter, and Marcus Vispanius Agrippa in B.C. 20. Julia gave birth to another son, Lucius, in B.C. 17. Immediately, Augustus adopted the two brothers as his sons to succeed him,

---

a Josephus, *Anitquities*, 17.9.5.

b "And Julia gave birth to a boy, who received the name Gaius; and a permanent annual sacrifice on his birthday was granted" (Dio, *Roman History*, 54.8.5).

The Timing of God's Visitations

believing that this would reduce the number of odious plots against him.ᵃ At the same time, the two boys could take on his family name, Caesar. Augustus devoted much of his time and energy to educating and training his grandchildren; he had three grandsons (Gaius, Lucius, and Agrippa) and two granddaughters (Julia and Agrippina).ᵇ

In 12 B.C., Augustus sent his best friend and son-in-law Marcus Agrippa to quell a rebellion in Pannonia, the modern-day region of Hungary and Austria. Agrippa advanced his army despite winter having already arrived. The Pannonians were terrified and abandoned their plans for rebellion. Agrippa then fell ill on his return to Rome and died. Augustus delivered the eulogy in the Roman Forum where Agrippa's body was laid before burial.ᶜ

In 8 B.C., Gaius accompanied Augustus in a campaign against the Germans. They both stayed behind the Roman side of the Rhine, while Tiberius, Augustus's

---

a "These were the occurrences of that year. In the consulship of Gaius Furnius and Gaius Silanus [17 B.C.], Agrippa again acknowledged the birth of a son, who was named Lucius; and Augustus immediately adopted him together with his brother Gaius, not waiting for them to become men, but appointing them then and there successors to his office, in order that fewer plots might be formed against him" (Dio, *Roman History*, 54.18.1).

b "He had three grandsons by Agrippa and Julia, namely, Caius, Lucius, and Agrippa; and two grand-daughters, Julia and Agrippina... Caius and Lucius he adopted at home, by the ceremony of purchase from their father, advanced them, while yet very young, to offices in the state, and when they were consuls-elect, sent them to visit the provinces and armies. In bringing up his daughter and grand-daughters, he accustomed them to domestic employments, and even spinning, and obliged them to speak and act everything openly before the family, that it might be put down in the diary. He so strictly prohibited them from all converse with strangers, that he once wrote a letter to Lucius Vinicius, a handsome young man of a good family, in which he told him, "You have not behaved very modestly, in making a visit to my daughter at Baiae." He usually instructed his grandsons himself in reading, swimming, and other rudiments of knowledge; and he laboured nothing more than to perfect them in the imitation of his hand-writing. He never supped but he had them sitting at the foot of his couch; nor ever travelled but with them in a chariot before him, or riding beside him" (Suetonius, *Twelve Caesars*, 2.64.1–3).

c "Meanwhile he increased the power of Agrippa, who had returned from Syria, by giving him the tribunician power again for another five years, and he sent him out to Pannonia, which was eager for war, entrusting him with greater authority than the officials outside Italy ordinarily possessed. And Agrippa set out on the campaign in spite of the fact that the winter had already begun (this was the year in which Marcus Valerius and Publius Sulpicius were the consuls [12 B.C.]); but when the Pannonians became terrified at his approach and gave up their plans for rebellion, he returned, and upon reaching Campania, fell ill. Augustus happened to be exhibiting, in the name of his sons, contests of armed warriors at the Panathenaic festival, and when he learned of Agrippa's illness, he set out for Italy; and finding him dead, he conveyed his body to the capital and caused it to lie in state in the Forum. He also delivered the eulogy over the dead, after first hanging a curtain in front of the corpse" (Dio, *Roman History*, 54.28.1–3).

stepson, crossed the river to go after the Germans. Augustus gave money to the soldiers because Gaius was with them for the first time.ᵃ

In 7 B.C., the Senate decided to hold a festival in honor of Augustus's return to Rome. Tiberius was in charge of organizing the event initially. When news of a disturbance in the province of Germany reached Rome, however, Tiberius immediately set out for the field. Gaius took over the task from Tiberius and had assistance from consul Piso.ᵇ

3.2 ARMENIA SOUGHT INDEPENDENCE

In 6 B.C., the people had elected Gaius consul before he was of military age. Gaius was only 15 years old based on Roman inclusive reckoning, one year short of the military age of 16. Augustus had decided that no man less than 20 years old should become consul. Even though the people insisted, he said that a person ought not to receive consulship until one was able not only to avoid error oneself but also to resist the ardent impulses of the people. Instead Augustus gave Gaius the priesthood and the right to attend the meetings and banquets of the Senate.ᶜ

In the meantime, he accepted the proposal from the Senate and the people that Gaius and Lucius be made consuls-designate (or consuls-elect). They would take their consulships automatically when they reached the age of 20 without the need of having to win regular elections. By the Senate's decree, they could

---

a "...the next year, when Asinius Gallus and Gaius Marcius were consuls [8 B.C.]... he made a campaign against the Germans. He himself remained behind in Roman territory, while Tiberius crossed the Rhine... Augustus granted money to the soldiers, not as to victors, though he himself had taken the title of imperator and had also conferred it upon Tiberius, but because then for the first time they had Gaius taking part with them in their exercises" (Dio, *Roman History*, 55.4.5–6).

b "Tiberius on the first day of the year in which he was consul with Gnaeus Piso [7 B.C.] convened the senate in the Curia Octaviae... A little later, when there was some disturbance in the province of Germany, he took the field. The festival held in honour of the return of Augustus was directed by Gaius, in place of Tiberius, with the assistance of Piso. The Campus Agrippae and the Diribitorium were made public property by Augustus himself" (Dio, *Roman History*, 55.8.1–3).

c "The next year, in which Gaius Antistius and Laelius Balbus were consuls [6 B.C.]... the people had elected Gaius consul before he was as yet of military age. All this, as I have said, vexed Augustus, and he even prayed that no compelling circumstances might arise, as had once occurred in his own case, such as to requisite that a man less than twenty years old should become consul. When even so the people insisted, he then said that one ought not to receive the office until one was able not only to avoid error oneself but also to resist the ardent impulses of the populace. After that he gave Gaius a priesthood and also the right to attend the meetings of the senate and to behold spectacles and be present at banquets with that body" (Dio, *Roman History*, 55.9.1–4).

take part in the counsels of state on the day they were introduced to the Forum.[a]

Due to the death of pro-Roman king Tigranes III in 6 B.C., the Armenians revolted and sought autonomy by affiliating with the Parthians (the Iranian Empire). Augustus wanted to send Tiberius to the East to restore Roman dominance in Armenia. He bestowed upon Tiberius the tribunician power for five years and assigned him in charge of Armenia. However, Tiberius declined the assignment.

According to Dio, Augustus wanted to give Tiberius a lesson, thus he sent him to the island of Rhodes.[b] Suetonius supported such a view.[c]

In contrast, Velleius offers a conflicting perspective. He wrote that Tiberius, who had now held two consulships and celebrated two triumphs, sought leave from Augustus himself in order that his own glory not stand in the way of the young men, Gaius and Lucius. Velleius also mentioned that Gaius had already celebrated the toga ceremony of manhood that year.[d]

In fact, Dio added other speculations as well, such as stating that Tiberius left for Rhodes because he could no longer stand his wife Julia, Augustus's daughter, who

---

a Augustus, *Res Gestae*, 14.

b "And wishing in some way to bring Gaius and Lucius to their senses still more sharply, he bestowed upon Tiberius the tribunician power for five years, and assigned to him Armenia, which was becoming estranged since the death of Tigranes. The result was that he needlessly offended not only his grandsons but Tiberius as well; for the former felt they had been slighted, and Tiberius feared their anger. At any rate he was sent to Rhodes on the pretext that he needed incidentally a bit of instruction; and he did not even take his entire retinue, to say nothing of friends, the object being that Gaius and Lucius should be relieved both of the sight of him and of his doings. He made the journey as a private citizen... when he reached Rhodes, he refrained from haughty conduct in both word and deed" (Dio, *Roman History*, 55.9.5–6).

c "He therefore continued at Rhodes much against his will, obtaining, with difficulty, through his mother, the title of Augustus's lieutenant, to cover his disgrace. He thenceforth lived, however, not only as a private person, but as one suspected and under apprehension, retiring into the interior of the country, and avoiding the visits of those who sailed that way, which were very frequent; for no one passed to take command of an army, or the government of a province, without touching at Rhodes" (Suetonius, *Twelve Caesars*, 3.12.1–2).

d "Soon afterwards Tiberius Nero, who had now held two consulships and celebrated two triumphs; who had been made the equal of Augustus by sharing with him the tribunician power; the most eminent of all Roman citizens save one (and that because he wished it so); the greatest of generals, attended alike by fame and fortune; veritably the second luminary and the second head of the state — this man, moved by some strangely incredible and inexpressible feeling of affection for Augustus, sought leave from him who was both his father-in-law and stepfather to rest from the unbroken succession of his labours. The real reasons for this were soon made plain. Inasmuch as Gaius Caesar had already assumed the toga of manhood, and Lucius was reaching maturity, he concealed his reason in order that his own glory might not stand in the way of the young men at the beginning of their careers" (Velleius, *Roman History*, 2.99.1–2).

had been widowed in 12 B.C. He was angry at not having been designated as Caesar, and so Augustus expelled him because he was plotting against Augustus's sons.[a]

Tiberius travelled to Rhodes as a private citizen and refrained from haughty conduct in both word and deed while living there. We may never know the real reason he lived in Rhodes for seven to eight years.[b]

In 5 B.C., when Gaius reached the military age of 16 years old, by Roman inclusive reckoning, Augustus took his twelfth consulship to introduce Gaius to the Senate. He declared Gaius *princeps iuventutis* ("prince of youth"), a title given by the Roman knights to Gaius and Lucius,[c] and appointed him commander of a division of cavalry.[d]

In other words, Gaius officially began his military training that year as a cavalry commander. At the same time, he could participate in the counsels of state affairs in the Forum, which was authorized by a Senate decree a year prior.

3.3 TRIP TO ARABIA

Velleius records that Gaius previously visited other provinces before he was sent to Syria.[e] [128] Suetonius also mentions that Augustus sent Gaius and Lucius to visit the provinces and armies.[f] Gaius had visited Germany in 8 B.C. at the age of 13, by inclusive reckoning, as mentioned earlier.

---

a "...there is also a story that he took this course on account of his wife Julia, because he could no longer endure her; at any rate, she was left behind in Rome. Others said that he was angry at not having been designated as Caesar, and yet others that he was expelled by Augustus himself, on the ground that he was plotting against Augustus' sons" (Dio, *Roman History*, 55.9.7).

b "Even in this brief epitome I ought to say that his stay of seven years in Rhodes was such that all who departed for the provinces across the sea, whether proconsuls or governors appointed by the emperor, went out of their way to see him at Rhodes, and on meeting him they lowered their fasces to him though he was but a private citizen — if such majesty could ever belong to a private citizen — thereby confessing that his retirement was more worthy of honour than their official position" (Velleius, *Roman History*, 2.99.4). "He returned to Rome after an absence of nearly eight years, with great and confident hopes of his future elevation, which he had entertained from his youth, in consequence of various prodigies and predictions" (Suetonius, *Twelve Caesars*, 3.14.1).

c Augustus, *Res Gestae*, 14.

d "The following year Augustus in the course of his twelfth consulship placed Gaius among the youths of military age, and at the same time introduced him into the senate, declared him princeps iuventutis, and permitted him to become commander of a division of cavalry" (Dio, *Roman History*, 55.9.9).

e "Only a short time passed after this when Gaius Caesar, having previously visited other provinces, was sent to Syria" (Velleius, *Roman History*, 2.101.1).

f Suetonius, *Twelve Caesars*, 2.64.1–3.

The Timing of God's Visitations

Gaius's visits to other provinces included a trip with King Juba II of Mauretania.[a] According to Pliny the Elder, Gaius and Juba II took a tour of Egypt and Arabia together, yet they got only a glimpse of that region.[b] Suetonius also mentions that they travelled through Judea and Jerusalem. Augustus commended Gaius for not paying any devotion at Jerusalem.[c]

No historical record has ever been found dating Gaius's trips to Egypt, Arabia, and Judea, but they must have taken place before Gaius was given command and sent to Syria, as Velleius noted. The spring or fall periods of 4 or 3 B.C. are the best candidates for this tour. Since there are no records about Gaius's movement in Italy and its neighboring countries for these two years, he could have taken a private trip abroad.

King Juba II and his entourage would have been the best tour guides and protectors for young Gaius in the Middle East and Africa. According to Pliny, Gaius and Juba went as far as the Arabian Gulf, which is likely the Persian Gulf today.[d] This implies that their trip took a considerable period of time, in the order of at least half to a full year.

---

a "Some say that the Mauretanians are Indians, who accompanied Hercules hither. A little before my time, the kings Bogus and Bocchus, allies of the Romans, possessed this country; after their death, Juba [II] succeeded to the kingdom, having received it from Augustus Cæsar, in addition to his paternal dominions. He was the son of Juba [I] who fought, in conjunction with Scipio, against divus Cæsar. Juba [II, 48 B.C.–23 A.D.] died lately, and was succeeded by his son Ptolemy, whose mother was the daughter of Antony and Cleopatra" (Strabo, *Geography*, 17.3.8).

b "It has not escaped my notice that Charax was the birthplace of Dionysius, the most recent writer dealing with the geography of the world, who was sent in advance to the East by the deified Augustus to write a full account of it when the emperor's elder son was about to proceed to Armenia to take command against the Parthians and Arabians; nor have I forgotten the view stated at the beginning of my work that each author appears to be most accurate in describing his own country; in this section however my intention is to be guided by the Roman armies and by King Juba, in his volumes dedicated to the above-mentioned Gaius Caesar describing the same expedition to Arabia" (Pliny, *Natural History*, 6.141). "Aelius Gallus [70 B.C.–25 A.D.], a member of the Order of Knights, is the only person who has hitherto carried the arms of Rome into this country; for Gaius Caesar son of Augustus only had a glimpse of Arabia. Gallus destroyed the following towns not named by the authors who have written previously - Negrana, Nestus, Nesca, Magusus, Caminacus, Labaetia; as well as Mariba above mentioned, which measures 6 miles round, and also Caripeta, which was the farthest point he reached" (Pliny, *Natural History*, 6.160). Note that Aelius Gallus led a military expedition into Arabia in 24 B.C. and retreated after destroying one township (Getzel M. Cohen, *The Hellenistic Settlements in Syriua, the Red Sea Basin, and North Africa* [Oakland, CA: University of California Press, 2006]).

c "…he [Augustus] likewise commended his grandson Gaius for not paying his devotions at Jerusalem in his passage through Judea" (Suetonius, *Twelve Caesars*, 2.93.1).

d "Indeed the greater part of it Alexander the Great's eastern conquests also explored as far as the Arabian Gulf; in which, when Augustus's son Gaius Caesar was operating there, it is said that figure-heads of ships from Spanish wrecks were identified" (Pliny, *Natural History*, 2.168).

As Pliny recalls, Augustus had sent Dionysius to the East to write a full account of the region in advance of Gaius going to Armenia to take command against the Parthians and Arabians. Possibly, Gaius and company followed the route described in Dionysius's report. King Juba II had dedicated to Gaius his volume *On Arabia*, describing their exploration in Arabia.[a] Juba's book is no longer available.

King Juba II could not have been a member of Gaius's advisory team to handle the revolt of Armenia around 1 A.D., because he had his own kingdom of Mauretania on the west coast of Africa to take care of, ever since Augustus had granted it to him in 25 B.C.[129] Gaius's Armenian campaign was expected to be a long one, lasting at least several years in Syria. It is illogical to suggest that Augustus would have requested Juba to leave his kingdom for someone else to govern and himself become one of Gaius's advisers.

Furthermore, their trip to Arabia was unlikely a military campaign, since none of the Roman historians—such as Dio, Tacitus, Velleius, and Suetonius—mentioned a word about Gaius's alleged war against the Arabs in 4 B.C. to 1 A.D.

Especially in the period of 1 B.C. to 1 A.D., although Roman military forces might have been strong in both Egypt and Syria, no military genius would have initiated two warfronts in close proximity, one against the Arabs and the other against the Armenians and Parthians. Furthermore, there would also have been the danger of other nations oppressed by the Romans joining the rebellion. Initiating two wars near the same time definitely wouldn't have been what Augustus wanted for the "young and inexperienced" teenager Gaius and his team.

In addition, Augustus's primary concern was the Armenian revolt, not Arabia. Arabia could well have been pro-Roman in that period, as evidenced by their assistance of Varus's suppression of the Jewish rebellion not long after Herod's death.[b] Gaius's urgent priority was to regain Armenia from the Parthians and not invade Arabia.

3.4 AUGUSTUS, FATHER OF THE COUNTRY IN 2 B.C.

On February 5, 2 B.C. Augustus was honored with the highest title "*Pater Patriae*, Father of the Country" by a formal Senate decree well supported by

---

a Pliny, *Natural History*, 6.141.

b "Aretas also, the king of Arabia Petrea, out of his hatred to Herod, and in order to purchase the favor of the Romans, sent him [Varus] no small assistance…" (Josephus, *Antiquities*, 17.10.9)

The Timing of God's Visitations

the people.[a] Augustus knew about this honor for quite some time, since many people had been addressing him as such, but he had refused to accept it until now.

3.5 TEMPLE OF MARS ULTOR DEDICATION

On January 1, 2 B.C., Augustus, in his thirteenth consulship, introduced Lucius, who was now 16 years old, by inclusive reckoning, to public life in the Senate.[b] In this same year, Augustus had planned to dedicate a new forum (Augustum) with a new temple of Mars Ultor (Avenger) for government operations such as magistracy, senatorial activities, and military ceremonies.

About 40 years earlier, Augustus had vowed to build a new temple of Mars if he were victorious in avenging his adoptive father Julius Caesar's death.[c]

---

a "While I was administering my thirteenth consulship the senate and the equestrian order and the entire Roman people gave me the title of *Father of my Country*, and decreed that this title should be inscribed upon the vestibule of my house and in the senate-house and in the Forum Augustum beneath the quadriga erected in my honour by decree of the senate. At the time of writing this I was in my seventy-sixth year" (Augustus, *Res Gestae*, 35); "He also was given the strict right to the title of 'Father'; for hitherto he had merely been addressed by that title without the formality of a decree" (Dio, *Roman History*, 55.10.10); "The whole body of citizens with a sudden unanimous impulse proffered him the title of *Father of his Country*: first the commons, by a deputation sent to Antium, and then, because he declined it, again at Rome as he entered the theatre, which they attended in throngs, all wearing laurel wreaths: the senate afterwards in the House, not by a decree or by acclamation, but through Valerius Messala. He, speaking for the whole body, said: 'Good fortune and divine favour attend thee and thy house, Caesar Augustus; for thus we feel that we are praying for lasting prosperity for our country and happiness for our city. The senate in accord with the people of Rome hails thee *Father of thy Country*.' Then Augustus with tears in his eyes replied as follows (and I have given his exact words, as I did those of Messala): 'Having attained my highest hopes, Fathers of the Senate, what more have I to ask of the immortal gods than that I may retain this same unanimous approval of yours to the very end of my life'" (Suetonius, *Twelve Caesars*, 2.58.1–2); and "Holy Father of thy Country, this title hath been conferred on thee by the people, by the senate, and by us, the knights" (Ovid, *Fasti*, 2:15).

b "...he [Augustus] asked of his own accord for a twelfth after a long interval, no less than seventeen years, and two years later for a thirteenth [2 B.C.], wishing to hold the highest magistracy at the time when he introduced each of his sons Gaius and Lucius to public life upon their coming of age" (Suetonius, *Twelve Caesars*, 2.26.2).

c "He [Augustus] built many public works, in particular the following: his forum with the temple of Mars the Avenger, the temple of Apollo on the Palatine, and the fane of Jupiter the Thunderer on the Capitol. His reason for building the forum was the increase in the number of the people and of cases at law, which seemed to call for a third forum, since two were no longer adequate. Therefore it was opened to the public with some haste, before the temple of Mars was finished, and it was provided that the public prosecutions be held there apart from the rest, as well as the selection of jurors by lot. He had made a vow to build the temple of Mars in the war of Philippi,

Augustus had renewed his pledge to build the temple of Mars Ultor in the capital in 20 B.C. It would house the Roman legion standards sent back by Parthian king Phraates. He took full credit for their return, as if he himself had conquered the Parthians in war. He rode into Rome on horseback and was honored with a triumphal arch. The year was marked by his daughter Julia giving birth to her first son Gaius.[a] The construction of a new forum and temple likely began shortly after.

The dedication date of the temple of Mars Ultor and the Forum Augustum has been debated for a long time.[130] Dio clearly states that the celebratory contests and dedication of the temple of Mars took place on August 1,[b] whereas sources such as Feriale Duranum (224/227 A.D.), Fasti Philocali (354 A.D.), and Ovid's *Fasti* (2 B.C.)[131] record that games in the Circus honoring Mars were conducted

---

which he undertook to avenge his father" (Suetonius, *Twelve Caesars*, 2.29.1–2). "…to Mars, and that he himself and his grandsons should go there as often as they wished, while those who were passing from the class of boys and were being enrolled among the youths of military age should invariably do so; that those who were sent out to commands abroad should make that their starting-point; that the senate should take its votes there in regard to the granting of triumphs, and that the victors after celebrating them should dedicate to this Mars their sceptre and their crown; that such victors and all others who receive triumphal honours should have their statues in bronze erected in the Forum; that in case military standards captured by the enemy were ever recovered they should be placed in the temple; that a festival should be celebrated besides the steps of the temple by the cavalry commanders of each year; that a nail should be driven into it by the censors at the close of their terms; and that even senators should have the right of contracting to supply the horses that were to compete in the Circensian games, and also to take general charge of the temple, just as had been provided by law in the case of the temples of Apollo and of Jupiter Capitolinus. These matters settled, Augustus dedicated this temple of Mars" (Dio, *Roman History*, 55.10.2–6).

a "Meanwhile Phraates, fearing that Augustus would lead an expedition against him because he had not yet performed any of his engagements, sent back to him the standards and all the captives, with the exception of a few who in shame had destroyed themselves or, eluding detection, remained in the country. Augustus received them as if he had conquered the Parthian in a war; for he took great pride in the achievement, declaring that he had recovered without a struggle what had formerly been lost in battle. Indeed, in honour of this success he commanded that sacrifices be decreed and likewise a temple to Mars Ultor on the Capitol, in imitation of that of Jupiter Feretrius, in which to dedicate the standards; and he himself carried out both decrees. Moreover he rode into the city on horseback and was honoured with a triumphal arch… And Julia gave birth to a boy, who received the name Gaius; and a permanent annual sacrifice on his birthday was granted" (Dio, *Roman History*, 54.8.3–5).

b "But, though he paid such reverence to his ancestors, he would accept nothing for himself beyond the titles belonging to his office. It is true that on the *first day of August*, which was his [Claudius's] birthday, there were equestrian contests, but they were not given on his account; it was rather because the temple of Mars had been dedicated on that day and this event had been celebrated thereafter by annual contests" (Dio, *Roman History*, 60.5.3).

The Timing of God's Visitations

on May 12. Augustus was the first to produce the games of Mars, which by decree took place annually.[a]

Dio's date of August 1 is supported by Velleius, who reports that the celebrations in Mars's honor happened in the consular year of Augustus and Caninius Gallus,[b] who started in July 1, 2 B.C. as a suffect consul (as inscribed on a tablet).[132]

In other words, the dedication took place after July 1 and not before.

Morawiecki proposes that the date of May 12 recorded by Ovid marks the beginning of all the games and ceremonies commemorating the temple of Mars's official consecration. They all ended with its dedication on August 1.[133] According to Suetonius, the Forum Augustum was opened to the public before the temple was finished.[c] The opening of the Forum likely took place on May 12. Once the temple was completed about 12 weeks later, it was dedicated on August 1.

Before the dedication of the temple of Mars, Augustus decreed that the Senate would consider wars and claims of triumphs in the new temple, and those who were sent to provinces with military commands should be escorted from there, the victors bearing their tokens of triumph to the temple. The recovered Roman standard eagles are housed in the temple.[d]

Gaius and Lucius were organizers of the Circensian games in honor of Mars, which included chariot races, battles of cavalry, gymnastic competitions, hunting, and sea battles.[134] Both brothers planned grand events which no doubt would have taken some time to prepare and execute. Their younger brother, Agrippa, took part in the equestrian exercise called "Troy," along with other boys from the first families. Circus performers slaughtered 260 lions. There was gladiator combat in the Saepta. A naval battle was staged between the "Persians" and the "Athenians". Afterwards, water was let into the circus Flaminius and 36 crocodiles were slain inside.[e]

---

a "In my thirteenth consulship [2 BC] I was the first to produce the games of Mars, which thereafter in each succeeding year have been produced by the consuls in accordance with a decree of the senate and by statute" (Augustus, *Res Gestae*, 22.2).

b "But in the city, in the very year in which Augustus, then consul with Gallus Caninius [suffect consul in July 1, 2 B.C.], had sated to repletion the minds and eyes of the Roman people with the magnificent spectacle of a gladiatorial show and a sham naval battle on the occasion of the dedication of the temple of Mars" (Velleius, *Roman History*, 2.100.2).

c Suetonius, *Twelve Caesars*, 2.29.1–2.

d Dio, *Roman History*, 55.10.2.

e Velleius, *Roman History*, 2.100.2; "...Augustus dedicated this temple of Mars, although he had granted to Gaius and Lucius once for all the right to consecrate all such buildings by virtue of a kind

3.6 JULIA'S EXILE

From February 5 to August 1, 2 B.C., the Caesar clan was busy with bashes on account of Augustus receiving the highest title in the land, "Father of the Country," the games, various performances, the consecration and opening of the Forum Augustum, and later the dedication of the temple of Mars Ultor.

Possibly near the end of all the celebrations in September/October, Augustus discovered that his only daughter Julia was living a dissolute life and taking part in revelries and drinking parties at night in the Forum and on the rostra (orator platform). He was exceedingly angry.

At the conclusion of a trial, Augustus banished Julia to the island of Pandateria, and her mother Scribonia (divorced by Augustus in 39 B.C.[a]) voluntarily accompanied her. Julia's acquaintances, such as Jullus Antonius, who was the son of Mark Anthony and Fulvia, and other prominent persons, were put to death, while others were banished to islands.[b] Julia's sentence probably happened when all her children were still in Rome to honor and celebrate their grandfather's achievements. No doubt they were all upset by the instance.

Some scholars have suggested that Gaius was sent on his way for training as the legate of legions in the fall of 2 B.C., which would have taken place at the Ister warfront when his mother Julia's affairs were discovered and she was put on trial in Rome. That timing for Gaius's departure and training isn't credible, though.

---

of consular authority that they exercised in the time-honoured manner. And they did, in fact, have the management of the Circensian games on this occasion, while their brother Agrippa took part along with the boys of the first families in the equestrian exercise called 'Troy.' Two hundred and sixty lions were slaughtered in the Circus. There was a gladiatorial combat in the Saepta, and a naval battle between the "Persians" and the "Athenians" was given on the spot where even today some relics of it are still pointed out. These, it will be understood, were the names given to the contestants; and the "Athenians" prevailed as of old. Afterwards water was let into the Circus Flaminius and thirty-six crocodiles were there slaughtered… These were the celebrations in honour of Mars" (Dio, *Roman History*, 55.10.6–9).

a "…when Lucius Marcius and Gaius Sabinus held the consulship [39 B.C.]… for he [Octavius] was already beginning to be enamored of Livia also, and for this reason divorced Scribonia the very day she bore him a daughter" (Dio, *Roman History*, 48.34.1–3).

b "…when he [Augustus] at length discovered that his daughter Julia was so dissolute in her conduct as actually to take part in revels and drinking bouts at night in the Forum and on the very rostra, he became exceedingly angry… As a result Julia was banished to the island of Pandateria, lying off Campania, and her mother Scribonia voluntarily accompanied her. Of the men who had enjoyed her favours, Iullus Antonius, on the ground that his conduct had been prompted by designs upon the monarchy, was put to death along with other prominent persons, while the remainder were banished to islands" (Dio, *Roman History*, 55.10.12–15).

After the magnificent spectacles that Gaius and Lucius had put together in honoring Mars, according to the chronological order of events described by Dio, they likely would have continued to celebrate their successes with their grandfather as a family. Wouldn't it then be reasonable for Augustus to give his crown prince Gaius a break rather than immediately expose him to the danger of war during this festive family time? The answer is naturally and logically negative. No historical record has thus been found to show that Gaius left Rome while his mother was on trial.

Furthermore, if Gaius were to have gone to Ister after all the celebrations in Rome had ended in October/November and during his mother's trial, it would have been time for the army at Ister to go into winter quarters. What would have been the point of arriving at the warfront when there wasn't much action?

Most likely, Gaius was still in Rome in the fall of 2 B.C. to support his mother.

3.7 GAIUS IN ROME IN 1 B.C.

In January or February of 1 B.C., after the Caesar family crisis caused by Julia had subsided somewhat, Gaius was sent to command the legions on the Ister front—along the Danube River in modern-day Hungary. The Romans were fighting a real war in the region, but Gaius wasn't engaged in the actual combat, since he was there to learn how to rule. The dangerous tasks were regularly assigned to others.[a]

No record has ever been found dating the duration of Gaius's legate field training. A rough estimation would be at least three to four months, including the time needed to travel back and forth from Rome.

It is important that young Gaius completed his military command training and returned to Rome alive from the warfront. That way, he could "prove" to the Roman people that he was a qualified general capable of taking full military command.

Augustus then gave Gaius proconsul authority in Syria, and he also arranged to have Gaius marry Claudia Livia (or Livilla) the same year. This way, Gaius, being now 20 years old by inclusive reckoning—19 years old in actuality—would have the identity and dignity of a mature married man.[b] Consequently, the likelihood

---

a "Gaius assumed command of the legions on the Ister with peaceful intent. Indeed, he fought no war, not because no war broke out, but because he was learning to rule in quiet and safety, while the dangerous undertakings were regularly assigned to others" (Dio, *Roman History*, 55.10.17).

b "When the Armenians revolted and the Parthians joined with them, Augustus was distressed and at a loss what to do. For he himself was not fit for campaigning by reason of age, while Tiberius, as has been stated, had already withdrawn, and he did not dare send any other influential man; as for Gaius and Lucius, they were young and inexperienced in affairs. Nevertheless, under the stress of necessity, he chose Gaius, gave him the proconsular authority and a wife,—in order that he might

of Gaius being in and around Rome in the summer/fall of 1 B.C. is very high.

Herod died around January 27, 1 B.C. His son Archelaus and company then set sail around April 23, 1 B.C. and arrived at the port of Ostia near Rome around June 17, 1 B.C., assuming an average of 55 days in sailing from Caesarea to Rome. They submitted their documents to Caesar, requesting a hearing for their inheritance. As mentioned, Gaius Caesar was available in Rome and was able to preside over the hearing.[a]

Since the death of King Tigranes III, the Armenians had allied with the Parthians. Augustus was distressed and not sure what to do. He had installed Artavasdes III on the throne in 6 B.C., but Artavasdes had been disposed shortly afterward by the Armenians and the Roman armies took heavy losses.[b] [135]

Augustus wanted to send Tiberius to regain Armenia, but Tiberius refused and left for Rhodes instead. According to Dio, Augustus dared not use another influential man for this task. Despite Gaius still being young and inexperienced, Augustus decided to send him to the East. Augustus appointed a delegation of advisors to go with Gaius.[c]

Ever since Tiberius's refusal of the assignment, Augustus had drawn up Gaius's path forward. First, he sent Dionysius to the East to map out the regions, including possibly Armenia, Arabia, Judea, and Syria.[d] Second, he trained Gaius to command a cavalry, and afterwards legions. Gaius's advisory team included Marcus Lollius and P. Sulpicius Quirinius.

In the meantime, Augustus had appointed Sentius Saturninus and Quintilius Varus as successive legates of Syria in the period between 6 B.C. and 1 A.D. Varus had the command of three legions, four troops of cavalry, and local auxiliary forces,[e] which amounted to possibly well over 20,000 soldiers.

In other words, Rome's dominance in Syria and the vicinity remained very

---

also have the increased dignity that attached to a married man, and appointed advisers to him" (Dio, *Roman History*, 55.10.18).

a Josephus, *Anitquities* 17.9.5.

b "Artavasdes was enthroned by order of Augustus and overthrown with heavy Roman losses" (Tacitus, *Annal*, 2.4.1).

c Dio, *Roman History*, 55.10.18.

d Pliny, *Natural History*, 6.141.

e "As soon as Varus was once informed of the state of Judea by Sabinus's writing to him, he was afraid for the legion he had left there; so he took the two other legions, (for there were three legions in all belonging to Syria,) and four troops of horsemen, with the several auxiliary forces which either the kings or certain of the tetrarchs afforded him, and made what haste he could to assist those that were then besieged in Judea" (Josephus, *Antiquities*, 17.10.9).

The Timing of God's Visitations

strong.

3.8 GAIUS'S DISPATCH TO SYRIA IN 1 A.D.

Gaius's date of departure from Rome to Syria has been debated for quite some time, because no definitive evidence has ever been found in this matter. Nonetheless, one fact is sure: when Gaius reached the age of 21, by inclusive reckoning, he became a consul by decree; A.D. 1 is the consular year of Gaius Caesar and L. Aemilius Paulius, as evidenced by inscriptions.[136]

According to tradition, the two consuls of the year would enter the Forum on January 1 and preside over the Senate.[137] In the same inscription, M. Herennius Picens was scribed as being the suffect consul[138] starting on July 1, 1 A.D., possibly replacing Gaius after he was dispatched to Syria.

There is no reason why Gaius should not have been in Rome in early 1 A.D. to fulfill his first consulship duty, at least in the early portion of the year. No historical record has ever been found to substantiate his absence in Rome, nothing that says he was consul *in absentia*. In fact, the inscription which names Picen as the suffect consul in that same year supports the interpretation that Gaius was likely still in Rome earlier that year. Consul substitution typically took place on July 1.

Furthermore, the ups and downs of the Armenia revolt had already lasted about six years. Roman military power remained very strong in Syria, as well as in Cappadocia. There was no sudden military urgency requiring the young and inexperienced Gaius to be there in 1 B.C. or early 1 A.D., or else Rome would lose control of the East. Augustus had waited six years for Gaius to grow up and take responsibility to regain Armenia and head Rome's eastern governance; a few more months of wait would not have had any significant effect.

It was a major historic moment for Gaius, the crown prince, to join the Senate formally in the Forum in his first consulship, and then to be commissioned from the temple of Mars Ultor, the Roman avenger god,[a] to recover Armenia from the Parthians with the blessings of the Senate, his grandfather Emperor Augustus, and the people of Rome.

This was perhaps one of the most major commissioning ceremonies to ever be held in the relatively new temple of Mars. By Augustus's own decree, those who were on their way to the provinces with military commands were to be escorted from the temple. It doesn't make sense that Augustus would violate his own decree by sending Gaius to Syria without being commissioned from the

---

a Suetonius, *Twelve Caesars*, 2.29.

temple of Mars.

Augustus, who was born on September 23, 63 B.C., presided over his first consulship in the Senate in August of 43 B.C. when he was also 20 years old. Why would he deny Gaius the same memorable experience by dispatching him to Syria just a few months, or even a year, before his first consulship? And what military urgency could have forced Augustus to send his young and inexperienced grandson to the field as early as possible?

The most probable and logical conclusion is that Gaius was commissioned from the temple of Mars and set sail to Syria in the spring/summer of 1 A.D. after his first consul appearance, and not in the summer or fall of 1 B.C., or even earlier, as some scholars have speculated.

Ovid, the Roman poet who lived from 43 B.C. to 17 A.D., hails Gaius as having Mars as his father and being the avenger for all the Roman soldiers slain by the Parthians. Evidently, Ovid was an eyewitness of Gaius's commissioning ceremony in the temple of Mars Ultor, for he wrote,

> Your avenger is at hand, and proves himself a general in his earliest years; and, while a boy, is conducting a war not fitted to be waged by a boy… Thou wilt wield the weapons of duty, the foe arrows accursed; before thy standard, Justice and Duty will take their post.[a] [139]

Ovid's poem contains his prayer asking the Roman avenger god to grant divine favor to Gaius's expedition to Syria and war against the Parthians. He pleaded,

> By the badness of their cause, the Parthians are conquered; in arms, too, may they be overcome; may my hero [Gaius] add to Latium the wealth of the East. Both thou, father Mars, and thou, father Caesar, grant your divine favour as he sets out; for the one of you is now a Deity, thou, the other, wilt so be.[b]

Ovid even prophesized that Gaius would be victorious over the Parthians. Likely, the general public would have had the same sentiment and expectation that Gaius indeed was the young avenger, son of Mars, who would triumph over their enemies.

The argument that Gaius was obliged under the law to take over the Syrian

---

a Ovid, *The Art of Love*, 1.4.
b Ibid.

The Timing of God's Visitations

governorship on January 1 A.D. is ludicrous. Gaius was the supreme imperial proconsul of Syria and thus his arrival date mattered to no one but himself; he was the boss. Varus, governor of Syria, had to wait until Gaius's arrival and would likely have served as a member of Gaius's advisory team as well.

When Gaius's team docked their ship at Chios, likely to replenish their supplies and take a break from the sea, Tiberius sailed from Rhodes to visit them. According to Dio, Tiberius humiliated himself and groveled at the feet of the delegation.[a] Suetonius adds that tutor Marcus Lollius had encouraged Gaius to quarrel with Tiberius. This instance was later reflected in a speech given by Caesar Tiberius in the Senate some 20 years later.[b]

In contrast, Velleius painted a completely different picture of the meeting. He reported that Gaius paid his respects to Tiberius, whom he treated with all honor as his superior.[c] Note that Velleius was part of Gaius's delegation to the East and was like a reporter of the Roman military chronicle. Obviously, Velleius contorted the truth about the meeting in Gaius's favor, for he knew that Augustus would someday read his report about Gaius's premature death.

After Gaius arrived in Syria around the late summer of 1 A.D., on an island in the Euphrates, he participated in a negotiation with the young Parthian king Phrataces V,[d] who had recently taken over the kingdom since the death of his father. King Phrataces suspected that people in his own court were disloyal to him, thus he relinquished his previous demands over keeping Armenia and recalling his brothers from Rome.

Gaius conceded to install a pro-Roman Mede (Iranian) named Ariobarzanes

---

a "Gaius accordingly set out and was everywhere received with marks of distinction, as befitted one who was the emperor's grandson and was even looked upon as his son. Even Tiberius went to Chios and paid court to him, thus endeavouring to clear himself of suspicion; indeed, he humiliated himself and grovelled at the feet, not only of Gaius, but also of all the associates of Gaius. And Gaius, after going to Syria and meeting with no great success, was wounded" (Dio, *Roman History*, 55.10.19).

b "The emperor now made all this known to the Senate, and extolled the good offices of Quirinius to himself, while he censured Marcus Lollius, whom he charged with encouraging Gaius Caesar in his perverse and quarrelsome behaviour" (Tacitus, *Annals*, 3.48).

c "On his way he first paid his respects to Tiberius Nero, whom he treated with all honour as his superior" (Velleius, *Roman History*, 2.101.1).

d "On an island in the Euphrates, with an equal retinue on each side, Gaius had a meeting with the king of the Parthians, a young man of distinguished presence. This spectacle of the Roman army arrayed on one side, the Parthian on the other, while these two eminent leaders not only of the empires they represented but also of mankind thus met in conference... As for the meeting, first the Parthian dined with Gaius upon the Roman bank, and later Gaius supped with the king on the soil of the enemy" (Velleius, *Roman History*, 2.101.1–3).

as king over Armenia with the approval of the Senate and Augustus.[a] Shortly after his enthronement in 2 A.D., Ariobarzanes died of a fatal accident. The Armenians refused Ariobarzanes's son as king and fought the Romans for their independence.

In the summer/fall of 3 A.D., Gaius's army reached the city of Artagira. An Armenian defender, Addon, then enticed Gaius to come close to the city wall to meet him, pretending that he would reveal to him some of the Parthian king's secrets. Instead he wounded Gaius seriously.[b]

Gaius became physically and mentally weak from his wound and immediately resigned all his duties and took a vessel back to Rome. He passed away at Limyra, Lycia on February 21, 4 A.D. His brother Lucius had died from a sudden illness about 18 months earlier at Massilia—now known as Marseille, France—on his way to Spain.[c] Tiberius had returned to Rome some time in 2 A.D.

The bodies of Gaius and Lucius were brought to Rome by the military

---

a "Nevertheless, war did not break out with the Parthians, either. For Phrataces, hearing that Gaius was in Syria, acting as consul, and, furthermore, having suspicions regarding his own people, who had even before this been inclined to be disloyal to him, forestalled action on their part by coming to terms with the Romans, on condition that he himself should renounce Armenia and that his brothers should remain beyond the sea. The Armenians, however, in spite of the fact that Tigranes had perished in a war with barbarians and Erato had resigned her sovereignty, nevertheless went to war with the Romans because they were being handed over to a Mede, Ariobarzanes, who had once come to the Romans along with Tiridates. This was in the following year, when Publius Vinicius and Publius Varus were consuls [2 A.D.]... Not only Augustus but Gaius also assumed the title of imperator, and Armenia was given by Augustus and the senate first to Ariobarzanes and then upon his death a little later to his son Artabazus" (Dio, *Roman History*, 55.10a.4–6, 7).

b "And though they accomplished nothing worthy of note, a certain Addon, who was holding Artagira, induced Gaius to come up close to the wall, pretending that he would reveal to him some of the Parthian king's secrets, and then wounded him, whereupon he was besieged. He held out for a long time but when he was at last captured" (Dio, *Roman History*, 55.10a.6–7). "...but later, in a parley near Artagira, to which he rashly entrusted his person, he was seriously wounded by a man named Adduus, so that, in consequence, his body became less active, and his mind of less service to the state" (Velleius, *Roman History*, 2.102.2).

c "So Gaius resigned at once all the duties of his office and took a trading vessel to Lycia, where, at Limyra, he passed away. But even before Gaius's death the spark of life in Lucius had been quenched at Massilia. He, too, was being trained to rule by being dispatched on missions to many places, it was his custom personally to read the letters of Gaius in the senate, whenever he was present. His death was due to a sudden illness" (Dio, *Roman History*, 55.10a.9–10). "But in the midst of all his joy and hopes in his numerous and well regulated family, his fortune failed him. The two Julias, his daughter and granddaughter, abandoned themselves to such courses of lewdness and debauchery, that he banished them both. Caius and Lucius he lost within the space of eighteen months; the former dying in Lycia, and the latter at Marseilles" (Suetonius, *Twelve Caesars*, 2.65.1).

The Timing of God's Visitations

tribunes and by chief men of each city.[a] According to Suetonius, Augustus punished all the tutor and attendants who had taken advantage of Gaius's illness and death in committing acts of arrogance and greed in Syria. They were thrown into a river with heavy weights about their necks.[b]

Table 3.1 presents the chronology of Gaius Caesar's life. The table presents two different lists of the governors of Syria from 20 B.C. to 4 A.D. Emil Schürer established a list of names based on various historical records, except from 3 to 2 B.C. He inserted Quirinius's name with a question mark to fill this void based on his own conviction that Herod had died in 4 B.C., not any authentic evidence, as he noted in his book.[c]

Table 3.1. Chronology of crown Prince Gaius Caesar's life.

Date	Consular[140] Year	Events	Dated Source	Governor of Syria	Governor of Syria Based on Herod's Death in 4 B.C.[141]
20 B.C.	M. Appuleius, P.S. Nerva	Gaius is born.	Dio, *RH*, 54.8.5	M.V. Agrippa	M.V. Agrippa
17	C. Furnius, C.I. Silanus	Lucius is born. Both brothers are adopted by Augustus as sons.	Dio, *RH*, 54.18.1	M.V. Agrippa	M.V. Agrippa
12	M. Valerius, P.S. Quirinius	Death of M.V. Agrippa.	Dio, *RH*, 54.28.1–3	M. Titius	M. Titius

---

a "The bodies of Lucius and Gaius were brought to Rome by the military tribunes and by the chief men of each city. And the golden targets and spears which they had received from the knights on entering the class of youths of military age were set up in the senate-house" (Dio, *Roman History*, 55.12.1).

b "Because the tutor and attendants of his son Gaius took advantage of their master's illness and death to commit acts of arrogance and greed in his province, he had them thrown into a river with heavy weights about their necks" (Suetonius, *Twelve Caesars*, 2.67.2).

c "P. Sulpicius Quirinius, b.c. 3–2 (?). During the period 3–2 B.C. there is no direct evidence about any governor of Syria" (Schürer, *A History of the Jewish People in the Time of Jesus Christ*, 351).

8	A. Gallus, G. Marcius	Augustus, Tiberius, and Gaius join the military campaign against Germany.	Dio, *RH*, 55.4.5–6	C.S. Saturninus	C.S. Saturninus
7	C.N. Tiberius, G. Piso	Gaius and Piso are put in charge of the celebration of Augustus's return to Rome.	Dio, *RH*, 55.8.1–3	C.S. Saturninus	C.S. Saturninus
6	C.V. Antistius, D.L. Balbus	Gaius and Lucius is made consuls-designate. Tiberius is exiled to Rhodes.	Dio, *RH*, 55.9.1–4	C.S. Saturninus	C.S. Saturninus
5	Augustus Caesar, L.C. Sulla	Augustus introduces Gaius to the Senate. Gaius takes *toga virilis*. Gaius begins his military training as a commander of the cavalry.	Dio, *RH*, 55.9.9	C.S. Saturninus	P.Q. Varus
4	C.C. Sabinus, L.P. Rufus	Gaius's military training continues.	-	C.S. Saturninus	P.Q. Varus
3	L.C. Lentulus, M.V. Messalinus	Gaius and Juba likely tour Arabia and Judea.	-	C.S. Saturninus	P.S. Quirinius?

The Timing of God's Visitations

2	Augustus Caesar, L.G. Caninius	Augustus introduces Lucius to the Senate. Augustus receives the highest title, "Father of the Country," on February 5. Gaius and Lucius are put in in charge of the celebration to honor Mars. He dedicates the temple of Mars on August 1. Gaius's mother Julia is banished to Pandateria.	Velleius, *RH*, 2.100.2; Augustus, *RG*,35[142]	P.Q. Varus	P.S. Quirinius?
1	C.C. Lentulus, L.C. Piso	Gaius begins his legate of legions training at the Ister warfront. Gaius receives his proconsul authority. The royal wedding of Gaius and Claudia Livia takes place in Rome.	-	P.Q. Varus	Gaius Caesar
1 A.D.	Gaius Caesar, L.A. Paullus	Gaius's first consulship in the Senate. Gaius is commissioned in the temple of Mars and sets sail to Syria. Picens replaces Gaius as consul starting on July 1. Tiberius visits Gaius at Chios. Gaius and Parthian king Phrataces negotiate on an island in the Euphrates.	Consul Inscription[143]	Gaius Caesar	Gaius Caesar

2	P. Vincius, P. Alfenius Varus	Gaius installs Ariobarzanes as king over Armenia. Tiberius returns to Rome. Lucius dies on his way to Spain.	Dio, *RH*, 55.10a.4–5	Gaius Caesar	Gaius Caesar
3	L.A. Lamia, M. Servilius	Ariobarzanes dies of an accident. Gaius installs Ariobarzanes's son as king over Armenia. Armenians revolt and war with the Romans for independence. Gaius is seriously wounded in Artagira by an Armenian soldier. Gaius resigns from all duties and takes a ship to return home.	-	Gaius Caesar	Gaius Caesar
4	S.A. Catus, C. Sentius Saturninus	Gaius dies on February 21 at Limyra, Lycia. The bodies of Gaius and Lucius reach Rome for burial.	Inscription[144]	L.V. Saturninus	L.V. Saturninus

Note the following abbreviations: RH (*Roman History*) and RG (*Res Gestae*). Note also that dated sources refer to events in Gaius's life.

3.9 SUMMARY

In 1 B.C., Gaius completed his training at the Ister warfront. He then came back to Rome alive, proving to the people in Rome and the Senate that he was capable of taking command in the East. Augustus gave him a proconsulship of Syria and also had him marry Claudia Livia to boost his mature image.

In the summer/fall of 1 B.C., when Herod's sons appeared before Augustus for a hearing related to their inheritance, Gaius also presided over the meeting because it concerned him as the proconsul of Syria, who oversaw the Middle Eastern region.

Evidently, Augustus had planned Gaius's and his brother Lucius's life courses when they were still in their teens. When Gaius reach the age of 21, by inclusive reckoning, Augustus sent him to the East as proconsul of Syria to regain Armenia from the Parthians in 1 A.D. Gaius played the role of a young avenger, son of Mars, who would avenge the deaths of the Roman legions slain by the Parthians in previous battles. Augustus also dispatched Lucius to Spain when he came of age. Likely, Augustus's plan was that Gaius would eventually rule the East and Lucius would ultimately command the West.

Based on a Roman inscription, Gaius Caesar and L. Aemilius Paulius were consuls in 1 A.D. Gaius's first consulship at the age of 21 was highly anticipated by the people of Rome and the Senate, because they had given him the title of consul-designate six years earlier.

After fulfilling his role as consul starting on January 1, 1 A.D., Gaius and his team of advisors were sent off by Augustus and the Senate in a ceremony at the new temple of Mars Ultor. Based on the inscription, M. Herennius Picens was a suffect consul starting on July 1, 1 A.D., possibly replacing Gaius.

Gaius was wounded seriously by an Armenian commander in the summer/fall of 3 A.D. He died on February 21, 4 A.D. at the age of 24, by inclusive reckoning, at Limyra, Lycia on his way back to Rome. His brother Lucius had died 18 months earlier at the age of 19 at Massilia on his way to Spain.

In his autobiography, Augustus remarked,

> My sons Gaius and Lucius Caesar, whom fortune snatched away from me in their youth, the senate and the Roman people to do me honour made consuls designate, each in his fifteenth year, providing that each should enter upon that office after a period of five years.[a]

Caesar Augustus, one of the most powerful persons on the earth in his era, remained helpless when it came to the deaths of his heirs. Although he had set in place great plans for them, he couldn't guarantee their safety and survival.

---

a Augustus, *Res Gestae*, 14.

Sulpicius Quirinius's Censuses

Chapter Four

Quirinius was born to the old patrician family of Sulpicii in Lanuvium in about 45 B.C.¹⁴⁵ However, he was "quite unconnected," meaning that he wasn't linked to any powerful aristocrats or clans.ª Instead he was a tireless soldier who earned a consulship under Augustus in 12 B.C., which typically lasted for one year.¹⁴⁶

Quirinius then received the honor of a triumph for capturing some fortresses of the Homonadenses in Cilicia and was appointed advisor to crown prince Gaius Caesar in the government of Syria and Armenia. Quirinius also counseled Tiberius at Rhodes.

Quirinius climbed the ranks of the Roman aristocracy step by step, and he wasn't popular with the people in Rome near his death. One of the reasons, according to Tacitus, a Roman historian who lived from 56–120 A.D., is that he had "meanness and dangerous power in his last years."¹⁴⁷

---

a "About the same time he [Tiberius] requested the Senate to let the death of Sulpicius Quirinus be celebrated with a public funeral. With the old patrician family of the Sulpicii this Quirinus, who was born in the town of Lanuvium, was quite unconnected. An indefatigable soldier, he had by his zealous services won the consulship under the Divine Augustus, and subsequently the honours of a triumph for having stormed some fortresses of the Homonadenses in Cilicia. He was also appointed advisor to Caius [Gaius] Caesar in the government of Armenia, and had likewise paid court to Tiberius, who was then at Rhodes. The emperor now made all this known to the Senate, and extolled the good offices of Quirinus to himself, while he censured Marcus Lollius, whom he charged with encouraging Caius Caesar in his perverse and quarrelsome behaviour. But people generally had no pleasure in the memory of Quirinus, because of the perils he had brought, as I have related, on Lepida, and the meanness and dangerous power of his last years" (Tacitus, *The Annals*, 3.48).

The Timing of God's Visitations

4.1 QUIRINIUS IN HISTORY (45 B.C.-21 A.D.)

In 21 A.D., Caesar Tiberius requested that the Senate pay tribute to Quirinius with a public funeral.[148] For some reason, Tacitus didn't even mention the highlight of Quirinius's career; he had served as the governor of Syria. Apparently Tacitus wasn't a fan of Quirinius either.

Furthermore, nowhere in Tacitus's books relevant to the first 70 years of the first century, *The Annals* and *The Histories*,[149] does he ever say that Quirinius was a proconsul of Asia, contrary to what Sir William M. Ramsay wrote in his book, *The Bearing of Recent Discovery on the Trustworthiness of the New Testament*.[a][150]

In fact, none of the ancient Roman historians in the first century—such as Florus, Strabo, Suetonius, Tacitus, Pliny the Elder, Dio, and Livy—mention explicitly and definitively that Quirinius was a proconsul or legate of Asia, Cilicia, Galatia, Crete, and Cyrene.

Florus records that Augustus dedicated the subjugations of the Marmarides and Garamantes, which is in modern-day Libya, to Quirinius, who triumphed in his mission.[151]

Strabo describes Quirinius's victory over the Homonadeis near Taurus, in southern Turkey, where he starved the people and captured alive 4,000 men.[152]

Suetonius writes about the period after Quirinius divorced his wife Lepida 20 years later, saying that he accused her of having attempted to poison him many years before.[153]

Tacitus documents Tiberius's speech in the Senate in which he requested a public funeral for Quirinius.[154]

Pliny reports what Strabo and Tacitus had already discussed the conquering of fortresses by Quirinius in Turkey.[155]

Dio mentions Quirinius's consular year only.[156]

Livy doesn't speak of Quirinius at all in his books available today.

Based on Florus's description of Quirinius's victories in Libya, Sir Ronald Syme was perhaps among the first to infer that Quirinius may have been a proconsul of Crete and Cyrene. In one footnote, he added a question mark to his speculation: "Date unknown: c. 15 B.C., as proconsul of Crete and Cyrene?"[157] In other footnotes regarding unknown dates, Syme didn't insert any question

---

[a] "The next office in his [Quirinius's] career mentioned by Tacitus is his proconsulship of Asia" (Ramsay, *The Bearing of Recent Discovery on the Trustworthiness of the New Testament*, 280). Tacitus mentioned a total of seven individuals with proconsulships of Asia in the remnants of his books available today, but Quirinius is not one of them.

mark at all. Thus, his intent was to question whether Quirinius was actually a proconsul of Crete and Cyrene, since Florus had said nothing of the sort.

Nonetheless, subsequent scholars have regarded Quirinius's proconsulship as a matter of fact,[a] assuming that any general who fought a war in the region should also have been governor there. Sadly, this is often how unproven inferences become "facts" in the study of ancient history.

4.2 ARCHELAUS'S DEPOSITION IN 6 A.D.

Archelaus was exiled to Vienne in Gaul (France) after Augustus found him guilty of some serious accusations from the "leading men in Judea and Samaria" and his brothers.[b] Subsequently, Judea, Samaria, and Idumea were annexed as parts of the Syrian province under direct Roman governance. Archelaus later died in exile in about 18 A.D.[158]

According to Dio, Archelaus was deposed as ethnarch of Judea in the consulship of Aemilius Lepidus and Lucius Arruntius (6 A.D.).[c] However, Josephus reported two different dates regarding this event. In *War* 2.7.3, Josephus wrote that Archelaus was banished to Vienne in the ninth year of government, whereas *Antiquities* 17.13.2 states that he was banished in his tenth

---

a For example, Hudson wrote, "Publius Sulpicius Quirinius held high office as the reward of proved ability and hard work. He came of an undistinguished family and had no connection, Tacitus says, with the patrician family of the Sulpicii. He was governor of Crete and Cyrene and proved himself a very competent and successful soldier in campaigns against nomad tribes in the deserts of Cyrene" (Egbert C. Hudson, "The Principal Family as Pisidian Antioch." *Journal of Near Eastern Studies*, 1956, volume 15, number 1, 103–107). Additionally, Stevenson commented, "Before the annexation of Moesia the proconsul of Macedonia was often in command of an army, and Quirinius when governor of Cyrene seems to have undertaken operations against the desert tribes" (G.H. Stevenson, "The Imperial Administration." *The Cambridge Ancient History*, 1934, volume X, 182–217). And Anderson stated that "Augustus resolved to deal with them. He entrusted the task to P. Sulpicius Quirinius, a man of humble birth who had forced his way up by his military talents. Among his services was the successful conduct of a campaign which he had been commissioned, no doubt as proconsul of Crete and Cyrene, to wage against two tribes of the Libyan desert, the Marmaridae and the Garamantes, which had menaced the security of the Cyrenic cities" (J.G.C. Anderson, "The Eastern Frontier Under Augustus." *The Cambridge Ancient History, 1934*, volume X, 239–283).

b "But in the tenth year of Archelaus' government, both his brethren, and the principal men of Judea and Samaria… accused him before Caesar… Caesar… banished him, and appointed Vienne, a city of Gaul, to be the place of his habitation, and took his money away from him" (Josephus, *Antiquities*, 17.13.2; Dio, Roman History, 55.27.6).

c "After this, in the consulship of Aemilius Lepidus and Lucius Arruntius [6 A.D.]… Herod of Palestine, who was accused by his brothers of some wrongdoing or other, was banished beyond the Alps and a portion of the domain was confiscated to the state" (Dio, *Roman History*, 55.25.1, 55.27.6).

The Timing of God's Visitations

year of government. Many scholars have pointed this out to be an error on Josephus's part.

Here, we propose a probable alternate interpretation of Josephus's alleged error.

In 79 A.D. Josephus finished *War of the Jews*, in which he mainly used the Syro-Macedonian calendar to date events.[a] He took the Syro-Macedonian months to be fully compatible with the Jewish ones, and he based all his chronologies on non-inclusive reckoning. Thus he reported that Archelaus had been deposed after nine actual years of rule from 5412 to 5421 JHY (or 4 B.C. to 6 A.D.).

Josephus presented his seven-book manuscript to emperor Caesar Titus, who venerated it highly and ordered it to be published. Subsequently, Josephus decided to expand the content of *War of the Jews* to include the history of creation up to his pertinent era. He completed *Antiquities of the Jews* in 20 books around 93 A.D. In this expanded edition, he appended Hebrew equivalent months alongside some of the Syro-Macedonian months to educate a wider audience about Jewish culture.

Possibly after he presented his new books to Caesar Domitian, his reviewers suggested that he use the common method of Roman inclusive reckoning in the cases of Pompey's and Herod's capture of Jerusalem and Archelaus's deposition. He decided to add Greek Olympiads and Roman consular years in dating some of the major events.[b]

In order to maintain the dates of Archelaus's rule between 5412 to 5421 JHY, he converted the nine actual years reported in *War* to inclusive reckoning of 10 years for his Roman audience in *Antiquities*. He did this on purpose, which is manifested in his contortion of Archelaus's dream to fit his narratives.

Josephus reports that Archelaus "seemed to see nine ears of corn," which represented the entire nine-year duration of his reign in Judea.[c] On the other hand, he later edited the same dream so that Archelaus saw 10 ears of corn.[d]

---

a This is discussed further in Chapter One (1.1).

b This is shown in Table 1.2 in Chapter One (Section 1.2.2).

c "...before he [Archelaus] was sent for by Caesar, he seemed to see nine ears of corn, full and large, but devoured by oxen... Simon... said that he thought the ears of corn denoted years, and the oxen denoted a mutation of things, because by their ploughing they made an alteration of the country. That therefore he [Archelaus] should reign as many years as there were ears of corn; and after he had passed through various alterations of fortune, should die" (Josephus, *War*, 2.7.3).

d "Now, before Archelaus was gone up to Rome upon this message, he related this dream to his friends: That he saw ears of corn, in number ten, full of wheat, perfectly ripe, which ears, as it seemed to him, were devoured by oxen... Simon... said that the vision denoted... a change of affairs, because that land which is ploughed by oxen cannot remain in its former state; and that the ears of corn being ten, determined the like number of years, because an ear of corn grows in one year; and that the time of Archelaus's government was over" (Josephus, *Antiquities*, 17.13.3).

Sulpicius Quirinius's Censuses

Clearly, the difference between the ninth and tenth year of Archelaus's rule in Judea was not caused by a slip of Josephus's pen or any transcription error, Josephus deliberately altered the text. In this particular case, to suit his Roman audience, he converted nine actual years presented in *War* to 10 inclusive years in *Antiquities* for the duration of Archelaus's reign. Furthermore, it looks like he did this in a hurry without putting too much thought into how to smooth out the rough edges in these two narratives.

Josephus reported Archelaus's deposition a second time.[a] Augustus sent Quirinius to dispose of Archelaus's assets and at the same time collect taxes in Syria.[b] The taxation was concluded on the thirty-seventh year from the victory at Actium on September 2, 31 B.C. In other words, it was completed sometime between September 2, 6 A.D. and September 2, 7 A.D.[159]

Due to Herod's chronic disease and declining health during Antipater's absence in 4 B.C., it is possible that Herod's sons, such as Archelaus, assisted in governing regions such as Judea, Samaria, and Idumea. The exact locations of his ruling exercises in 4/1 B.C. are immaterial. The inference regarding Archelaus's rulings is substantiated by Josephus's account of Caesar's hearing of Herod's sons in Rome, in which Archelaus's cousin Antipater accused him of long exercising royal authority before his father's death and being granted any title and power by Caesar. Antipater backed up all his accusations with witnesses.[c] Steinmann and Young are the first to point this out.[160]

There is one noteworthy example that relates to the Roman convention of using inclusive reckoning.

The Julian calendar was decreed to replace the Roman Republic's AUC calendar in 46 B.C., with 90 days being added to ensure that the following new year would start on January 1, 45 B.C. Thus, the year 46 B.C. had 445 days and was called by many the *annus confusionis*, or year of confusion.[161] A leap day was supposed to be added in the fourth year of a four-year-cycle afterwards.

For the first 36 years of the Julian calendar, the pontiffs who were responsible for declaring the leap year added the extra day every three years instead of four. The error was only discovered in B.C. 8. The exact cause of the mistake is unknown, but the confusion is commonly thought to be caused by the Roman

---

a Josephus, *Antiquities*, 18.2.1.

b "When Cyrenius [Quirinius] had now disposed of Archelaus's money, and when the taxings were come to a conclusion, which were made in the thirty-seventh year of Caesar's victory over Antony at Actium, he deprived Joazar of the high priesthood" (Josephus, *Antiquities*, 18.2.1).

c Josephus, *War*, 2.2.5–6.

convention of inclusive reckoning.¹⁶² The phrase in the decree "every fourth year" (*quarto quoque anno*) was misinterpreted as meaning inclusively by the priests. Augustus corrected the mistake by ordering the next 12 years to pass without any intercalation.[a]

However, one must keep in mind that the practice of inclusive reckoning in Italy during Roman times wasn't universal or conclusive, as one would like. There is evidence that non-inclusive reckoning was used also.¹⁶³

4.3 QUIRINIUS'S SECOND CENSUS IN 6 A.D.

Augustus appointed Quirinius promptly to be the governor of Syria and sent him to settle Archelaus's account in 6 A.D. At the same time, he took a taxation census of the region. Luke cited this census in quoting Gamaliel, a rabbi of the law: *"After this man, Judas of Galilee appeared in the days of the census and drew away some people after him; he also perished, and all those who followed him were scattered"* (Acts 5:37).

Josephus corroborated Luke's account in his record of a revolt led by Judas of Galilee while this census was being taken.[b] Based on Luke's account, this would have been Quirinius's second census.

4.4 QUIRINIUS'S FIRST CENSUS IN 2 B.C.

Quirinius conducted his first census in the year of Jesus's birth, which would have been in the 3/2 B.C. period, according to Luke (Luke 2:2).

There were three Roman censuses on record in the two decades closest to the period of Jesus's birth in Judea—namely, in 8 B.C.,¹⁶⁴ 2 B.C. (Luke 2:2),¹⁶⁵ and 6 A.D. (Acts 5:37). However, the census in 8 B.C. was too remote from the possible years when Herod could have died, and thus it is irrelevant here.

Apparently, Caesar Augustus accepted the highest honor of *Pater Patriae*, meaning "Father of the Country," in 2 B.C., at a time when he had also planned

---

a "Thus Caesar, having held the civil year, made it known by edict that the dimensions of the moon had been established. And the error could have remained hitherto had it not been for the priests to have made a new error by the amendment itself. For when it was necessary for the day to be completed, the fourth year, before the fifth began to intercalate; This error continued for thirty-six years, during which years twelve days were intercalated, when nine had to be intercalated. But Augustus also corrected this error, which was lately discovered, and ordered that twelve years should be passed without intercalation; After this one day, according to Caesar's ordinance, the fifth intercalari in the beginning of the year he ordered, and ordered all this order of brass tablets to be kept in order for everlasting engraving" (Macrobius, *Satunalia*, 1.14.13–15).

b Josephus, *War*, 2.8.1.

to dedicate the Forum Augustum and the temple of Mars Ultor. He had declined such a title for quite some time.[a]

According to Josephus, an oath of allegiance was required from all Jews around that same period:

> When all the people of the Jews gave assurance of their good-will to Caesar, and to the king's [Herod's] government, these very men did not swear, being about six thousand; and when the king imposed a fine upon them, Pheroras' wife paid their fine for them.[b]

Pheroras, Herod's younger brother, was tetrarch of Galilee.

Orosius, a Spanish historian and theologian who lived from 385 to 420 A.D., wrote about an oath tied to a Roman census that took place in 2 B.C. He wrote,

> Seven hundred and ten years after the foundation of the City [710 AUC], after Julius Caesar was killed, Octavian, to whom his uncle had bequeathed in his will both his estate and name, and who was later, after he had assumed power, called Augustus, came to Rome and, though he was but a youth, devoted himself to waging civil war...
>
> So in the seven hundred and fifty two years after the foundation of the City [752 AUC], Caesar Augustus... ordered that the first census be taken in each and every province and that every man be recorded, God deemed it right to be seen as, and become, a man. Christ was therefore born at this time and at his birth was immediately recorded on the Roman census. This census in which he who made all men wished to be listed as a man and numbered among men was the first and clearest statement which marked out Caesar as the lord of all and the Romans as masters of the world...
>
> This was when the first and greatest census was held, when all God's creation of great nations unanimously swore loyalty to Caesar alone, and at the same time, by partaking of the census were made into one community.[166]

Orosius wrote that Julius Caesar died in the year 710 AUC after the foundation of the city, which corresponds to 44 B.C. Thus, year 752 AUC equates to 2 B.C.,

---

a Dio, *Roman History*, 55.10.10; and Suetonius, *Twelve Caesars*, 2.58.1–2.
b Josephus, *Antiquities*, 17.2.4.

in which Augustus ordered a census that was to be accompanied by the swearing of loyalty across the Roman Empire.

The census in 2 B.C. that Orosius referred to is likely the same one described by Josephus and Luke (Luke 2:2). Jesus's name was registered in this census in 2 B.C., according to Orosius.[167]

> *Now in those days a decree went out from Caesar Augustus, that a census be taken of all the inhabited earth. This was the first census taken while Quirinius was governor of Syria. And all the people were on their way to register for the census, each to his own city.* (Luke 2:1–3)

A direct translation of Luke 2:2 from the original Greek reads this way: "This registration first took place was governing (procurator, proconsul or governor) Syria Quirinius."[168] The same Greek word used here, *hégemoneuóntos* (ἡγεμονεύοντος), means "governing of procurator, proconsul, or governor."[169] It was used only twice by Luke, once in reference to Quirinius and the other to Pontius Pilate (Luke 3:1). This same word isn't used elsewhere in the Bible.

Matthew, Mark, Luke, and Peter used other words from the same root, *hégemón* (ἡγεμών), to describe someone in a ruling position. These words appear a total of 20 times in the New Testament and they are translated mainly as governor, ruler, or prince.

However, this root word has a much broader meaning. It can refer to a chief, commander, guide, general, leader, prefect, prince, ruler, president, procurator, governor, or sovereign.[170]

Many Bible translations say that Quirinius *"was governor"* (Luke 2:2). However, the English word for governor, which is equivalent to a proconsul or legate of a province, implies the highest-ranking officer in a country or province. But that's likely not how it was intended to be used here for Quirinius.

In 1961, a first-century stone was discovered that dedicated a building to Emperor Tiberius in Caesarea. The inscribed Latin phrase reads "…Tiberievm… [Po]ntivs Pilatvs… [Praef]ectvs Ivda[ea]…"[a] [171] This text in English says "… Tiberieum… Pontius Pilate… Prefect Judea…"

This stone, known as the Pilate Stone, reveals that Pontius Pilate was once a prefect of Judea, and during this time he dedicated a building called Tiberieum to honor Caesar Tiberius.

---

a The letters in brackets aren't legible on the stone itself but were mended by the archeologists who interpreted the ancient inscription. The name of the building being dedicated was called the Tiberieum.

On the other hand, the Roman historian Tacitus attested that Pilate was a procurator: "Christ, from whom the name had its origin, suffered the extreme penalty during the reign of Tiberius at the hands of one of our procurators, Pontius Pilate... in Judea."[a]

In addition, Josephus also referred Pilate as a procurator of Judea.[b]

Likely, Pontius Pilate was appointed initially as a prefect of Judea and later promoted to procurator.

Historically, Judea was well known to be a troublesome place for foreign political powers. Any Roman procurator governing Judea would have needed strong military might. Pilate probably had four to five infantry cohorts and a cavalry regiment with a total of about 2,500 to 5,000 soldiers under his command. In many ways, he acted like a Roman legate of legion, or general. At the same time, he ruled as a procurator who administered the judiciary and presided in the Roman court in Jerusalem. He also collected taxes for Rome in Judea, Samaria, and Idumea.

A Roman prefect, procurator, and legate of legion were all subordinate to a proconsul or governor, the top Roman officer in the province. Pilate was appointed as a prefect and later procurator of Judea from 26 to 36 A.D. During his 10-year tenure, he had to report to three proconsuls or legates of Syria—namely, L. Aelius Lamina (21–32 A.D.), L. Pomponius Flaccus (32–35 A.D.), and L. Vitellius (35–39 A.D.).[172] Vitellius was the one who dismissed and ordered Pilate to go to Rome to face accusations against him for ordering his troops to slay many innocent Samaritans.[c]

Clearly, Luke was saying in Luke 2:2 that Quirinius was a general/procurator in Syria, similar to what Pilate was in Judea some years later. Likely, Augustus deployed Quirinius to Syria as a legate of legion to assist Saturninus in controlling the rebellious neighboring countries, such as Armenia and Cilicia. One legion comprised about 5,000 soldiers.[173] Quirinius would have reported to the governor or legate of Syria, Sentius Saturninus, who was consul in 19 B.C.[174] and seven years senior in consulship to Quirinius. The Roman administration in Syria likely received Augustus's decree in early 2 B.C. to take a census in both Syria and Judea.

---

a Tacitus, *The Annals*, 15.44.

b Josephus, *Antiquities*, 18.3.1; and Josephus, *War*, 2.9.2.

c Josephus, *Antiquities*, 18.4.2.

Justin Martyr, a Christian apologist from 100–165 A.D., referred to both Pilate and Quirinius as procurator (επιτροπου, *epitropou*[175]).[a][176] Similarly, Philo of Alexandria, the Jewish philosopher and contemporary of Jesus who lived from 20 B.C.–50 A.D, used an equivalent word, *epitropos* (επίτροπος),[b] to describe Pilate's appointment as procurator in Judea.[177]

Above all, Justin Martyr identified Quirinius as the procurator, or lieutenant, who took the census when Jesus was born, resonating with Luke's statement in Luke 2:2.

In taking the census, Quirinius performed the role of a procurator. He was not the proconsul or legate of Syria at the time of Jesus's birth, and therefore there is no conflict between Luke and Tertullianus regarding who the governor of Syria was. The confusion was created solely by the translation error of the word ἡγεμονεύοντος in Luke 2:2 and 3:1. Instead of "was governor," this should have been translated as "was governing as a general/procurator."

Scholars have written scores of papers and articles attempting to assign to Quirinius the undated and unnamed inscription on a tombstone discovered near Tivoli in 1764. The inscription identified as "Titulus Tiburtinus CIL XIV 3613 ILS 918"[178] refers to a person being proconsul of Syria twice. Some people have taken this conjecture as proof, as though it were a well-established historical fact that Quirinius was proconsul of Syria twice.

This subject has remained debatable for a long time, and the debate will likely continue well into the future because the inscription is undated and unnamed. Scholars can speculate as much as they want. However, the most probable candidate for the person referred to on the tombstone is Sentius Saturninus.[179] Quirinius should be disqualified because the tombstone doesn't mention another important highlight of his career, which is being an advisor to Gaius Caesar in Syria.

King Herod's Judean kingdom was always under the oversight of the governor of Syria, as demonstrated on many occasions in Josephus's work. Herod was stricken with serious chronic illness, and possibly mental diseases, in his last years. Saturninus, proconsul of Syria, then sent one of his legion generals, Quirinius,

---

a "Our teacher of these things is Jesus Christ, who also was born for this purpose, and was crucified under Pontius Pilate, procurator [επιτροπου] of Judaea, in the times of Tiberius Caesar" (Martyr, *Apologies*, 1:13).

b "This is a village in the land of the Jews, thirty-five stadia from Jerusalem, in which Jesus Christ was born, as you can learn from the census which was taken under Quirinius, who was your first procurator [επιτροπου] or in Judea" (Martyr, *Apologies*, 1:34). Note: the Greek word επίτροπος was translated as "lieutenant" by F.H. Colson in Philo's *The Embassy to Gaius*.

to conduct Caesar Augustus's census in Herod's Judean kingdom in the year of Jesus's birth in 2 B.C. Herod's eldest son Antipater was probably on his way back to Judea from Rome during the census period.

There were probably several prefects, procurators, and generals in Syria, because it was a sizable province. Saturninus would have sent them all to perform the census in different regions under his jurisdiction. After all the data and/or taxes were collected, the results could have been sent on to Rome. Thus, it is correct to say that either Saturninus, legate of Syria, or Quirinius, legion general of Syria, took the census in Judea in 2 B.C.

This census was different from the previous ones, though, because it required everyone to go back to their hometown to register. It might not have been a tax collection census, though the information from the registration could have been used for tax collection purposes later. People who had left their birthplaces or ancestral lands had to return to take part in family reunions if their relatives were still alive. They took time off from work and spent money to travel.

Caesar Augustus fulfilled his vow of constructing and dedicating the temple of Mars Ultor in Rome on August 1, 2 B.C. Earlier, he had accepted the highest honor of being named "Father of the Country," on February 5.[a] Likely, he wanted all his subjects across the empire to vow loyalty to him, not just the Italians. Thus in early 2 B.C., he decreed to take a registration of all who would swear their goodwill allegiance to him.[180]

Historically, there is evidence of other such registrations being performed by Rome, in terms of requesting citizens to return to their hometowns.[181]

The Judean kingdom was under the jurisdiction of Herod the Great. Most likely, the legion general/procurator Quirinius went to Herod and requested his collaboration. Herod would have been glad to comply in administering the census through local Jewish officials. He wasn't going to miss this golden opportunity to secure the Jews' assurance of goodwill submission towards not only Caesar but also his local government, as noted by Josephus. Jews who wouldn't swear allegiance to Caesar were fined by Herod.[b]

4.5 QUIRINIUS IN ARCHAEOLOGY

Young crown prince Gaius Caesar was appointed by Augustus and the Senate to be the imperial proconsul of Syria in 1 B.C. at the actual age of 19 years old.[182]

---

a Suetonius, *Twelve Caesars*, 2.58.1–2.

b Josephus, *Antiquities*, 17.2.4.

The Timing of God's Visitations

Augustus assigned Quirinius to be one of Gaius's advisors[a] in Middle Eastern affairs because he had valuable experience in Syria, Cilicia, and Galatia as a legion general.

Quirinius would have been grateful to Augustus for such a promotion. On the other hand, if Quirinius had been a legate of Syria earlier, this would have been a demotion for him. He was a middle-aged general in his forties and nowhere near retirement. Logically, Augustus would not have selected a demoted officer to advise his heir in the province of Syria, because no one knew what grudges such an individual might hold.

Young Gaius died on February 21, 4 A.D. from a wound afflicted earlier by an Armenian commander named Addon.[183]

According to Caesar Tiberius, a tutor named Marcus Lollius encouraged Caesar Gaius "in his perverse and quarrelsome behaviour" when they met at Chios.[b] Young Gaius could have been quite argumentative and not listened to Quirinius's advice. He rashly trusted strangers and suffered the dreadful consequence of eventually losing his life.

Addon enticed Gaius to come close to the city wall, pretending that he would reveal some of the Parthian king's secrets. Instead he wounded him seriously.[184] Gaius resigned from his proconsulship and later took a vessel home but died at Limyra.

Quirinius had done his job properly as one of Gaius's advisors. When Archelaus was exiled in 6 A.D., Augustus promoted Quirinius to be the legate of Syria and commissioned him to secure Archelaus's assets in Judea, Samaria, and Idumea, as well as conduct a taxation census in the Syrian region, as noted earlier.

The famous Aemilius Secundus's tombstone, which was acquired in Beirut in 1674 by the Venetian merchants who subsequently brought it to Venice, was engraved with the following translated message:

> Quintus Aemilius Secundus s[on] of Q[uintus], of the tribe Palatina, who served in the camps of the divine Aug[ustus] under P. Sulpicius Quirinius, legate of Caesar in Syria, decorated with honorary distinctions, prefect of the 1st cohort Aug[ustus], prefect of the cohort II Classica, Besides, by order of Quirinius I made the census in Apamea of citizens male 117 thousand. Besides, sent on mission by Quirinius against the Itureans, on Mount Lebanon I took their citadel…[185]

---

a Tacitus, *The Annals*.
b Ibid., 3.48.

This inscription confirms the historical record of the census conducted by Quirinius as the governor or legate of Syria.

According to Josephus, the census was completed in the thirty-seventh year of Caesar's victory over Antony and Cleopatra at Actium, which happened on September 2, 31 B.C.[a] In other words, the census was taken in 6/7 A.D. This corroborates the date given by Dio for Archelaus's exile in 6 A.D.

Furthermore, the designation of "legate of Augustus Caesar of Syria (*legato Augusti Caesaris Syriae*)" in the inscription to Quirinius could mean that Quirinius was a special envoy of Caesar[186] directly under Augustus's command, similar to Sabinus, who was Caesar's Steward for Syrian Affairs,[b] or Caesar's procurator. Augustus needed someone like his right-hand man and best friend, Marcus V. Agrippa, who wasn't connected to any powerful aristocrats or clans. He was someone Augustus could trust. Quirinius fit the requirement of being unconnected.

Two other undated inscriptions were discovered by Sir William M. Ramsay in 1912 and 1913 in Pisidian Antioch, in modern-day Turkey,[187] mentioning Quirinius as a duumvir, meaning "one of two people jointly holding power, or one of two officers or magistrates constituting a board or court."[188]

No details were ever found to pinpoint what kind of civic power Quirinius held, with whom, or for where. Probably, legion general Quirinius was commissioned by the Senate to serve as a duumvir,[c] one of the two chief magistrates for the region of Pisidian Antioch.[189] He would have been one of two judges in charge of the administration of justice for the region.

Duumvirs had limited power within their jurisdiction and were subordinate to the proconsul[190]—in this case, of Asia. Quirinius was not a proconsul or legate of Cilicia or Galatia; instead he was a duumvir and legion general. His duumvir title would have been dismissed once he had left Pisidian Antioch.

The first inscription[d] was translated by Ramsay to read as follows:

To Gaius Caristanius, son of Gaius, of Sergian tribe, Fronto Caesainus Julius, chief [or prefect] of engineers, pontifex, priest, prefect of P.

---

a Josephus, *Antiquities*, 17.13.2, 18.1.1, 18.2.1.

b Josephus, *Antiquities*, 17.9.3, 17.10.1.

c It was fairly common to designate high-ranking Roman officers and their sons as duumvirs throughout the Roman Empire (Eric M. Orlin, *Temples, Religion, and Politics in the Roman Republic* [Boston, MA: Brill Academic, 2002]).

d The artifact was registered as #9502 in Hermann Dessau's book, *Inscription Latinae Selectae, Volume III* (Berlin, Germany: Apud Weidmannos, 1916).

The Timing of God's Visitations

Sulpicius Quirinius duumvir, prefect of M. Servilius, To him first of all men at state expense by decree of the decuriones [local council], a statue was erected.[191]

The second inscription[a] reads:

To C Caristanius Fronto Caesiaus Iulius, son of Gaius, from the tribe of Sergia, prefect of civil engineers, military tribune of the twelfth legion, prefect of Bosporan cohort, priest, prefect of P. Sulpicius Quirinius Duumvir, prefect of Marcus Servilius, prefect...[192]

Caristanius had a long military career which likely started when he was a young foot soldier to a prefect of engineers. He went on to serve as a tribune of the twelfth legion, prefect of the Bosporan cohort in Greece, a priest in the army, and a prefect under general Quirinius duumvir. Caristanius also served as a prefect of Marcus Servilius.

Aelius Lamia and Marcus Servilius were the elected consuls in 3 A.D.[193] Marcus Servilius was 15 years junior in consulship than Quirinius. Normally, Servilius would have served one full year in the Roman Senate as consul leader before taking some kind of military command in the field. According to the Fasti inscription, Lamia and Servilius were substituted by suffect consuls P. Silius and Volusius Saturninus in 3 A.D.[194]

The earliest time that Caristanius could have switched from serving under Quirinius to Servilius is 3/4 A.D. This is the period when Gaius Caesar was wounded and on his way back to Rome. All of Gaius's servants, tutors, and team of advisors were liable for their failure in protecting him. Obviously Quirinius had been forced to give up his legate of legion power and report to Caesar Augustus personally. Marcus Servilius was possibly sent by an edict of the Senate or Augustus in the summer/fall of 3 A.D. to replace Quirinius in Syria so that Quirinius could return to Rome for a hearing.

Quirinius might have accompanied Gaius on the same vessel heading back to Rome. According to Suetonius, Augustus punished all the tutor and attendants who took advantage of Gaius's illness and death in committing acts of arrogance and greed in Syria. They were thrown into a river with heavy weights about their necks.[b]

---

a This artifact was registered as #9503 in Hermann Dessau's book, *Inscription Latinae Selectae, Volume III*.

b Suetonius, *Twelve Caesars*, 2.67.2.

As a brief summary of Quirinius's military career, first he subjugated the Marmarides and Garamantes in Libya around 15 B.C.[195] This victory probably earned him the consulship in 12 B.C.[196]

In the period from 11 B.C. to about 6 B.C., Quirinius earned the honor of a triumph for having stormed some fortresses of the Homonadenses in Cilicia.[197] These and other military successes earned him the rank of duumvir at Pisidian Antioch.

In 6 B.C., King Tigranes III died and the Armenians revolted and sought autonomy by affiliating with the Parthians. They installed Tigranes's sons as joint rulers without seeking approval from Rome.[198] Augustus was distressed by this, possibly due to the increasing potential of war with Parthia.

In 5 B.C., "Artavasdes was next appointed (Armenian) king by command of Augustus and subsequently expelled, but only after a disaster to the Roman arms."[199]

Augustus may have sent Quirinius, his special legate of legion, to Syria after Rome's disastrous losses in 5 B.C. His mission would have been to reinforce military power in the region in preparation for a potential war with Armenia and Parthia. Quirinius would have served under Saturninus, governor of Syria, up until their replacement in the fall of 2 B.C. by Quinctilius Varus and his troops. By then, the censuses in Syria and Judea were completed by Saturninus, who reported it back to Rome.

From 1 A.D. to 4 A.D., Quirinius was one of the advisors to Gaius Caesar. In other words, his highest military rank before 1 A.D. was most likely a duumvir and legion general, as engraved in Caristanius's inscriptions. He became the governor of Syria when Archelaus was deposed in 6 A.D. and Judea, Samaria, and Idumea were annexed as part of Syria.

4.6 SEQUENCE OF EVENTS AROUND JESUS'S BIRTH

The major historical events surrounding Jesus's birth are summarized chronologically in Table 4.1. These events paint a vivid picture of the political circumstances in and around Judea during the period when Jesus Christ was born into the world. The dates in the table are computed or inferred based on information provided mainly by Josephus and other pertinent sources.

Table 4.1. Chronological events around the time of Jesus's birth.[200]

Year Estimated	Event	Source
5 B.C.	Saturninus, Pedanius, Volumnius, and other Roman officials preside in the parricide trial of Alexander and Aristobulus. Both brothers are executed by the order of their father, Herod.	*War*, 1.27.2
5/4 B.C.	Herod's eldest son, Antipater, co-reigns unofficially as king with him in Judea. Herod names Antipater as his successor.	*Antiquities*, 17.1.1, 17.2.4,
Fall 4 B.C.	Antipater sails to Rome with Herod's testament designating him to succeed the client kingship. Caesar Augustus validates Herod's testament. Officially Herod retires in 4 B.C. and Antipater becomes the new king of the Jews.	*Antiquities*, 17.3.2
3 B.C.	Antipater plans to stay away until his father is murdered, as intended, or dies of his chronic diseases. He is fearful of Herod finding out about his murderous plot against his two half-brothers, who were executed a couple of years earlier. From Rome, he applies the same trick to accuse his other two half-brothers, Archelaus and Philip.	*Antiquities*, 17.4.3

Early 2 B.C.	Augustus decrees to take a census across the Roman Empire. Sentius Saturninus, legate of Syria, sends legion general Quirinius to take the census in Herod's kingdom. Herod collaborates with Quirinius in the exercise and orders free Jews to return to their hometowns to register and swear assurance of goodwill to Caesar and Herod's government. This is general Quirinius's first census.	Luke 2:2; *Antiquities*, 17.2.4 [201]
Spring 2 B.C.	In the spring of 2 B.C., Joseph and Mary go to Bethlehem to take part in the census and Mary gives birth to Jesus in a manger, where the shepherds visit. The family of three then move into a house and stay in Bethlehem.	Luke 2:7–8
Spring 2 B.C.	After the death of Pheroras (Herod's younger brother, tetrarch of Galilee), Herod discovers Antipater's parricide plot. Josephus writes, "Seven months had intervened between his [Antipater] conviction and return." Essentially, Antipater is convicted *in absentia* after his parricide scheme is exposed. Herod sends Antipater a benevolent letter, urging him to return quickly.	*War*, 1.30.1–1.31.2; *Antiquities*, 17.5.1
Fall 2 B.C.	Earlier, the Magi in Mesopotamia tracked the movement of a bright star in the night sky for quite some time. They likely searched the literature and determined that the star signified the birth of a Jewish king. They head for Jerusalem in the fall of 2 B.C. to pay tribute to this newborn king of the Jews.	Matthew 2:1–2

Late Fall 2 B.C.	Antipater arrives in Jerusalem in early November of 2 B.C. and faces trial before Quinctilius Varus, who replaced Sentius Saturninus as legate of Syria. Antipater is found guilty and jailed to await the final verdict from Rome.	*War*, 1.31.5, 1.32.5
December, 2 B.C.	Herod meets the Magi in Jerusalem to inquire about the precise time when they first saw the star. He tells the Magi to look for the child in Bethlehem and report back after they find him. The star becomes visible again in the night sky, having stopped above the general location where Jesus was staying. (Note: planets such as Jupiter in retrograde motion relative to the earth do appear to stop in the sky for a period of time.) The Magi present their gifts and worship the child Jesus.	Matthew 2:1–11
December, 2 B.C.	The Magi are told in a dream not to go back to Herod, so they return to their country by another route. That same night, an angel instructs Joseph in a dream to take Mary and Jesus to Egypt. Herod is furious when he realizes that the Magi left without reporting to him, so he sends his army to kill all the boys two years and under in Bethlehem and its vicinity.	Matthew 2:12–16 [202]
January 10, 1 B.C.	Earlier, Herod had erected a golden eagle over the great gate of the temple. The eagle is broken into pieces by a group of young Jews. Herod then orders some to be burnt alive, along with the two rabbis who instigated the incident. The rest are slain by soldiers. A lunar eclipse occurs that night.	*War*, 1.33.2; *Antiquities*, 17.6.4

Sulpicius Quirinius's Censuses

January 27, 1 B.C.	Herod's health deteriorates further from terrible chronic disease. He orders Antipater's execution after receiving permission from Augustus five days prior to his own death on January 27 of 1 B.C. The date of Herod's death is inferred from the date Shebat 2 for a festival in the Jewish Megillat Taanit. News of Herod's death is sent to Rome the next day.	*War*, 1.33.8 203
April 6, 1 B.C.	After Herod's funeral is complete, a furor breaks out at the temple prior to the Passover on April 7, 1 B.C., with the Jews inciting revenge for the death of those killed by Herod's armies on January 10. Archelaus sends in his troops to subdue the unrest. As a result, 3,000 Jews are killed by soldiers. Archelaus cancels Passover and orders the Jews to go home.	*Antiquities*, 17.9.3
April 23, 1 B.C.	Archelaus, family members, and government officials sail to Rome to seek Caesar Augustus's approval of Herod's last testament. Varus goes to Jerusalem to punish the imprisoned Jews who revolted on Passover. He advises Philip to go to Rome for his inheritance hearing.	*War*, 2.2.3; *Antiquities*, 17.10.1, 17.11.1
May 29, 1 B.C.	Caesar's procurator Sabinus and his troops provoke a Jewish uproar, and fighting breaks out. Roman soldiers burn the porticoes and plunder the temple treasury on the day before Pentecost. Sabinus and his troops are trapped within the palace by angry Jews who came for the festival.	*War*, 2.3.2–3

The Timing of God's Visitations

June 9, 1 B.C.	Varus takes control of Jerusalem after returning from his march back to Antioch. Sabinus and his troops slip away promptly. Varus crucifies 2,000 Jews to end the unrest.	*War*, 2.5.2
Fall 1 B.C.	Archelaus is appointed ethnarch of Judea, Samaria, and Idumea by Augustus in Rome. Antipas is made tetrarch of Galilee and Perea. Philip II is made tetrarch in Panea, Batanea, Auranitis, Gaulanitis, and Trachonitis.	*Antiquities*, 17.11.4
Late 1 B.C.	Joseph returns with Jesus and Mary from Egypt to live in Nazareth of Galilee in late 1 B.C., after Herod died earlier in the year, and after hearing the news that Archelaus reigns in Judea.	Matthew 2:19–23
1 B.C. /4 A.D.	Crown prince Gaius Caesar is appointed imperial proconsul of Syria in 1 B.C. He arrives in Syria in mid-1 A.D. with Quirinius as one of his advisors. Gaius is tricked and injured by an Armenian soldier in the summer of 3 A.D., and he later dies from the wound on February 21, 4 A.D. at Limyra, Lycia on his way back to Italy.	Dio, *RH*, 55.10, 55.10a.6–7
4/6 A.D.	Lucius Volusius Saturninus is appointed legate of Syria by Augustus from 4 to 6 A.D.	[204]
Early 6 A.D.	Archelaus is deposed and exiled to Vienne in Gaul 6 A.D. by Augustus. The regions of Judea, Samaria, and Idumea are annexed into Syria.	*Antiquities*, 17.13.3

Early 6 A.D.	Caesar Augustus promotes Quirinius to governor of Syria in 6 A.D. and sends him to secure Archelaus's assets and at the same time take a taxation census in the province. This is Quirinius's second census. Judas the Galilean and his followers revolt during the time of this census. In the end, Judas is killed and his followers are scattered.	*War*, 2.7.3, 2.8.1; *Antiquities*, 17.13.5, Acts 5:37
September, 9 A.D.	Quinctilius Varus overestimates the fighting strength of his troops and moves into dangerous Germanic territory. His armies are ambushed by the Germanic tribes in the Battle of the Teutoburg Forest in September 9 A.D. Varus loses his life together with three Roman legions and support personnel. In total, between 15,000 and 20,000 men meet their demise. Augustus is traumatized by the news and repeatedly utters the famous saying, "Quintili Vare, legiones redde," meaning "Quinctilius Varus, give me back my legions," while banging his head against the door.	Suetonius, *TC*, 2.23 [205]

Note the following abbreviations: RH (*Roman History*) and TC (*The Lives of the Twelve Caesars*).

History clearly shows that none of the people who engaged in power struggles, pursuit of glory, land conquest, or quests for fame and fortune gained anything in the end. This includes people such as Julius Caesar, Magnus Pompey, Sextus Pompey, Mark Antony, Caesar Augustus, Herod the Great, Antipater, Archelaus, Quinctilius Varus, and Pontius Pilate. All that's left of them are records of their atrocities. They are accountable for shedding much innocent blood. They came into the world emptyhanded but managed to create extreme pain and suffering for others, and at the end they left emptyhanded. Most of their skeletal remains are nowhere to be found; only their infamous names are left.

When Rome was sacked by King Alaric of the Visigoths in 410 A.D., they broke into the mausoleum of Caesar Augustus, dumped his and his successor's ashes on the floor, and took the golden urns as trophies.[206]

In later decades, Augustus's mausoleum was converted into a castle which was bombed, and eventually made into a theatre for circuses, bullfighting, and concerts. It has been abandoned to ruins for a long time.[207] Restoration work on the mausoleum for tourism purpose has only recently begun.

4.7 SUMMARY

Based on the information provided by Josephus, Luke, Dio, Appian, Tertullianus, Orosius, Justin Martyr, and the Jewish Mishnah, we can conclude that Herod was appointed king of the Jews by the Roman Senate around October 39 B.C., that he captured Jerusalem in September 36 B.C., and that he died around January 27 of 1 B.C.

In early 2 B.C., Caesar Augustus decreed that a census be taken across the entire Roman Empire. People were required to return to their ancestral towns to register and vouch their goodwill and loyalty to Caesar. Likely, Augustus had planned this for some time. He accepted the title "Father of the Country" and dedicated the temple of Mars Ultor, which he had pledged around 44/43 B.C. to build. He renewed his vow again in 20 B.C., and construction of the temple began shortly after.

Sentius Saturninus, legate of Syria, sent legion general Quirinius to request Herod's assistance in taking the census in Judea. It was Quirinius's first census, as noted by Luke (Luke 2:1–3) and Justin Martyr.[208]

Archelaus was deposed as ethnarch of Judea and exiled to Gaul in 6 A.D. by Caesar. Judea, Samaria, and Idumea were annexed into the province of Syria. Augustus promoted Quirinius to legate of Syria and ordered him to take a taxation census in the Syrian regions.[a] This was Quirinius's second census (Acts 5:37).

Jesus was most likely born in the spring, summer, or fall of 2 B.C. at Bethlehem. After growing up in Nazareth, he was baptized by John the Baptist in the River Jordan in the summer of 29 A.D. (Luke 3:1–2). By then, Jesus had turned 30 years old, but not yet 31, as Luke reported (Luke 3:23).

---

a Josephus, *Antiquities*, 17.13.2, 18.1.1, 18.2.1.

Debate Over the Date of Herod's Death

Chapter Five

5.1 HEROD'S SONS MEETING PRINCE GAIUS CAESAR IN 1 B.C.?

In the article "The Date of Herod's Death," Timothy Barnes wrote,

> Although temporal indications are completely lacking for Gaius's movements between his being in Rome in 2 B.C. and his presence in Syria in A.D. 1, the time needed for the operations on the Danube and in Arabia requires him to have left Rome early spring 1 B.C. at the very latest. That he did not return to Rome from the northern frontier before going to Egypt seems to be indicated by the fact that he travelled there by way of the Ionian islands; the voyager from Rome was carried very swiftly by the prevailing winds direct from the straits of Messina to Alexandria.[209]

Barnes assumes that Gaius didn't return to Rome after his legate training at Ister in 1 B.C. Instead he sailed directly to Alexandria, Egypt by way of the Ionian islands. He then operated in those regions and arrived in Syria in A.D. 1.

There are a few pertinent questions associated with Barnes's assumption which he did not address.

1. When did Gaius receive his commissioning ceremony in the temple of Mars Ultor in Rome? By Augustus's decree, all those who were dispatched to the provinces with military commands should have been escorted from the temple of Mars in a send-off ceremony.[a]

---

a Suetonius, *Twelve Caesars*, 2.29.

2. When did the royal wedding of Gaius Caesar and Claudia Livia take place?

3. What kind of operation or expedition did Gaius undertake in Egypt and Arabia before arriving in Syria?

4. If Gaius left Rome in the spring of 1 B.C. without fulfilling his duty as consul-elect by decree in the Senate on January 1, 1 A.D., why was his name inscribed together with Aemilius Paulius's in a tablet as consuls-elect that year?

5. Why did Gaius's replacement suffect consul, Herennius Picens,[a] join the Senate in July 1 A.D. and not January 1, 1 A.D. if Gaius had already left for Syria a year earlier?

According to Dio's chronology, Augustus gave Gaius proconsul authority of Syria and a wife after he completed his command training.[b] Gaius was "young and inexperienced in affairs."[c] This probably reflects the general public's view of all 19-year-old boys, including Gaius. To counter such a popular opinion, Augustus gave him a wife so he might have the dignity attached to a married man. After that, Gaius would have received his commissioning ceremony in the temple of Mars before setting out for Syria.

If Barnes's interpretation were correct, then Gaius's commissioning ceremony in the temple of Mars must have taken place just before Gaius was sent to the Ister warfront for command training. Also, Gaius's marriage with Claudia Livia must have happened prior to his departure. The question naturally arises of whether a student going for legion command school training could be fit to be commissioned by Augustus in the temple of Mars. However, if Gaius had graduated and come back to Rome, it would be a different story. No one would question his ability.

---

a Degrassi, *Fasti Capitolini*; and Liebenam, *Fasti Conslares Imperii Romani*.

b "Gaius assumed command of the legions on the Ister with peaceful intent. Indeed, he fought no war, not because no war broke out, but because he was learning to rule in quiet and safety, while the dangerous undertakings were regularly assigned to others... as for Gaius and Lucius, they were young and inexperienced in affairs. Nevertheless, under the stress of necessity, he [Augustus] chose Gaius, gave him the proconsular authority and a wife — in order that he might also have the increased dignity that attached to a married man — and appointed advisers to him. Gaius accordingly set out and was everywhere received with marks of distinction, as befitted one who was the emperor's grandson and was even looked upon as his son" (Dio, *Roman History*, 55.17–19).

c Ibid.

Debate Over the Date of Herod's Death

Ovid praised Gaius in saying, "Your avenger is at hand, and proves himself a general in his earliest years; and, while a boy, is conducting a war not fitted to be waged by a boy."[a]

How did Gaius prove himself to be a qualified boy-general to the people of Rome? The minimum requirement would have been to successfully complete his command training and return alive. Whether he actually engaged in hand-to-hand combat wouldn't be important. In fact, Dio said that Gaius stayed safe while he was at Ister. The critical matter is that he returned to Rome after having commanded the army with success.

Ovid was possibly an eyewitness to Gaius's commissioning ceremony at the temple of Mars Ultor in Rome sometime in the summer before July 1, 1 A.D. Gaius had proved himself ready and worthy of being commissioned to take command in Syria in the temple of Mars with all the glory, fanfare, and blessings from Augustus, the Senate, and the people in Rome. Ovid pleaded for the Roman god Mars Ultor to grant his divine favor as Gaius set out. Ovid even prophesized that Gaius would be victorious over the Parthians.[b]

Gerald Gertoux has suggested that Ovid's poem describing Gaius's mission to the East was written in response to the announcement made by Augustus at the dedication of the temple of Mars Ultor on May 12, 2 B.C.[210]

Firstly, Augustus dedicated the temple on August 1, 2 B.C., according to Dio.[c] The temple of Mars was not finished until August 1.[d]

Secondly, Ovid was probably describing the general Roman sentiment for Gaius's campaign against the Parthians in the commissioning ceremony in the temple of Mars, not during the temple dedication performed earlier. The reasons are simple. Who would announce to the world a year in advance that they were going to embark on a military campaign against an enemy? That way, the enemy would be able to prepare for it. That is, unless it was intended as a hoax in order for the Romans to come across as overconfident.

Typically, plans of military campaigns are highly classified, both in ancient and modern times. Many foreigners lived in Rome. Undoubtedly, there was no

---

a Ovid, *Art of Love*, 1.737.

b Ibid.

c "It is true that on the first day of August, which was his [Claudius's] birthday, there were equestrian contests, but they were not given on his account; it was rather because the temple of Mars had been dedicated on that day and this event had been celebrated thereafter by annual contests" (Dio, *Roman History*, 60.5.3).

d See Chapter Three (3.5) for a further discussion of the two different possible days for the temple's celebration and dedication.

lack of informers, spies, and assassins in the city. Furthermore, for the safety of the commanders being sent into the field, it's possible that such announcements were made known only on the same day that the troops were sent off from the temple.

Barnes's idea of Gaius travelling through Ister, Egypt, Arabia, and Judea before arriving at Syria in a single trip between 1 B.C. and 1 A.D. conflicts with Velleius's record. Velleius wrote, "Breve ab hoc intercesserat spatium, cum C. Caesar ante aliis provinciis ad visendum obitis in Syriam missus,"[a] which is translated as "Only a short time passed after this, when Gaius Caesar, having previously visited other provinces, was sent to Syria."[211] Velleius did not say, "Gaius having visited other provinces prior, arrived at Syria"; however, this is what Barnes contorts Velleius's statement to convey.

What was Gaius doing in Arabia before reaching Syria? Barnes believed that Gaius was there not for tourism but to conduct an expedition into Arabia. What kind of expedition was it? Barnes does not elaborate.

Did Gaius conduct a military expedition into Arabia? Although Augustus had plans to take Arabia much like he had taken Syria, the timing wouldn't have been right for a military campaign. It is illogical for anyone to request that the "young and inexperienced" teenager Gaius and his team start two potential warfronts in close proximity, one against the Arabs and the other against the Armenians and Parthians. There would have been a real risk of other nations joining in the revolt as well.

Taking control of Arabia was no swift task. No one knew how long this kind of war would last. In fact, the Romans had suffered heavy losses in previous military campaigns against the Arabs.

So the logical answer is that Gaius didn't conduct any military expedition in Arabia. Evidently, none of the Roman historians—such as Dio, Tacitus, and Suetonius—mentioned a word about Gaius's alleged war against the Arabs in 1 B.C. to 1 A.D. Especially Velleius, who accompanied Gaius in this trip to Syria; he made no remark about ever having visited Arabia at all. His silence on this matter speaks volumes.

Pliny comments that Aelius Gallus (70 B.C.–25 A.D.) is the only person who had conducted a military campaign of any depth in Arabia.[b] According to Dio, the

---

a Velleius, *Roman History*, 2.101.1.

b "Aelius Gallus, a member of the Order of Knights, is the only person who has hitherto carried the arms of Rome into this country; for Gaius Caesar son of Augustus only had a glimpse of Arabia. Gallus destroyed the following towns not named by the authors who have written previously - Ne-

expedition of Gallus, governor of Egypt, took place in 24 B.C. when Augustus became consul for the tenth time together with consul Gaius Norbanus.[a] In Strabo's description, Gallus's army included 130 vessels carrying about 10,000 infantry. Gallus made the mistake of trusting his Nabataean guide, Syllaeus, who deceitfully led them through treacherous routes. The Roman army suffered heavy losses through calamities such as hunger, fatigue, and disease. They managed to destroy some tribes and cities, but at the end it was a disaster for the Romans. Syllaeus was tried, convicted, and beheaded in Rome.[b]

If Gaius Caesar was in Arabia neither for tourism nor military expedition in 1 B.C., then what was he doing there? Does Barnes or anyone else know?

Furthermore, if it had been so urgent for Gaius to leave Rome for Syria after taking his command training in Ister and skipping his first consul appearance in the Senate in 1 A.D., he could not have taken this alleged roundabout trip from Ister to Alexandria, Arabia, Judea, and Syria. He should have sailed from the Adriatic Sea to either Beirut, Ptolemais, or Tripoli directly, then marched to Antioch, Syria.

Barnes's interpretation of Gaius leaving Rome in the spring of 1 B.C. was fabricated by his opinionated conviction rather than any logical reasoning. He acknowledged the fact that, in his own words, "temporal indications are

---

grana, Nestus, Nesca, Magusus, Caminacus, Labaetia; as well as Mariba above mentioned, which measures 6 miles round, and also Caripeta, which was the farthest point he reached" (Pliny, *Natural History*, 6.160).

a "Augustus now became consul for the tenth time, with Gaius Norbanus as colleague, and on the first day of the year the senate confirmed his acts by taking oaths… While this was going on, another and a new campaign had at once its beginning and its end. It was conducted by Aelius Gallus, the governor of Egypt, against the country called Arabia Felix, of which Sabos was king" (Dio, *Roman History*, 53.28.1, 53.29.3).

b "…he [Gallus] built one hundred and thirty vessels of burden, on which he set sail with about ten thousand infantry… Syllaeus treacherously out-generalled Gallus in every way, and sought, as I think, to spy out the country and, along with the Romans, to destroy some of its cities and tribes, and then to establish himself lord of all, after the Romans were wiped out by hunger and fatigue and diseases and any other evils which he had treacherously contrived for them… On his return he [Gallus] accomplished the whole journey within sixty days, although he had used up six months in his first journey. Thence he carried his army across the Myus Harbour within eleven days, and marched by land over to Coptus, and, with all who had been fortunate enough to survive, landed at Alexandria. The rest he had lost, not in wars, but from sickness and fatigue and hunger and bad roads; for only seven men perished in war. For these reasons, also this expedition did not profit us to a great extent in our knowledge of those regions, but still it made a slight contribution. But the man who was responsible for this failure, I mean Syllaeus, paid the penalty at Rome, since, although he pretend friendship, he was convicted, in addition to his rascality in this matter, of other offences too, and was beheaded" (Strabo, *Geography*, 16.4.23–24).

completely lacking for Gaius's movements between his being in Rome in 2 B.C. and his presence in Syria in A.D. 1."[212] Yet he insisted that Gaius had made a single trip from Ister to Alexandria, Arabia, Judea, and then Syria, thus providing the definitive proof that Herod's sons could not have met Gaius Caesar in Rome in 1 B.C. Gaius was in Arabia and could not have presided over the hearing of Herod's will. Consequently, Herod could not have died in 1 B.C. but in 4 B.C. instead.

Contrary to this interpretation, though, it is highly likely that Gaius was present in Rome in the summer of 1 B.C., as expounded earlier. In other words, Gaius would have been available to preside over the hearing of Herod's will in 1 B.C.

Barnes wrote,

> Historians and works of reference have long accepted the view that Herod of Judaea, surnamed the Great, died in the spring of 4 B.C. Recently, however, this date has been called in question by W. E. Filmer. Lest another such attempt ever be made to deny it, the evidence that Herod died in 5/4 B.C. will here be set out in detail.[213]

Barnes genuinely believed that his questionable interpretation of Gaius's trip from Ister to Syria did indeed provide the decisive evidence showing Herod died in 5/4 B.C. How could he be so certain that his interpretation was indeed the truth, even though—again, in his own words—the temporal indications were completely lacking? At best, his conviction in Gaius's single uninterrupted trip from Ister to Syria was only conjecture, equally probable as any other logical interpretation.

Some interpretations, speculations, hypotheses, and conjectures are more and less logical, probable, and reasonable than others. Barnes seems to have had real difficulty distinguishing speculation from proven truth, which is well substantiated by the evidence. In fact, anyone who supports Barnes's argument fails to see this as well, yet unsurprisingly there is no lack of supporters of Barnes—for example, Douglas Johnson, Louis Feldman, and Nadav Sharon, to name a few.[214]

Barnes and his supporters seem to deliberately ignore the evidence, such as the inscriptions in which Gaius Caesar and L. Aemilius Paulius are named as consuls in 1 A.D. and Herennius Picens became suffect consul starting on July 1, 1 A.D., possibly replacing Gaius after he was dispatched to Syria.[215]

Apparently, Barnes and his supporters know that such an authentic truth inscribed in stone would disprove their hypothesis that Gaius left Rome for Syria before 1 A.D. Their eagerness to confirm their own view rather than discover the truth behind the historical event causes them to experience tunnel vision; they see only their own conviction and nothing else factual.

5.2 SCHÜRER CONSENSUS SUPPORTERS

Douglas Johnson states,

> Filmer's theory had already been thoroughly discredited by T. D. Barnes in 1968.[216] In a 1983 follow-up article to Barnes, P. M. Bernegger[217] further undermined the position of Filmer and Martin by proving that, according to Josephus's narrative concerning Herod's regnal years, the death of Herod must have occurred no later than 4 B.C.[218]

Johnson's support for Barnes's conclusions and Bernegger's so-called proofs are based on superficial reasoning alone, not on the fine details of the real issues.

5.3 BERNEGGER'S VERSION OF JOSEPHUS'S INCLUSIVE RECKONING

Bernegger writes,

> The evidence presented by Barnes weighs heavily in putting this issue to rest, but as long as there are conflicting interpretations of the principal evidence, there will continue to be advocates of the opposing view. The debate can only be settled by demonstrating precisely where the error lies among the facts and figures recorded by Josephus. This paper will explain the discrepancy and confirm that Herod died no later than 4 B.C.[219]

Obviously, Bernegger is another supporter of the Schürer consensus, just like Barnes, Johnson, and others.

It is noteworthy that Bernegger acknowledges the fact that Barnes's argument did not prevent others from advocating the opposing view. Why? Because Barnes did not demonstrate precisely where the "error," as Bernegger put it, lay among the facts and figures recorded by Josephus.

According to Bernegger, the main point of contention between Filmer and Schürer (or Barnes) can be summarized as follows:

The discrepancy in question is revealed by the conflicting interpretations presented by these views. On the one hand, the consular dates situate Antigonus' deposition in 37 B.C., whereas, the reigns of Hyrcanus and Antigonus place the event in 36 B.C. The figures reported for the reigns of the high priests directly contradict the consular dates of Herod's accession. Either the consular dates are wrong, or the reigns of the high priests are inaccurate. This is the crux of the issue. If the correct date of Antigonus' deposition can be determined, then the error can be identified and the true chronology of Herod's reign established.[220]

Bernegger then cites a couple of examples to demonstrate the point that Josephus's chronology of the reigns of the high priests should be interpreted as using inclusive reckoning. As a result, the consular dates are correct, whereas the reigns of the high priest years are not.

In the following, we will examine Bernegger's examples in detail.

5.3.1 ROMAN TAXATION CENSUS IN 6 A.D.

Bernegger wrote,

> One such example is Josephus's discussion about the Roman tax registration in Syria during A.D. 6. Josephus stated that the registration was completed in the thirty-seventh year after Actium. The battle of Actium took place in 31 B.C., thirty-six factual years before the completion of the Syrian registration. In this instance, Josephus counted inclusively, and without any ambiguity.[221]

In response to Bernegger's example of Josephus using inclusive reckoning in this case, Andrew Steinmann explains:

> Bernegger then calculates this way: The Battle of Actium took place in 31 BCE. Therefore, one must add only thirty-six years to arrive at 6 CE. However, Bernegger's reasoning only works if one forgets about the date of the Battle of Actium, September 2, 31 BCE. Years after Actium commenced on September 3, not on the following January 1, as Bernegger's calculations assume. This is confirmed by the Actian Games, which were founded by Augustus in honor of his victory at

Debate Over the Date of Herod's Death

Actium and held on September 2 every four years. Josephus states that the census "happened during the thirty-seventh year of Caesar's victory over Antony at Actium"... Since the first year after Actium ran from September 2, 31 BCE to September 1, 30 BCE, the thirty-seventh year ran from September 2, 6 CE to September 1, 7 CE. Thus, in this case Josephus was not counting inclusively, since one-third of the thirty-seventh year after Actium took place in 6 CE.[222]

5.3.2 HIGH PRIESTHOOD FROM DAYS OF HEROD TO TEMPLE DESTRUCTION

Bernegger then lays out his second example:

> The siege and destruction of Jerusalem by Titus occurred in A.D. 70. Counting back 107 factual years from A.D. 70 results in the date 38 B.C. for the deposition of Antigonus, but 38 B.C. is two years earlier than the date proposed by Filmer. In fact, Filmer's date, 36 B.C., cannot be derived from the 107-year figure by any system of counting or chronology. Moreover, 38 B.C. is too early for the deposition of Antigonus. This further complicates Filmer's position because the 107-year figure cannot possibly be expressed in terms of factual years as one might expect from Filmer's assumptions.[223]

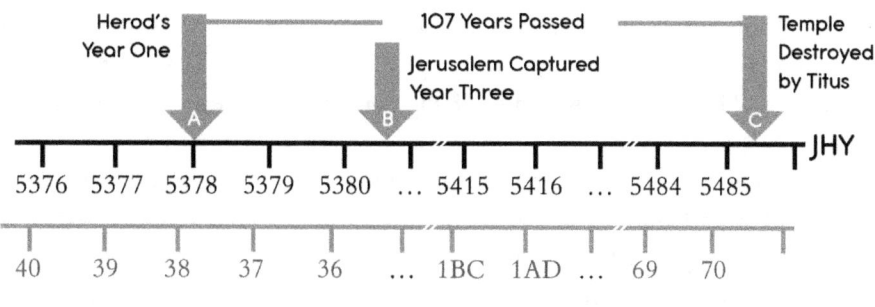

Figure 5.1. The start of Herod's first regnal year in Nisan 1 (A). Herod's capture of Jerusalem in year three (B). The temple is destroyed by Titus in 70 A.D. (C).

127

The Timing of God's Visitations

The second temple was destroyed by Titus on August 5, 70 A.D. Counting 107 actual non-inclusive years backward from 5485 JHY leads to year 5378 (5485 − 107), which is Herod's first regnal year, starting on Nisan 1, 5378 (March/April 38 B.C.), as shown in Figure 5.1. About 10 months earlier, around May/July 39 B.C., Antigonus became the high priest after deposing Hyrcanus in Jerusalem.

As Steinmann pointed out, Bernegger did not address the number of high priests at all. Counting high priests beginning with Herod's appointment of Anonel and ending with Pannias in the year of the second temple's destruction, there were 27.[224] Yet according to Josephus,

> the number of the high priests, from the days of Herod until the day when Titus took the temple and the city, and burnt them, were in all twenty-eight; the time also that belonged to them was a hundred and seven years.[a]

In other words, Josephus included Antigonus as one of the high priests to reach the total of 28 in the days during which Herod began his reign in 38 B.C. A total of 107.3 actual years passes, as shown in Figure 5.1. Josephus used a year as the basic unit, thus the decimal portion of 0.3 year was dropped, as he commonly practiced in his writings.

On the other hand, if one uses the Julian calendar, as Schürer and Bernegger do, then starting from the deposition of Antigonus in 37 B.C. to 70 A.D. there are only 27 high priests in 107 years, contrary to the 28 reported by Josephus.

If Antigonus were to be included as one of the high priests, then starting from the ascension year (the first regnal year in inclusive reckoning) of Herod in 40 B.C. to 70 A.D., there would be 28 high priests in 110 years—three years too many.

Either way, the Schürer consensus contradicts Josephus's tallies regarding the number of high priests and the total number of years from the reign of Herod to the day on which the temple was destroyed by Titus. This leads to the logical conclusion that Herod's ascension year was not 40 B.C. but 39 B.C., and his capture of Jerusalem occurred not in 37 B.C. but instead 36 B.C.

---

a Josephus, *Antiquities*, 20.10.1.

5.4 COULD HEROD HAVE CAPTURED JERUSALEM IN 38 B.C.?

Herod assisted Antony in taking the city of Samosata near the Euphrates during the consulship of Claudius and Norbanus in 38 B.C.[a] Because Antony, Sosius, and Herod were busy capturing Samosata in 38 B.C., there was no spare time or army to take Judea that year.

Afterwards, Antony gave Gaius Sosius command of Syria and Cilicia. He then set out for Italy. In fact, he went first to Egypt, based on Josephus's account.[b] Likely, Antony spent some time in Egypt with Cleopatra and their children before sailing to Athens.

In Athens, Antony and Octavia, who was pregnant with their child, sailed with 300 ships to Tarentum, Italy to meet Octavius.[c] Octavius agreed to provide two legions for 100 bronze-beaked galleys from Antony. In addition, Antony gave Octavius 20 light sailing crafts and in return Octavius gave Antony 1,000

---

a "...when he [Herod] heard that he [Antony] was besieging Samosata with a great army, which is a strong city near to Euphrates, he made the greater haste; as observing that this was a proper opportunity for showing at once his courage, and for doing what would greatly oblige Antony. Indeed, when he came, he soon made an end of that siege, and slew a great number of the barbarians, and took from them a large prey; insomuch that Antony, who admired his courage formerly, did now admire it still more. Accordingly, he heaped many more honors upon him, and gave him more assured hopes that he should gain his kingdom; and now king Antiochus was forced to deliver up Samosata" (Josephus, *War*, 1.16.7). "This, to be sure, took place at a later period; at the time under consideration Antony attacked Antiochus, shut him up in Samosata and proceeded to besiege him... This was the course of events in the consulship of Claudius and Norbanus [38 B.C.]; during the following year [37 B.C.] the Romans accomplished nothing worthy of note in Syria. For Antony spent the entire year in reaching Italy and returning again to the province" (Dio, *Roman History*, 49.22.1–23.1).

b "...after the taking of Samosata, and when Antony had set Sosius over the affairs of Syria, and had given him orders to assist Herod against Antigonus, he departed into Egypt; but Sosius sent two legions before him into Judea to assist Herod, and followed himself soon after with the rest of his army" (Josephus, *War*, 1.17.2).

c After settling some trivial matters in Syria, he returned to Athens, and sent Ventidius home, with becoming honours, to enjoy his triumph... But Antony himself, once more irritated against Caesar by certain calumnies, sailed with three hundred ships for Italy; and when the people of Brundisium would not receive his armament, he coasted along to Tarentum. Here he sent Octavia, who had sailed with him from Greece, at her own request, to her brother. She was with child, and had already borne Antony two daughters... Antony entertained Caesar first, who consented to it for his sister's sake. And after it had been agreed that Caesar should give to Antony two legions for his Parthian war, and Antony to Caesar one hundred bronze-beaked galleys, Octavia, independently of this agreement, obtained twenty light sailing craft from her husband for her brother, and one thousand soldiers from her brother for her husband" (Plutarch, *Life of Antony*, 34.4, 35.1,4).

The Timing of God's Visitations

soldiers. Afterwards, Antony sailed to Syria. Antony took the entirety of 37 B.C. to reach Italy and return again to Syria.[a]

According to Dio, after Antony had left Syria, Sosius did nothing in 37 B.C., because he didn't want to advance Antony's interest but his own.[b] Thus, Herod and Sosius could not have captured Jerusalem in either 38 or 37 B.C.

In addition, Josephus said that Herod took Jerusalem in the third year from his being appointed king of the Jews in Rome,[c] either in 37 B.C. (from 40 B.C.) or 36 B.C. (from 39 B.C.), but not 38 B.C. The year in which Sosius and Herod seized Jerusalem was a sabbatical year. Historic evidence shows that 36 B.C. was a sabbatical year, and conclusively 38 and 37 B.C. were not, as discussed in Chapter One.

Table 5.1 presents the chronology from Antigonus capturing Jerusalem by deceit shortly after Pentecost to Herod recapturing it. The ethnarch and high priest Hyrcanus was carried to Parthia, but he later returned to Jerusalem after Herod's victory over Antigonus.

Antigonus reigned three years and three months.[d] Hyrcanus could never have been a high priest again, because Antigonus had bitten off his ears to blemish him. Later, Herod murdered both Hyrcanus and Mariamne's younger brother Aristobulus in order to secure his rule over the Jews.[e]

---

a Dio, *Roman History*, 49.23.1.

b "Sosius, because anything he did would be advancing Antony's interests rather than his own, and he therefore dreaded his jealousy and anger, spent the time in devising means, not for achieving some success and incurring his enmity, but for pleasing him without engaging in any activity" (Dio, *Roman History*, 49.23.2).

c "Now as winter was going off, Herod marched to Jerusalem, and brought his army to the wall of it; this was the third year since he had been made king at Rome; so he pitched his camp before the temple, for on that side it might be besieged, and there it was that Pompey took the city" (Josephus, *War*, 1.17.8).

d "…made Antigonus, the son of Aristobulus, king; and when he had reigned three years and three months, Sosius and Herod besieged him, and took him, when Antony had him brought to Antioch, and slain there" (Josephus, *Antiquities*, 20.10.1).

e "But Mariamne's hatred to him was not inferior to his love to her. She had indeed but too just a cause of indignation from what he had done, while her boldness proceeded from his affection to her; so she openly reproached him with what he had done to her grandfather Hyrcanus, and to her brother Aristobulus; for he had not spared this Aristobulus, though he were but a child" (Josephus, *War*, 1.22.2).

Table 5.1. Chronology from Antigonus's seizure of Jerusalem to Herod's recapture.

Season	B.C.	JHY	Event	Source
Summer May/June	39	5377	Pentecost	*War*, 1.13.3
May/June	39	5377	The peace treaty of Misenum is reached between Octavius, Antony, and Sextus Pompey. After the treaty, Antony sends Ventidius in August/September to Syria to halt the advancement of the Parthians.	Plutarch, *LA*, 32.1–2, 33:1
May/June	39	5377	Antigonus's soldiers combat Herod, Phasaelus, and the guards in Jerusalem at Pentecost. Antigonus proposes to use the Parthian prince Pacorus (his secret ally) as a reconciler.	*War*, 1.13.3
June/July	39	5377	Phasaelus is killed, and Herod and his family flee to Masada. Antigonus bites off Hyrcanus's ears with his own teeth so that Hyrcanus might never be high priest again. He's taken to Parthia. Antigonus rules as king and high priest in Jerusalem.	*War*, 1.13.7–11

August/ October	39	5377	Herod sails from Alexandria, Egypt, likely in August, and reaches Rome in October due to a storm. He is appointed king of the Jews by the Senate and is tasked with taking Judea from the Parthians. Herod leaves Rome and lands on Ptolemais. Generals Silo and Ventidius arrive to assist him.	*War*, 1.14.4
Winter	39	5377	Herod returns to Judea, takes Joppa, and frees Masada. General Silo and the Roman army rest in winter quarters.	*War*, 1.15.3; *Antiquities*, 14.15.1
Winter	39	5377	Antony abides at Athens with Octavia.	*War*, 1.16.4; Appian, *RH*, 58.75–76
Winter	38	5377	Herod besieges Jerusalem but leaves shortly after.	*War*, 1.15.4
Winter	38	5377	Herod takes Sepphoris.	*War*, 1.16.1–2
Spring	38	5378	Ventidius and Silo combat the Parthians.	*War*, 1.16.4; Dio, *RH*, 49.19.4
Spring	38	5378	Herod clears out the cave robbers in Galilee. Herod's general Ptolemy is killed by robbers.	*War*, 1.16.5

Summer	38	5378	Prince Pacorus is slain by Ventidius's army. The Parthians retreat from Syria. Antony returns to Syria and relieves Ventidius of command.	*War*, 1.16.6; Dio, *RH*, 49.20.1–3, 49.21.1
Summer	38	5378	Herod helps Antony subdue Samosata near the Euphrates. Ventidius receives an honor of triumph in Rome in 38 B.C.[a]	*War*, 1.16.7; Dio, *RH*, 49.22.1–2, 49.23.1[i]
Summer/ Fall	38	5378	Herod's younger brother Joseph is slain by Antigonus's general Pappus near Jericho.	*War*, 1.17.1
Winter	38	5378	Antony goes to Egypt, Athens, and Italy. Sosius is given command of Syria and Cilicia. Sosius does nothing in 37 B.C. the following year.[b]	*War*, 1.17.2; Dio, *RH*, 49.22.2, 49.23.1–5; Plutarch, *LA*, 34.1–4
Winter	37	5378	Herod marches from Daphne, near Antioch, to Galilee to avenge his brother.	*War*, 1.17.3
Winter/ Spring	37	5378 /5379	Herod is wounded at Jericho.	*War*, 1.17.4
Summer	37	5379	Antigonus sends Pappus and his army to fight Herod's army.	*War*, 1.17.5
Fall/ Winter	37	5379	Herod marches to Jerusalem after defeating and killing Pappus.	*War*, 1.17.6

a Degrassi, *Fasti Capitolini*.
b During the consulship of Agrippa and Gallus in 37 B.C.

The Timing of God's Visitations

Winter/Spring	36	5379/5380	In the third year after Herod was appointed king, he besieges Jerusalem when winter is about to end.	*War*, 1.17.8
Spring	36	5380	Sosius sends two legions to assist Herod. Herod marries Mariamne. Antony arrives in Antioch, Syria.	*War*, 1.17.2, 1.17.9
Spring	36	5380	Sosius joins Herod with a large army.	*War*, 1.17.9
September 22/23	36	5380	After a siege of five months, Herod and Sosius capture Jerusalem on the day of the Fast. Herod sends Antigonus to Antony for execution at Antioch.	*War*, 1.18.2, *Antiquities* 20.10.1

Note the following abbreviations: RH (*Roman History*) and LA (*Life of Antony*).

First Visitation as Lamb of God

Chapter Six

The Orthodox Church celebrates Christmas on January 6,[225] while Catholic and Protestant churches have adopted December 25 as Jesus's birthday. Historically, the celebration of Jesus's birth did not start until the third century A.D.[226]

Dionysius Exiguus, who lived from 470–544 A.D., invented the Easter table for dates celebrating the crucifixion and resurrection of Jesus Christ. He placed the incarnation on March 25, 1 B.C., and so nine months later Jesus was supposed to have been born on December 25, 1 B.C. at Bethlehem.[227]

The above dates for Jesus's birth have been debated among scholars for a long time because they remain unconvincing. Christians and non-Christians alike ask the same questions about the Bible regarding Jesus's day of birth.

6.1 YEAR OF JESUS'S BIRTH

Does the Bible mention the year of Jesus's birth?

The answer is yes. Luke clearly tells us that Jesus was born in a year when Caesar Augustus decreed a census to be taken over the entire Roman Empire. If the Roman Empire were to have continued until the modern day, then the date of the decree would have served as a historical anchor point for Jesus's birthday, known to all.

The Timing of God's Visitations

In fact, Tertullianus refers twice in his book to the record archived in Rome for Jesus's enrollment in the census of Augustus.[a] The question of whether Tertullianus saw these records himself would be a subject for other research. Yet it is possible that he might have seen the records because he lived in Rome for some time, and that's where he was introduced to Christianity.[228] He strongly believed that such a census record did exist and was kept in Rome.

Due to the ruins of war, these records have been lost and destroyed. All we can do now is to make an educated assessment for the day of Jesus's birth based on the historical clues we can find.

King Herod most probably died around January 27, 1 B.C. between the full lunar eclipse visible in Judea on January 10, 1 B.C. and Passover on April 7, 1 B.C. Jesus was born within the two years prior to Herod's death. In addition, Luke said that Jesus was about 30 years old when he started his ministry right after his baptism by John in the River Jordan. Jesus would have been 30 in 29 A.D., the fifteenth year of Tiberius's reign. Thus Jesus was born in 2 B.C. This is well supported by the early Christian consensus.[b]

6.2 TIME OF YEAR WHEN JESUS WAS BORN

Does the Bible allude to the time of year when Jesus was born? Again, the answer is yes—yet indirectly. Luke said the following:

> *Now Joseph also went up from Galilee, from the city of Nazareth, to Judea, to the city of David which is called Bethlehem, because he was of the house and family of David, in order to register along with Mary, who was betrothed to him, and was pregnant. While they were there, the time came for her to give birth. And she gave birth to her firstborn son; and she wrapped Him in cloths, and laid Him in a manger, because there was no room for them in the inn.*
>
> *In the same region there were some shepherds staying out in the fields and keeping watch over their flock at night. And an angel of the Lord suddenly stood near them, and the glory of the Lord shone around them; and they were terribly*

---

a "And yet how could He have been admitted into the synagogue—one so abruptly appearing, so unknown one, of whom no one had as yet been apprised of His tribe, His nation, His family, and lastly, His enrolment in the census of Augustus—that most faithful witness of the Lord's nativity, kept in the archives of Rome?... But there is historical proof that at this very time a census had been taken in Judea by Sentius Saturninus, which might have satisfied their inquiry respecting the family and descent of Christ" (Tertullianus, *Against Marcion*, 4.7.7, 4.19.10).

b See Appendix A.

First Visitation as Lamb of God

frightened. And so the angel said to them, "Do not be afraid; for behold, I bring you good news of great joy which will be for all the people; for today in the city of David there has been born for you a Savior, who is Christ the Lord. And this will be a sign for you: you will find a baby wrapped in cloths and lying in a manger." And suddenly there appeared with the angel a multitude of the heavenly army of angels praising God and saying, "Glory to God in the highest, and on earth peace among people with whom He is pleased."

When the angels had departed from them into heaven, the shepherds began saying to one another, "Let's go straight to Bethlehem, then, and see this thing that has happened, which the Lord has made known to us." (Luke 2:4–15)

Luke told us that when Mary gave birth to Jesus in a manger at night, the shepherds from the field near Bethlehem came to see the baby after they were notified by the angels.

The average nighttime temperature from December to February in Bethlehem and its vicinity is about 6°C. Snow could have even fallen in Galilee and Judea, as Josephus mentioned on several occasions.[a] Snowfall in Judea, and specifically Bethlehem, is rare but quite possible. The winter months bring the most precipitation in the Bethlehem region, with February being the wettest.[229]

The Jewish oral traditions, the Mishnah (Skekalim 7.4), state:

> If cattle are found between Jerusalem and as far as Migdal Eder, or within the like distance in any direction, males must be deemed to be Whole-offerings and females Peace-offerings. R. Judah says: If fitted to be Passover-offerings, they must be deemed to be Passover-offerings [if they are found during] thirty days before the Feast.[b]

Alfred Edersheim was the first to infer from Shekalim 7.4 the following:

> That the Messiah was to be born in Bethlehem, was a settle conviction. Equally so was the belief, that He was to be revealed from Migdal Eder, "the tower of the flock." This Migdal Eder was not the watch-tower for the ordinary flocks which pastured on the barren sheep-ground beyond Bethlehem, but lay close to the town, on the road to Jerusalem. A passage in the Mishnah [Shekalim 7.4] leads to the conclusion, that

---

a Josephus, *War*, 1.16.2, 4.8.3; *Antiquities* 8.6.6.
b Danby, *Mishnah*, Shekalim, 7.4.

the flocks, which pastured there, were destined for Temple-sacrifices, and, accordingly, that the shepherds, who watched over them, were not ordinary shepherds... The same Mishnic passage also leads us to infer, that these flocks lay out all the year round, since they are spoken of as in the fields thirty days before Passover—that is, in the month of February, when in Palestine the average rainfall is nearly greatest. Thus, Jewish tradition in some dim manner apprehended the first revelation of the Messiah from that Migdal Eder where shepherds watched the Temple-flocks all the year round. Of the deep symbolic significance of such a coincidence, it is needless to speak.[230]

Regarding the temple flocks in the field, Edersheim further explains:

In fact the Mishnah (Baba K. vii.7[a]) expressly forbids the keeping of flocks throughout the land of Israel, except in the wildernesses – and the only flocks otherwise kept, would be those for the Temple-services (Baba K. 80a).

The passage of Baba Kama 7.7 says,

They may not rear small cattle [or domesticated animals, i.e., sheep and goats] in the land of Israel, but they may rear them in Syria or in the wildernesses that are in the land of Israel.[b]

The permitted grazing area for flocks includes wildernesses, forests,[c] [231] and fields around the edges of forests and streams where there are no cultivated crops.

According to Edersheim, Migdal Eder—meaning "tower of the flock"—is located close to Bethlehem on the road to Jerusalem. Bethlehem is about 10 kilometers (6.2 miles) southwest of the Jerusalem temple mount.

There are other possible interpretations of Shekalim 7.4 above. Some scholars[232] point out that the Babylonian Talmud renders it as a policy for

---

a Danby, *Mishnah*, Baba Kama 7.7.

b Ibid.

c "That one may pasture his cattle in the forest of another" (Rodkinson, *Babylonian Talmud*, Tracts Baba Kama 81a.1); and "The conditions are that people shall have the right to graze their animals in forests, even on private property; and that they shall have the right to gather wood from each other's fields, to be used as animal fodder" (Davidson Digital Edition of the Koren Noé Talmud, Bava Kamma 81a.1).

First Visitation as Lamb of God

finding stray, unclaimed cattle and sheep within a radius of about 10 kilometers from Jerusalem encompassing Migdal Eder. The cattle would be assessed for burnt offerings, with the male yearlings without blemish being considered for Passover offerings if they were found more than 30 days before the feast. These animals could only be sacrificed as peace offerings and they weren't fit for human consumption for the Passover Seder. The reason given in the Babylonian Talmud was that the owners' intentions for the stray animals were unknown. The Passover yearling for consumption had to be intended for a stipulated number of persons.[a]

Edersheim's inference from Shekalim 7.4 has since been quoted and adopted by a great number of scholars. Some propose that Mary gave birth to Jesus inside Migdal Eder, fulfilling Micah's prophecy (Micah 4:8[b]).[233]

One major problem with Edersheim's claim—"the only flocks otherwise kept [in the field], would be those for the Temple-services"—is that this exemption or tradition cannot be found anywhere in the Baba Kama 80a or the entire book of Tract Baba Kama.[234] Since Edersheim's statement is out of context with his source reference, we can only view it as his own assumption.

Legally and logically, the Jewish tradition of the Mishnah Baba Kama 7.7 should apply to everyone including the temple priests and their hired shepherds for their flocks and the temple flocks. Without exemption, Jews were not permitted to raise sheep and goats in residential areas and agricultural fields because the animals would graze on the cultivated vegetation and thereby steal the farmer's crops. If that happened, the owner of the animals had to pay restitution to the owner of the crop.[c] During the winter months, crops such as herbs, legumes, barley, and wheat grew in the fields and shepherds would keep their flocks away from them.

Most of the Passover yearlings, if not all, were brought in by Jewish families across Israel a day or two prior to Passover. They would arrange with their relatives, friends, and neighbors to decide who would bring and slay the yearling, who would carry or buy the wood for the fire pit, who would bring flour to make

---

a "Mishna d. R. Jehudah states, that if the animal found was a yearling and a male, it is considered a Passover-offering, but may be sacrificed only as a peace-offering, because a Passover-offering must be intended for a stipulated number of persons." (Rodkinson, *Babylonian Talmud*, Tract Shekalim 7).

b "As for you, tower of the flock [Migdal Eder], Hill of the daughter of Zion, To you it will come— Yes, the former dominion will come, The kingdom of the daughter of Jerusalem" (Micah 4:8).

c "If the animal fell into a garden and derives benefit from produce there, its owner pays for the benefit that it derives and not for other damage caused. If the animal descended into the garden in its usual manner and caused damage there, its owner pays for what it damaged" (Davidson Digital Edition of the Koren Noé Talmud, Bava Kamma 55b.5).

unleavened bread, and how many people would be sharing the Passover Seder in Jerusalem. Some likely bought life lambs or goats in the temple mount market.

Josephus wrote about the Passover feast in the early first century A.D.:

> So these high priests, upon the coming of that feast which is called the Passover, when they slay their sacrifices, from the ninth hour (3 p.m.) till the eleventh (5 p.m.), but so that a company not less than ten belong to every sacrifice, (for it is not lawful for them to feast singly by themselves,) and many of us are twenty in a company, found the number of sacrifices was two hundred and fifty-six thousand five hundred.[a]

Roughly three to four million Jews ate the Passover Seder at Jerusalem annually during that period.

According to the Mishnah Skekalim 3.1, Jewish farmers and herders would send their tithes of livestock, such as cattle, sheep, goats, and yearlings, to the temple at least 15 days before the festivals of Passover, Pentecost, and Tabernacle.[b]

Two male lambs would be offered daily by the priests in the temple, one in the morning and one in the evening year-round.[c] In other words, the temple priests required a constant supply of lambs. Most likely they hired professional herders in the vicinity of Jerusalem to raise lambs and take care of the tithes of livestock people offered.

Some shepherds in Bethlehem were likely members of a large-scale temple service operation for livestock, while other shepherds and farmers raised oxen, doves, lambs, and kids for wholesaling to merchants who resold them at the temple mount (John 2:13–15[d]). This was big business at the temple mount marketplace.

---

a Josephus, *War*, 6.9.3.

b "Three times in the year did they take up Terumah [offering to priests] out of the Shekel-chamber: a half month before Passover, a half month before Pentecost, and a half month before the Feast [of Tabernacles]; and these same are the appointed seasons for the Tithe of Cattle" (Danby, *Mishnah*, Skekalim 3.1).

c "And you shall say to them, 'This is the offering by fire which you shall offer to the Lord: two male lambs one year old without defect as a continual burnt offering every day. You shall offer the one lamb in the morning, and the other lamb you shall offer at twilight'" (Numbers 28:3–4).

d "The Passover of the Jews was near, and Jesus went up to Jerusalem. And within the temple grounds He found those who were selling oxen, sheep, and doves, and the money changers seated at their tables. And He made a whip of cords, and drove them all out of the temple area, with the sheep and the oxen; and He poured out the coins of the money changers and overturned their tables" (John 2:13–15).

Shortly before the new year on Nisan 1, about 15 days prior to the Passover based on Skekalim 3.1, the temple livestock of cattle, sheep, goats, lambs, and kids increased drastically due to people's tithes. The temple service cattle herders and shepherds needed to take care of all the animals. They likely separated the temple livestock into small groups to be fed at many different locations to minimize the risk of cross infection.

A flock of the yearlings earmarked for Passover together with a herd of local sheep and goats likely appeared in the fields near Bethlehem as early as mid-March.[a] This was when shepherds and their flocks went outdoors more frequently than in the winter months.

The story of the most famous shepherd in Bethlehem needs to be mentioned here, for it illustrates a couple of important points. When God sent the priest and judge Samuel to Jesse's family to anoint a new king to replace Saul, Samuel didn't find the chosen one among the seven sons who passed before him.

> *Then Samuel said to Jesse, "Are these all the boys?"*
> *And he said, "The youngest is still left, but behold, he is tending the sheep."*
> *So Samuel said to Jesse, "Send word and bring him; for we will not take our places at the table until he comes here."*
> *So he sent word and brought him in. Now he was reddish, with beautiful eyes and a handsome appearance. And the Lord said, "Arise, anoint him; for this is he."*
> (1 Samuel 16:11–12)

David was tending sheep in a field likely at the edge of a forest or stream close to Bethlehem. The place was within walking distance of his house.

In order to bring David back as soon as possible, Jesse would have sent at least two people on donkeys to fetch him. They would have ridden to the field where David usually pastured the sheep. One person would have looked after the flock and led it back while the other brought David in to meet Samuel.

The whole fetching process would have taken a couple of hours, but unlikely half a day. Samuel would still have needed time to anoint David, offer the sacrifice, and partake of dinner at the table with Jesse's family and the elders of the town.

David's conversation with Saul and his fight with Goliath allude to where he might often have pastured his flock.

---

[a] The vernal equinox typically appears on March 20/21. Nisan 1 is always designated to be the day with the first new moon after the vernal equinox. Assuming Nisan 1 lands on March 20 at the earliest, then the fifteenth day before Nisan 14 (April 2) Passover Feast would be March 18.

The Timing of God's Visitations

> *But Saul said to David, "You are not able to go against this Philistine to fight him [Goliath]; for you are only a youth, while he has been a warrior since his youth."*
>
> *But David said to Saul, "Your servant was tending his father's sheep. When a lion or a bear came and took a sheep from the flock, I went out after it and attacked it, and rescued the sheep from its mouth; and when it rose up against me, I grabbed it by its mane and struck it and killed it. Your servant has killed both the lion and the bear; and this uncircumcised Philistine will be like one of them, since he has defied the armies of the living God."*
>
> *...Then he took his staff in his hand and chose for himself five smooth stones from the brook, and put them in the shepherd's bag which he had, that is, in his shepherd's pouch, and his sling was in his hand; and he approached the Philistine.* (1 Samuel 17:33–36, 40).

In David's era, lions and bears roamed mainly in the forests where they had secret hideouts far from humans. Naturally, a lion or bear would grab a sheep when the flock ventured too close to its hunting territories. To reduce the risk of encountering lions and bears, David likely led his flock to graze in the green open fields next to a forest or stream but away from cultivated lands. Likely, this is where he practiced his slingshots with smooth stones from the stream. He could scare away beasts such as lions, bears, jackals, and wolves from a distance. He later killed Goliath with his first shot of a smooth stone.

During Jesus's era, shepherds from Bethlehem probably took their flocks to the same fields next to the forest or streams as where David had gone centuries earlier. Yet these fields were within walking distance and relatively close to the town of Bethlehem.

The coldest and wettest winter months coincide with the lambing season from December to January/February[235] in Bethlehem. If the weather was cold, rainy, and windy, it would have made sense to keep the flock in caves and mangers for warmth and dryness. The average wind in winter around Bethlehem is about 10 kilometers per hour. Even though mature ruminants have furs to protect themselves against the elements, the newly born yearlings would have been susceptible to hypothermia.[236] They were most vulnerable in the open fields in the cold and wet months of December to February.

In general, shepherds would bring their flocks into shelters until all the yearlings were born and their health was stable. They may have brought the animals out in the winter months to graze, but not for long and not in distant pastures.

When the weather turned drier and warmer in March and April, shepherds even let the flock stay in the fields overnight.

Starting around mid-March, the temple service shepherds all around Jerusalem, not just Bethlehem, would have needed a lot more space to keep the tithes of livestock offered by common Jews. They would likely have stayed outdoors most of the time. Possibly the ones tending sheep in the fields near Bethlehem were the temple service shepherds whom the angels notified of the Messiah's birth.

After the destruction of Jerusalem and the second temple in 70 A.D., the feast of Passover stopped—and it hasn't resumed to this day. For most religious Jews, they are forbidden to eat lambs or goats roasted over a fire pit for Passover Seder until the temple and altar are rebuilt.[237]

The Roman census required a sizable Jewish population to return to their hometowns. It is unlikely that such an event would have taken place in the winter, when traveling and camping outdoors was so much more difficult. Needless to say, it would have been especially strenuous and dangerous for any pregnant woman near full term to journey over a long distance in the winter. Joseph with his good common sense would probably have waited until the weather turned before taking Mary on the relatively long trip to Bethlehem.

When we put together all of the above, they concur that the birth of Jesus likely happened in the spring, summer, or fall—March to October—but unlikely in the winter.

6.3 DAY OF JESUS'S BIRTH

Does the Bible disclose the day of Jesus's birth? The answer is evidently yes. Listen to what Luke says:

> *His parents went to Jerusalem every year at the Feast of the Passover. And when He was twelve years old, they went up there according to the custom of the feast; and as they were returning, after spending the full number of days required, the boy Jesus stayed behind in Jerusalem, but His parents were unaware of it. Instead, they thought that He was somewhere in the caravan, and they went a day's journey; and then they began looking for Him among their relatives and acquaintances. And when they did not find Him, they returned to Jerusalem, looking for Him. Then, after three days they found Him in the temple, sitting in the midst of the teachers, both listening to them and asking them questions* (Luke 2:41–46)

The Timing of God's Visitations

Joseph and the family lived in Nazareth and travelled to Jerusalem annually for the Passover festival. Nazareth is about 85 miles (137 kilometers) north of Jerusalem. An ordinary person's walking speed ranges from two to four miles per hour (3.2 to 6.4 kilometers per hour).[238] It would take about 21 to 43 hours to reach Jerusalem by foot. For a crowd of people travelling with young and old, it would likely take about three to six days.

If they wanted to arrive in Jerusalem in time for Passover on Nisan 14 or earlier, folks at Nazareth must have started walking around Nisan 10. Likely, young children and older folks in the travelling company could ride on carts drawn by donkeys or horses to make the trip easier and avoid delays. Obviously they would bring along their Passover lambs and goats as well.

After the Jews occupied Canaan, God chose Jerusalem to be the dwelling place of his name.[a] The Passover animals had to be slaughtered annually between the evenings of Nisan 14 and 15 in Jerusalem and nowhere else.[b]

Luke says that Jesus went up to Jerusalem when he was 12 years old. Note that Luke doesn't say, "And when he [Jesus] was *about* twelve years old, they went up there according to the custom of the feast," like he did in reporting Jesus's baptism. In that instance, Luke says that Jesus was about 30 years old when he was baptized,[c] because his birthday and baptismal day did not coincide.

However, in the case of travelling to Jerusalem for Passover when Jesus was 12, his birthday coincided precisely with the day when the family started walking from Nazareth to Jerusalem. That's why Luke doesn't say Jesus was *about* 12 years old, because he was *exactly* 12.

Luke's original Greek writing says, "καὶ ὅτε ἐγένετο ἐτῶν δώδεκα, ἀναβαινόντων αὐτῶν κατὰ τὸ ἔθος τῆς ἑορτῆς." This can be translated literally

---

a "But I have chosen Jerusalem, that my name might be there; and have chosen David to be over my people Israel" (2 Chronicles 6:6, KJV).

b "You shall sacrifice the Passover to the Lord your God from the flock and the herd, in the place where the Lord chooses to establish His name... You are not allowed to sacrifice the Passover in any of your towns which the Lord your God is giving you; but only at the place where the Lord your God chooses to establish His name, you shall sacrifice the Passover in the evening at sunset, at the time that you came out of Egypt" (Deuteronomy 16:2, 5–6).

c "Now in the fifteenth year of the reign of Tiberius Caesar, when Pontius Pilate was governor of Judea, and Herod was tetrarch of Galilee and his brother Philip was tetrarch of the region of Ituraea and Trachonitis, and Lysanias was tetrarch of Abilene, in the high priesthood of Annas and Caiaphas... Now when all the people were baptized, Jesus also was baptized, and while He was praying, heaven was opened, and the Holy Spirit descended upon Him in bodily form like a dove, and a voice came from heaven: "You are My beloved Son, in You I am well pleased." When He began His ministry, Jesus Himself was about thirty years old..." (Luke 3:1–2, 21–23).

this way: *"...and when he became twelve years old, they having gone up to Jerusalem, according to the custom of the feast..."* (Luke 2:42, YLT).

In fact, the 1995 NASB version reads similarly: *"And when He became twelve, they went up there according to the custom of the Feast"* (Luke 2:42).

Luke uses the Greek word ἐγένετο (*egeneto*, became), which is more meaningful than ἦν (*en*, was). The Greek word ἐγένετο (*egeneto*) can mean "come into being, am born, become, come about, happen."[239] Luke uses the word ἐγένετο 69 times in his gospel and 54 times in the book of Acts. For example: *"And it happened (ἐγένετο) that on the eighth day they came to circumcise the child [John], and they were going to call him Zechariah, after his father"* (Luke 1:59). A second example: *"While they were there, the time came (ἐγένετο) for her [Mary] to give birth"* (Luke 2:6). In the above examples, Luke uses the word ἐγένετο in the sense that the event happened immediately, within the same day.

Most English Bible translations use the phrase "When he was twelve years old..." instead of "When he became twelve years old..." However, the latter phrase is what Luke intended. Luke clearly tells us when Jesus became 12 years old, the family went up for the Feast. In other words, the day when Jesus turned 12, the family started their hiking trip towards Jerusalem.

There is another pertinent event in Luke that substantiates the above interpretation:

And a man named Jairus came, and he was an official of the synagogue; and he fell at Jesus' feet, and began urging Him to come to his house; for he had an only daughter, about twelve years old, and she was dying. But as He went, the crowds were pressing against Him. (Luke 8:41–42)

Luke reports that Jairus's daughter was *about* 12 years old on the day when Jesus went to heal her. He doesn't say this because he was guessing her age. Remember that Luke states clearly that he investigated everything carefully,[a] which would include the girl's date of birth. To believe otherwise would mean Luke was lying.

All Luke needed to do was ask her, her family, her friends, her relatives, or anyone who knew about her date of birth. It would have been an easy thing

---

a "Since many have undertaken to compile an account of the things accomplished among us, just as they were handed down to us by those who from the beginning were eyewitnesses and servants of the word, it seemed fitting to me as well, having investigated everything carefully from the beginning, to write it out for you in an orderly sequence, most excellent Theophilus; so that you may know the exact truth about the things you have been taught" (Luke 1:1–4).

for him to do. She was a well-known person because Jesus had resurrected her from the dead (Luke 8:49–56). There were only three young people whom Jesus revived, as recorded in the gospels, so likely her date of birth was known to many. The day on which she was resurrected was not her birthday, so Luke says she was *about* 12 years old.

Again, Luke was a meticulously detailed writer and he investigated the matter carefully. Evidently he interviewed Mary, the mother of Jesus. It is highly likely that Mary told him about the events and timing surrounding Jesus's birth (Luke 2:41–46).

Passover took place on Nisan 14, according to Exodus 12:3–8. A one-year-old unblemished male lamb or goat for the Passover meal would have needed to be selected four days prior, on Nisan 10. Jesus is the Lamb of God who takes away the sin of the world,[a] so it makes perfect sense that Jesus would have been presented to the world on Nisan 10 for the salvation of mankind. In other words, Jesus was born on Nisan 10 in 2 B.C.

Likely, it was an annual custom for Joseph's family to start walking with friends and relatives from Nazareth to Jerusalem for the Passover festival on Jesus's birthday. In the year when Jesus turned 12, he decided to stay behind Jerusalem after the festival without telling anyone. Joseph and Mary went back to Jerusalem and looked for him for three days.

The month of Nisan always begins with a new moon after the vernal equinox. Priests in Jerusalem would observe not only the new moon[240] in the sky to identify the beginning of the month but also examine the crop of barley to see if any were ripe enough to harvest in about two weeks.[241]

The word Nisan has no Jewish meaning, because it was adopted from the Babylonians. Moses called the first Jewish month Abib/Aviv (אָבִיב),[b] [c] which means "fresh," "young ears," or "young green ears of grain."[242] Jews were to celebrate the Passover during this month. Once the month of Abib was declared in Jerusalem and relayed to the nation via a network of communication, in about two weeks' time the farmers would have to offer sheaves of ripened barley for the wave sheaf offering. The wave sheaf offering took place on the Sunday after Passover, following which the Jews could begin their harvest.

---

a "The next day he saw Jesus coming toward him, and said, 'Behold, the Lamb of God, who takes away the sin of the world!'" (John 1:29, ESV)

b "On this day in the month of Abib, you are about to go out from here" (Exodus 13:4).

c "Observe the month of Abib and celebrate the Passover to the Lord your God, for in the month of Abib the Lord your God brought you out of Egypt by night" (Deuteronomy 16:1).

From numerical calculations of the lunar phases in 2 B.C., the new moon right after the vernal equinox on March 21 appeared on the night of April 4 at about 10:44 p.m., Jerusalem local time.[243] Thus, April 4 would have been designated as Nisan 1. In other words, Jesus was born at night on April 13, 2 B.C., corresponding to Nisan 10, 2 B.C. Note that Hebrew days are reckoned from sundown to sundown.

The earlier new moon on March 6, 2 B.C. would have been too early for barley to be ready to harvest for the wave sheaf offering, and it came before the vernal equinox (March 21), so this date for Nisan 1 can certainly be dismissed.

The timing of April 13 fits well with the season in which the shepherds would have been in their fields tending sheep. Shepherds were the ones chosen to hear the announcement of the arrival of the Lamb of God by angels. Jesus was also the chief shepherd of the world, for he said, *"I am the good shepherd. The good shepherd lays down his life for the sheep"* (John 10:11, ESV).

Gérard Gertoux has proposed that Jesus was born on Tishri 1 or September 29 of 2 B.C.,[244] whereas Holly Snead has suggested Tishri 1 or September 11 of 3 B.C.[245] Colin Humphrey mentions the possibility of Jesus having been born on either Nisan 10 or 14 in 5 B.C.,[246] while Mimpriss recommends a date of Nisan 10 in 4 B.C.[247] However, none of these scholars provide supporting arguments for Jesus's birthday having been Nisan 10 in 2 B.C.

Behold! Luke has told us the date of Jesus's birth all along.

6.4 ANNUNCIATION AND INCARNATION

When did the annunciation and incarnation of Jesus take place?

Using Jesus's day of birth on April 13, 2 B.C. and assuming a full-term gestation of 280 days, the incarnation of Jesus would have occurred on July 7, 3 B.C. The day of annunciation, when the angel Gabriel brought the message to Mary, must have taken place earlier, possibly on July 6, 3 B.C.

In the first instance, Mary would have told Joseph about her meeting with Gabriel and informed him about her divine pregnancy. Naturally, Joseph's primal human reaction would have been disbelief. Undoubtedly, he would have struggled hard over what to do with Mary.

Gabriel had also told Mary that her relative Elizabeth was pregnant and in her sixth month (Luke 1:36). Elizabeth was well known to have been infertile up till her old age, but now she was pregnant.

Wanting to see if it was true, Mary left Nazareth to visit Elizabeth and Zechariah in a town in the hill country of Judea, where she stayed for *"about three*

The Timing of God's Visitations

months" (Luke 1:56) before returning home. Note once again that Luke uses the word "about," faithfully reporting what he heard from Mary. If the timing wasn't exactly three months, he would have said that it was about three months.

Mary heard the news of Elizabeth having been pregnant for six months on July 6. She likely helped out when Elizabeth gave birth to John around October 6, 3 B.C. Thus, John the Baptist was about six months older than Jesus. The two might have met each other in Jerusalem for some of the festivals while growing up, such as Passover, Pentecost, and Tabernacle.

After John's birth, Mary went back to Nazareth to see what final decision Joseph had made.

> *Because Joseph her husband was faithful to the law, and yet did not want to expose her to public disgrace, he had in mind to divorce her quietly.*
>
> *But after he had considered this, an angel of the Lord appeared to him in a dream and said, "Joseph son of David, do not be afraid to take Mary home as your wife, because what is conceived in her is from the Holy Spirit. She will give birth to a son, and you are to give him the name Jesus, because he will save his people from their sins."* (Matthew 1:19–21, NIV)

After the angel of the Lord appeared and brought God's message to Joseph in a dream, Joseph discarded his idea of divorcing Mary quietly. He obeyed God's instruction to take Mary as his wife. They likely celebrated their wedding in mid-October of 3 B.C.

Near the end of winter (February/March) in 2 B.C., the Nazareth community received Herod's order that all the people had to go back to their ancestral town to register in Caesar Augustus's census. Joseph could not leave Mary behind since her pregnancy was near full-term, so he put her on a donkey and they slowly travelled to Bethlehem, the town of David, both being descendants of David.

When they arrived in Bethlehem, the time came for Mary to give birth. Since there was no guest room available for them in the inn, Mary gave birth to Jesus, wrapped him in cloths, and laid him in a manger (Luke 2:4–7).

6.5 PASSOVER LAMB CHOSEN ON NISAN 10

Why did the Passover lamb have to be chosen on Nisan 10?

First Visitation as Lamb of God

Now the Lord said to Moses and Aaron in the land of Egypt, "This month shall be the beginning of months for you; it is to be the first month of the year for you. Speak to all the congregation of Israel, saying, 'On the tenth of this month they are, each one, to take a lamb for themselves, according to the fathers' households, a lamb for each household. Now if the household is too small for a lamb, then he and his neighbor nearest to his house are to take one according to the number of persons in them; in proportion to what each one should eat, you are to divide the lamb. Your lamb shall be an unblemished male a year old; you may take it from the sheep or from the goats. You shall keep it until the fourteenth day of the same month, then the whole assembly of the congregation of Israel is to slaughter it at twilight. Moreover, they shall take some of the blood and put it on the two doorposts and on the lintel of the houses in which they eat it. (Exodus 12:1–7)

Before the Israelites left Egypt, God's instruction about Passover was very clear. The man of the family would select a one-year-old unblemished male lamb or goat on Nisan 10 and keep it until Nisan 14. More than one family could share a lamb for Passover meal.

On Nisan 14 at midnight, God visited the land of Egypt (Exodus 12:1–13). When God saw the blood of the lambs on the sides and tops of the doorframes of the houses where Jews had eaten the roasted lambs or goats, he passed over them without killing the firstborn inside.

Technically, it made no difference if the lamb were to be chosen on Nisan 14 rather than Nisan 10 since it was the same lamb to be slain. So why did the Passover lamb have to be selected on Nisan 10 and not Nisan 14 or some other day?

Obviously, the Passover lamb serves as a prophetic sign. It symbolizes the true Passover Lamb of God, Jesus, who takes away the sin of the world[a] and his blood shields all believers from God's judgment. God commands that the Passover lamb be selected on Nisan 10. After the selection, the owner must mark the lamb or set it aside somehow so that family, friends, and neighbors would know its identity and purpose for the Passover. If the lamb was not marked, it could be sold, traded, or consumed in the following days.

On Nisan 10, Jesus appeared in the world and was introduced first to the shepherds. The angel announced to them:

I bring you good news of great joy which will be for all the people; for today in the city of David there has been born for you a Savior, who is Christ the Lord. And this

---

a John 1:29; 1 Corinthians 5:7; 1 Peter 1:19.

> *will be a sign for you: you will find a baby wrapped in cloths and lying in a manger.* (Luke 2:10–12)

A manger is a place where livestock are born other than in the field. Not only did Jesus humble himself to be born as a baby, but he identified himself with a baby lamb born in a manger.

The Passover lamb was not slain on the same day that it was chosen. Rather, it would live four more days. About 30 years after his birth, Jesus was introduced once again to the world as the Lamb of God in 29 A.D. by John the Baptist: *"The next day he saw Jesus coming to him, and said, 'Behold, the Lamb of God who takes away the sin of the world!'"* (John 1:29)

Right after his baptism, Jesus began his ministry. The four days from Nisan 10 to 14 symbolize the last four years of Jesus's life, in which he healed the sick, resurrected the dead, trained his disciples, cleansed the temple a few times, and preached the message of the kingdom of God to the people.

At the end of about four years, Jesus was crucified by the priests, scribes, elders, members of the Sanhedrin, and the Romans on Nisan 14, the Passover day, corresponding to April 3, 33 A.D.[248]

6.6 JESUS, THE LAMB OF GOD

God has given the world a clear description of Jesus's life and mission in Isaiah 53, which was written about 700 years before his birth. Isaiah 53 is often called the Servant Song, which was composed as a poem around 700 B.C. To aid our focus and appreciation of this brilliant passage, let's rearrange Isaiah's verses in a chronological manner.

> *Who has believed what he has heard from us?*
> *And to whom has the arm of the Lord been revealed?*
> *For he grew up before him like a young plant,*
> *and like a root out of dry ground;*
> *he had no form or majesty that we should look at him,*
> *and no beauty that we should desire him.*
> *He was despised and rejected by men,*
> *a man of sorrows and acquainted with grief;*
> *and as one from whom men hide their faces*
> *he was despised, and we esteemed him not.*

First Visitation as Lamb of God

Although he had done no violence,
  and there was no deceit in his mouth,
By oppression and judgment he was taken away;
  and as for his generation, who considered
that he was cut off out of the land of the living,
  stricken for the transgression of my people?
and like a sheep that before its shearers is silent,
  so he opened not his mouth.
He was oppressed, and he was afflicted,
  yet he opened not his mouth;

Like a lamb that is led to the slaughter,
  and was numbered with the transgressors;
Yet he bore the sin of many,
  and makes intercession for the transgressors.
And they made his grave with the wicked
  and with a rich man in his death,

When his soul makes an offering for guilt,
  he shall see his offspring; he shall prolong his days;
The will of the Lord shall prosper in his hand,
  out of the anguish of his soul he shall see and be satisfied.

All we like sheep have gone astray;
  we have turned—every one—to his own way;
and the Lord has laid on him
  the iniquity of us all.
Surely he has borne our griefs
  and carried our sorrows;
yet we esteemed him stricken,
  smitten by God, and afflicted.
But he was pierced for our transgressions;
  he was crushed for our iniquities;
upon him was the chastisement that brought us peace,
  and with his wounds we are healed.
Yet it was the will of the Lord to crush him,
  he has put him to grief.

> *By his knowledge shall the righteous one, my servant,*
>   *make many to be accounted righteous,*
>   *and he shall bear their iniquities.*
> *Therefore I will divide him a portion with the many,*
>   *and he shall divide the spoil with the strong,*
>   *because he poured out his soul to death.* (Isaiah 53:1–12, ESV)

Isaiah 53 is the Old Testament gospel to the Jewish nation—and Jesus precisely fulfilled this salvation plan of God. He was born of the virgin Mary[a] as the seed of a woman (Genesis 3:15). Yet he was not alone, for he was the incarnated Son of God. The image of a root arising from the dry ground and growing into a tender shoot depicts the development of Jesus's life, his divinity being connected to God the Father and God the Holy Spirit.

Jesus had no beauty and majesty to attract people to him. He was a man of sorrow and familiar with pain and suffering. People had a low esteem of him. They even despised and rejected him.

Even though Jesus had done no violence and said nothing deceitful, he was nonetheless arrested for a religious trial by the Sanhedrin and the high priests. Jesus stood silent like a sheep before them. Then they took him to Pilate, before the Roman court for a civil trial, and after being whipped and bruised he remained silent. Note that Isaiah prophesied twice that he *"did not open His mouth"* (Isaiah 53:7). These two prophecies were separately and precisely fulfilled—once in the Jewish religious trial, and the other in the Roman civil trial.

Jesus was sentenced for crucifixion along with two other criminals on the day of Passover. Thus, he was numbered among transgressors. On the cross, Jesus prayed, *"Father, forgive them, for they do not know what they are doing"* (Luke 23:34, NIV). His prayer was for all the sinful people around him, including his murderers and executioners.

After he died, if nobody had collected his body he would have been buried together with the wicked criminals in a mass grave. Yet a rich man, Joseph of Arithmathea, took and buried Jesus's body in his own brand-new garden tomb.

Many people of the day misunderstood Jesus. Some thought he was being punished by God for his own iniquities. While he hung on the cross, others passed by and hurled insults at him:

---

a "Therefore the Lord himself shall give you a sign; Behold, a virgin shall conceive, and bear a son, and shall call his name Immanuel" (Isaiah 7:14, KJV).

Those who passed by hurled insults at him, shaking their heads and saying, "You who are going to destroy the temple and build it in three days, save yourself! Come down from the cross, if you are the Son of God!"

In the same way the chief priests, the teachers of the law and the elders mocked him. "He saved others," they said, "but he can't save himself! He's the king of Israel! Let him come down now from the cross, and we will believe in him. He trusts in God. Let God rescue him now if he wants him, for he said, 'I am the Son of God.'" (Matthew 27:39–43, NIV)

These people were all wrong about Christ. God allowed everything that happened to Jesus as a way to provide salvation for mankind because he loves us.

For God so loved the world, that he gave his only begotten Son, that whosoever believeth in him should not perish, but have everlasting life. (John 3:16, KJV)

This is God's will, to bruise Jesus and allow him to go through suffering and death. God laid on Jesus the iniquity of us all. He took our punishment so that we might have peace. Through trusting Jesus as personal Savior and Lord, penitents are justified, redeemed, and given eternal life by God.

After Jesus offered his soul as an offering for sin, he was resurrected on the third day. Ever since, he sees all who believe in him as his offspring for eternity, which is the result of the outpouring of his soul unto death as the Lamb of God.

For to us a child is born, to us a son is given, and the government will be on his shoulders. And he will be called Wonderful Counselor, Mighty God, Everlasting Father, Prince of Peace. (Isaiah 9:6, NIV)

Jesus is the Mighty God and Prince of Peace who was born to redeem mankind. He is the creator who humbled himself to take on the form of a creature.

As Paul pointed out,

Have this attitude in yourselves which was also in Christ Jesus, who, as He already existed in the form of God, did not consider equality with God something to be grasped, but emptied Himself by taking the form of a bond-servant and being born in the likeness of men. And being found in appearance as a man, He humbled Himself by becoming obedient to the point of death: death on a cross. For this reason also God highly exalted Him, and bestowed on Him the name which is above every

> name, so that at the name of Jesus every knee will bow, of those who are in heaven and on earth and under the earth, and that every tongue will confess that Jesus Christ is Lord, to the glory of God the Father. (Philippians 2:5–11)

A self-sacrificing Creator whose love is truly unconditional deserves all honor and glory from the entirety of creation forever. On the Day of Judgment, when Jesus will appear as a Lion and not just a Lamb, every knee shall bow and every tongue shall confess that Jesus Christ is Lord, to the glory of God the Father.

> And I saw between the throne (with the four living creatures) and the elders a Lamb standing, as if slaughtered, having seven horns and seven eyes, which are the seven spirits of God sent out into all the earth. And He came and took the scroll out of the right hand of Him who sat on the throne. (Revelation 5:6–7)

In his vision, John recognized the Lamb who was slain. Likely, he saw the scars on Jesus's hands and head. Undoubtedly, Jesus could have erased these scars on his resurrected body, but instead he chose to keep them. Why? Because Jesus was proud to carry them for all eternity as proof of his absolute and unconditional love for mankind. They also proved the truth of his death and resurrection, just as he had promised.

6.7 SUMMARY

In summary, Jesus's birth and death precisely fulfilled the prophetic signs of the Lamb of God in the festival of Passover. Jesus was born during the night of Nisan 10 (April 13), 2 B.C., revealing to the shepherds and the world that he was the true designated Lamb of God. He was slain on Passover Nisan 14 (April 3), 33 A.D. When Jesus was crucified, he was 34 years and four days old, according to the Hebrew calendar.

Second Visitation as Lion from Judah

Chapter Seven

The book of Revelation reveals many names and titles that illustrate the unique divinity and humanity of Jesus. These names and titles are summarized in Table 7.1.

Firstly, Jesus in his humanity is the Christ (or Messiah), the firstborn of the dead, the ruler of kings, the Amen, the faithful and true Witness, the Lion, the Root of David, and the Lamb.

Secondly, Jesus in his divinity is the Word of God, the Alpha and the Omega, the Almighty, the first and the last, the beginning and the end, the Son of God, the Origin of creation of God, Faithful and True, Lord of lord and King of kings, and the bright morning star.

Table 7.1. Names and titles of Jesus in the book of Revelation.

	Name/Titles	Revelation
Humanity		
1	Christ	1:1, 20:4–6
2	the firstborn of the dead	1:5
3	the ruler of kings	1:5
4	the Amen, the faithful and true Witness	3:14, 1:5
5	the Lion	5:5
6	the Root of David	5:5, 22:16
7	the Lamb	5:6–13, 6:16

Divinity		
8	The Word of God	19:13
9	the Alpha and the Omega	1:8, 21:6, 22:13
10	the Almighty	1:8
11	the first and the last, the beginning and the end	2:8, 21:6, 22:13
12	the Son of God	2:18
13	the Origin of creation of God	3:14
14	Faithful and True	19:11
15	Lord of lords and King of kings	17:14, 19:16
16	the bright morning star	22:16

In contrast to Jesus's first visitation as the Passover Lamb of God that was slain, he will appear as the Lion from Judah and God Almighty in his second advent. He will return to judge the earth of its evil and destroy those who destroy the earth.[a] The earth includes the people, not just the material part of the planet.

In the Old Testament, the time of God's coming judgment of the world is often referred to as "the Day of the Lord." For example, Isaiah 13:9–11:

> *Behold, the day of the Lord is coming, cruel, with fury and burning anger, to make the land a desolation; and He will exterminate its sinners from it. For the stars of heaven and their constellations will not flash their light; the sun will be dark when it rises and the moon will not shed its light. So I will punish the world for its evil and the wicked for their wrongdoing; I will also put an end to the audacity of the proud and humiliate the arrogance of the tyrants.*

"The Day of the Lord" in the Old Testament is essentially the same as "the great day of the wrath of God and the Lamb" in Revelation.[b] God is the creator of

---

a "And the nations were enraged, and Your wrath came, and the time came for the dead to be judged, and the time to reward Your bond-servants the prophets and the saints and those who fear Your name, the small and the great, and to destroy those who destroy the earth" (Revelation 11:18).

b "...and they said to the mountains and the rocks, 'Fall on us and hide us from the sight of Him who sits on the throne, and from the wrath of the Lamb; for the great day of Their wrath has come, and who is able to stand?'" (Revelation 6:16–17).

Second Visitation as Lion from Judah

everything.[a] Certainly, he has the right to judge all. The main theme of the book of Revelation is Christ's return to judge humans and demons.

7.1 SEVEN SEALS, SEVEN TRUMPETS, AND SEVEN BOWLS

> *I saw in the right hand of Him who sat on the throne a scroll written inside and on the back, sealed up with seven seals. And I saw a strong angel proclaiming with a loud voice, "Who is worthy to open the scroll and to break its seals?" And no one in heaven or on the earth or under the earth was able to open the scroll or to look into it. Then I began to weep greatly because no one was found worthy to open the scroll or to look into it. And one of the elders said to me, "Stop weeping; behold, the Lion that is from the tribe of Judah, the Root of David, has overcome so as to be able to open the scroll and its seven seals."* (Revelation 5:1–5)

John saw the slain Lamb who came and took the scroll from God. Many angels, the four living creatures, and the elders praised the Lamb by loudly proclaiming, *"Worthy is the Lamb that was slaughtered to receive power, wealth, wisdom, might, honor, glory, and blessing"* (Revelation 5:12).

Jesus is the Lamb of God, and at the same time he is also the Lion from the tribe of Judah who is worthy to open the scroll and break the seven seals. The seven seals extend into seven trumpets, which in turn expand into seven bowls of God's wrath.

Table 7.2 lists the scenes that John witnesses in his visions when the seals are broken, the trumpets are blown, and the content of the bowls are poured out.

Table 7.2. Events associated with the seven seals, the seven trumpets, and the seven bowls.

Item	Content	Revelation
First seal	A white horse rider with a bow is given a crown and conquers.	6:1–2
Second seal	A red horse rider is given a large sword to take away peace on the world.	6:3–4

---

[a] "Worthy are You, our Lord and our God, to receive glory and honor and power; for You created all things, and because of Your will they existed, and were created" (Revelation 4:11).

Third seal	A black horse rider holds a pair of scales and food becomes very expensive.	6:5–6
Fourth seal	Death rides a pale green horse, followed by Hades, to kill people with sword, famine and plague, and animals.	6:7–8
Fifth seal	White robes are given to souls who were killed for their testimonies for the word of God.	6:9–11
Sixth seal	There is an earthquake, the sun is blackened, the moon reddens, stars fall to the earth, a great wind breaks out, and people hide in caves.	6:12–16
Seventh seal	Seven trumpets blow.	8:1
First trumpet	Hail and fire mixed with blood are hurled to the earth and one-third of the earth burns, along with one-third of trees and all the green grass.	8:7
Second trumpet	A great mountain burning with fire is hurled into the sea and one-third of the sea turns bloody, one-third of sea creatures die, and one-third of ships are destroyed.	8:8–9
Third trumpet	A great star named Wormwood falls and turns one-third of waters bitter, causing many people to die.	8:10–11
Fourth trumpet	One-third of the sun, moon, and stars are struck and darkened.	8:12
Fifth trumpet	An angel is given the key to open the bottomless pit and let out locusts to hurt people for five months.	9:1–11

Sixth trumpet	Loosened four angels kill one-third of an army comprising two hundred thousand thousand people.	9:13–19
Seventh trumpet	Seven bowls are poured out.	11:15
First bowl	Bad and grievous sores develop in people with the mark of the beast.	16:2
Second bowl	The sea turns to blood and every creature in the sea dies.	16:3
Third bowl	The waters in springs and rivers turns to blood.	16:4–7
Fourth bowl	People are scorched by the sun.	16:8–9
Fifth bowl	The beast's kingdom is full of darkness and people endure pains and sores.	16:10–11
Sixth bowl	The Euphrates dries up and three unclean spirits gather kings of the whole world to battle God at Armageddon.	16:12–16
Seventh bowl	A great earthquake causes cities to fall, islands and mountains to disappear, and great hail to come down.	16:17–21

When Jesus opens the first seal, a white horse rider with a bow is given a crown to conquer. There has been all kinds of speculation about the identity of this white horse rider and what he represents.

Death is the pale green horse rider, who appears after the fourth seal is broken by Jesus. Similarly, the first three riders—white, red, and black—likely aren't human but rather non-physical entities, substances, or phenomena; for example, Christianity, war, plague, and famine.

The scenes described in the wake of the six seals match fairly closely to the initial end-time events that Jesus spoke of in Matthew 24:6–8:

The Timing of God's Visitations

And you will be hearing of wars and rumors of wars. See that you are not alarmed, for those things must take place, but that is not yet the end. For nation will rise against nation, and kingdom against kingdom, and there will be famines and earthquakes in various places. But all these things are merely the beginning of birth pains.

The first sign that Jesus mentions has to do with rumors of wars, nation against nation. Today, there are all sorts of conflicts between nations such as China/India, Israel/Palestine, Bangladesh/Myanmar, and Armenia/Azerbaijan. These could easily escalate into full-scale wars between rival nations, much like Ukraine and Russia.

A kingdom represents a group of countries bound together, such as the Roman Empire which controlled many nations, or an alliance of several countries, such as the Arab League, European Union, or NATO. The three principal destructive allies during World War II were Germany, Italy, and Japan. These countries caused the death of millions from September 1939 to September 1945.

According to World Food Programme (WFP), the world is facing the largest global food crisis ever. Millions of people are at risk of experiencing worsening hunger. About 49 million people in 49 countries are on the verge of famine.[249]

The year 2022 saw a great deal of volcanic activity, such as the eruptions on Hunga Tonga in January, Stromboli in March, Sicily in June, Sakurajima in July, and Kilauea in September. These and many other volcanoes will likely remain active. According to the United States Geological Survey (USGS),[250] there were 1,684 earthquakes of magnitude 5.0 or greater in 2022, an increase of about 29% from 2002, which saw 1,308 quakes of similar magnitudes.

These are merely the opening scenes of a much more extensive drama to follow (Matthew 24:8).

The breaking of the seventh seal will bring about the natural disasters associated with the blowing of the seven trumpets. The first four will account for physical destruction through hail and fire, volcanic eruptions in the sea, a meteorite strike that turns freshwater bitter, and astrophysical changes to the sun, moon, and stars as observed from the earth. The fifth and sixth trumpets will engage insect-like locusts to hurt people for five months, and the killing of one-third of a large human army by four angels.

The blowing of the seventh trumpet will lead to the seven bowls of wrath of God being poured out onto the earth. These bowls will cause people with the mark of the beast to develop bad and painful sores, the sea and other waters to turn red, the sun to scorch people, three evil spirits to entice kings to battle God, a great earthquake to devastate cities and cause islands and mountains to disappear, and great hail to fall from the sky.

Ever since Jesus was resurrected from the dead as the Lamb 2,000 years ago, this scroll has been open. The seals have been broken. In other words, the scenes that John witness have already taken place.

In fact, the last days began when Jesus was born into this world, grew up, and preached about God's kingdom of heaven. This is confirmed by Hebrews 1:1–2:

God, after He spoke long ago to the fathers in the prophets in many portions and in many ways, in these last days has spoken to us in His Son, whom He appointed heir of all things, through whom He also made the world.

Some time ago, in about 540 B.C., an angel told Daniel,

But you, Daniel, shut up the words and seal the book, until the time of the end. Many shall run to and fro, and knowledge shall increase… Go your way, Daniel, for the words are shut up and sealed until the time of the end. (Daniel 12:4, 9, ESV)

Our present era is situated within the end-times. This is an age of communication through multimedia, with the majority of people in the world having devices such as smart TVs, computers, and mobile phones. Our knowledge in the world today has been increasing by leaps and bounds compared to that of Daniel's era.

The once-sealed words and apocalyptic prophecies in Daniel have already been unsealed by Jesus. A huge volume of eschatological literature is available for our study nowadays. Yet no one knows exactly where we stand on the end-times timeline and when Jesus will return—except God.

In the past three and a half years, we have seen an unprecedented global plague result in the death of 6.6 million people.[251] At the same time, we have seen the legislation of mandatory vaccine passports to allow for travel and dining by certain countries around the world. The cost of food, goods, and services have gotten significantly more expensive after the pandemic, and their prices will likely remain high.

A number of major conflicts have been playing out over the past five years, such as Ukraine versus Russia, Turkey versus Kurdish groups, Armenia versus

Azerbaijan, and the civil war in Syria. Many lives have been lost in these wars. However, they are only a foretaste of what is to come.

At this point in time, it is fair to say that we aren't in the bowls of God's wrath period, because the Antichrist hasn't risen and no one yet bears the mark of the beast. People with the mark of the beast will be the first targets of God's wrath. Roughly, our present age may be somewhere along the initial stage of the black horse rider period.

7.2 GOSPEL PREACHED IN THE WHOLE WORLD

Jesus said, *"This gospel of the kingdom shall be preached in the whole world as a testimony to all the nations, and then the end will come"* (Matthew 24:14). A group of all-male Jewish missionaries, evangelists, teachers, and preachers will be formed for the purpose of sharing the gospel in unreached locations of the world, so that all nations will get at least one chance to hear the gospel. This group will number 144,000 (Revelation 14:1–5).

There will be a big harvest, as illustrated in John's vision of Jesus wearing a golden crown and swinging his sharp sickle to reap the crop over the earth (Revelation 14:14–16). That crop represents all the believers who will be saved.

In the meantime, the Antichrist and the false prophet will rise and take control of a group of nations (Revelation 12:1–18). Satan will empower them himself. The kingdom they control will require all its citizens to carry the mark of the beast—which will have the number or name "666"—in order to buy and sell. The mark of the beast will be stored inside a nanochip which will likely replace credit, bank, citizenship, and health cards.

These events will happen before the bowls of God's wrath are poured out onto the earth.

After all the bowls of God's wrath are poured out, Jesus will ride a white horse, leading his armies upon white horses to return to the earth: *"And on His robe and on His thigh He has a name written: 'KING OF KINGS, AND LORD OF LORDS'"* (Revelation 19:16).

After losing their battle to Jesus, the Antichrist and the false prophet will be seized and thrown into a lake of fire, and Satan will be bound in the abyss for 1,000 years. Jesus Christ will then establish a millennial kingdom upon the earth (Revelation 20:1–6).

7.3 JESUS, PRINCE OF PEACE

After Isaiah prophesized the Messiah's mission in Isaiah 53, the Old Testament gospel, God instructed him to write down something seemingly paradoxical in Isaiah 55:

> *Come, everyone who thirsts, come to the waters; and he who has no money, come, buy and eat! Come, buy wine and milk without money and without price. Why do you spend your money for that which is not bread, and your labor for that which does not satisfy? Listen diligently to me, and eat what is good, and delight yourselves in rich food. Incline your ear, and come to me; hear, that your soul may live; and I will make with you an everlasting covenant, my steadfast, sure love for David.* (Isaiah 55:1–3, ESV)

God is asking people without money to buy good and rich food of wine, milk, and bread. Those who thirst are to come to the waters and drink. The paradox here is that the food has no price. What God asks people to do seems self-contradictory, because one cannot buy anything when one doesn't have money. Furthermore, the items are priceless. Yet God invites all to come, to buy, to eat, and to drink. Why?

The reason is that God has already paid for these things. No one has the kind of money needed to buy food, because the money required is the innocent blood of the Lamb of God. No one can pay except Jesus. God is generous and loving to all. The bread and wine are not cheap, but they are free for all who are willing to accept and participate in God's invitation.

Jesus is the bread of life[a] who gives life to the people of the world. Anyone who partakes of the bread of God will not go hungry. Jesus also gives living water to those who are thirsty.[b] Those who drink the living water will never be thirsty again.

---

a "Jesus then said to them, 'Truly, truly, I say to you, it was not Moses who gave you the bread from heaven, but my Father gives you the true bread from heaven. For the bread of God is he who comes down from heaven and gives life to the world.' They said to him, 'Sir, give us this bread always.' Jesus said to them, 'I am the bread of life; whoever comes to me shall not hunger, and whoever believes in me shall never thirst'" (John 6:32–35, ESV).

b "Jesus answered her, 'If you knew the gift of God, and who it is that is saying to you, "Give me a drink," you would have asked him, and he would have given you living water.' The woman said to him, 'Sir, you have nothing to draw water with, and the well is deep. Where do you get that living water? Are you greater than our father Jacob? He gave us the well and drank from it himself, as did his sons and his livestock.' Jesus said to her, 'Everyone who drinks of this water will be thirsty again, but whoever drinks of the water that I will give him will never be thirsty again. The water that I will give him will become in him a spring of water welling up to eternal life'" (John 4:10–14, ESV).

God's salvation is free to all. Jesus has already paid with his own blood for the forgiveness of mankind's sins.[a] All we need to do is repent of our sins, believe, and accept Jesus Christ as our personal Savior and Lord. Then, spiritually, we will never again be hungry or thirsty.

It is worth noting that Jesus once told the Jews,

> *Truly, truly, I say to you, unless you eat the flesh of the Son of Man and drink His blood, you have no life in yourselves. The one who eats My flesh and drinks My blood has eternal life, and I will raise him up on the last day. For My flesh is true food, and My blood is true drink. The one who eats My flesh and drinks My blood remains in Me, and I in him. Just as the living Father sent Me, and I live because of the Father, the one who eats Me, he also will live because of Me. This is the bread that came down out of heaven, not as the fathers ate and died; the one who eats this bread will live forever.* (John 6:53–58)

Jesus's teaching in this passage refers to true believers who participate in holy communion by eating the bread and drinking the wine, where the bread and wine symbolize Jesus's body and blood.

However, the action of eating and drinking these elements doesn't guarantee eternal life. Anyone can eat and drink these, but they won't necessarily be saved. Only people who truly believe Jesus are saved. Thus, the eating and drinking symbolize true belief and trust in Jesus as the Passover Lamb of God who took away the sin of the world.

God promises in Isaiah 55:3 (ESV), *"Incline your ear, and come to me; hear, that your soul may live."* If we listen to God and do what he asks, our souls will live, meaning that he will give us eternal life. As we read in John 3:16, *"For God so loved the world, that he gave his only Son, that whoever believes in him should not perish but have eternal life"* (ESV).

The passage found in Revelation 21:5–6 echoes this truth, revealing that God will freely give the water of life to all who are thirsty:

> *And He who sits on the throne said, "Behold, I am making all things new." And He said, "Write, for these words are faithful and true." Then He said to me, "It is done. I am the Alpha and the Omega, the beginning and the end. I will give water to the one who thirsts from the spring of the water of life, without cost."*

---

a "Indeed, under the law almost everything is purified with blood, and without the shedding of blood there is no forgiveness of sins" (Hebrews 9:22, ESV).

Isaiah encourages all to listen to God's calling:

Seek the Lord while He may be found; call upon Him while He is near. Let the wicked abandon his way, and the unrighteous person his thoughts; and let him return to the Lord, and He will have compassion on him, and to our God, for He will abundantly pardon. (Isaiah 55:6–7)

As Jesus says, "*Behold, I stand at the door and knock; if anyone hears My voice and opens the door, I will come in to him and will dine with him, and he with Me*" (Revelation 3:20).

Don't wait any longer. Our loving and gracious God is waiting for you to turn to him. He will abundantly pardon you when you confess your sins before him. You can have a wonderful personal relationship with the creator redeemer forever.

The Lord bless you and keep you; the Lord make his face to shine upon you and be gracious to you; the Lord lift up his countenance upon you and give you peace. (Numbers 6:24–26, ESV)

Early Christian Consensus

Appendix A

Jack Finegan tabulated a list of early Christian sources from the second to the sixth centuries dating the birth of Christ.[252]

Some scholars assume that Octavius (Augustus) started reigning right after the assassination of his adopted father, Julius Caesar, on March 15, 44 B.C., like Finegan did. Such an assumption would hold true if Rome had been an autocratic country like the rest of the world at that time. However, it was not. The empire's governance right after Julius Caesar's death was extremely chaotic.

Certainly, Mark Antony would have been the first to object to the 19-year-old Octavius claiming the empire in 44 B.C. He kept and spent a fair amount of Julius Caesar's money, which was supposed to have been Octavius's inheritance. The Roman Senate didn't help, either, because it was trying hard to stop both Antony and Octavius from becoming the next dictator.

Instead of 44 B.C., it is more legitimate and appropriate to date Augustus's reign as beginning in 43 B.C. because he was officially granted real military and political power as propraetor (commander) on January 2, a suffect consul on August 19, and a triumvir on November 27 by the Senate in 43 B.C.[253] Indisputably, Octavius had firmed up his power and privilege in Roman governance only when he became one of three leaders of the triumvirate with Antony and Lepidus. Thus, it makes perfect sense to regard Augustus's reign as having started on November 27 of 43 B.C.

Table A.1 presents the dates for the birth of Jesus given by early Christian scholars and historians in the first eight centuries A.D. Finegan was the first to establish a similar table for the dates of Christ's birth.

In general, of the 15 authoritative sources, 12 of them affirm that Jesus was born during the period of 3/2 B.C., and at least six of these vouch for 2 B.C. At the same time, they substantiate the case that Herod died in 1 B.C. We refer to this—Jesus's birth taking place in 3/2 B.C. and Herod dying in 1 B.C.—as the early Christian consensus.

It is important to point out that none of these ancient sources in the first eight centuries A.D. designate 6/5 B.C. as the potential years for Jesus's birth. Only two indicate 4 B.C. The Schürer consensus, which advocates for Jesus's birth taking place in 6/4 B.C., is a modern-day invention which obviously contradicts the majority of the 15 historical records.

Luke, Tertullianus, Irenaeus,[254] Origen,[255] and Africanus travelled to Rome and lived there for some time. Most likely, they were familiar with using Roman regnal years to date events.

For example, Irenaeus dated Jesus's birth to the forty-first year of Augustus's reign. Using 43 B.C. as Augustus's accession year, his forty-first year corresponds to 2 B.C. (43 − 41).

Tertullianus, Eusebius, and Clement of Alexandria date the birth of Jesus to the twenty-eighth year after the death of Antony and Cleopatra.

After Antony and Cleopatra lost the Battle of Actium to Octavius on September 2, 31 B.C., they returned to Alexandria, Egypt. Octavius regrouped and pursued them. Eventually, most of Antony's legions deserted to Octavius, and both Antony and Cleopatra committed suicide in August of 30 B.C.[256] Octavius formally annexed Egypt under Roman rule, and he became the undisputed Roman emperor. His accession year in Egypt is 30 B.C. Therefore, the twenty-eighth year of Augustus's reign in Egypt is 2 B.C. (30 − 28).

Table A.1. Dates for Jesus's birth provided by early Christian scholars and historians.

Source	Lived (A.D.)	Year of Jesus's Birth	B.C.	Reference
Luke	1–100	Jesus was about 30 at his baptism in the fifteenth year of Tiberius's reign.	3/2	Luke 3:1–3, 23
Alogi group	~180	The fortieth year of Augustus's reign.	4/3	Panarion 51:3–2[257]
Irenaeus of Lyon	120/140–200/203	About the forty-first year of Augustus's reign.	3/2	Against Heresies 3.21.3[258]

Tertullianus of Carthage	155/160–after 220	The twenty-eighth year after the death of Cleopatra.	2	*Answer to the Jews* 8[259]
Clement of Alexandria	150–211/215	The twenty-eighth year of the reign of Augustus.	2	*Stromata* 1.21.145[260]
Julius Africanus	170–240	Year 5500 from creation and the second year in the 194th Olympiad.	3/2	*Chronography* 3.1[261]
Hippolytus of Rome	170–236	Year 5500 from creation.	3/2	*Commentaries On Daniel* 2.4[262]
Origen of Alexandria	185–253	The forty-first year of Augustus's reign.	2	*Homilies on Luke*[263]
Eusebius of Caesarea	265–340	The twenty-eighth year after the death of Antony and Cleopatra.	2	*Ecclesiastical History* 1.5.2[264]
Epiphanius of Salamis	315–403	The consular year of Augustus XIII and Silanus.	2	*Panarion* 22:3–4
Sulpicius Severus of France	363–425	The thirty-third year of Herod's reign, during the consulship of Sabinus and Rufinus, on December 25.	4	*Sacred History II*[265]
Paulus Orosius	385–420	752 AUC, when Augustus ordered that the first census be taken.	2	*Against Pagans* VI.22.6–7[266]
Dionysius Exiguus	475–554	753 AUC.	1	Easter Table[267]
Cassiodorus Senator	490–585	The consular year of C. Lentulus and M. Messala.	3	List of consuls Note[268]
Hippolytus of Thebes	650–750	The forty-second year of Augustus's reign.	3	Fragments[269]

Flavius Josephus's Hebrew Calendar

Appendix B

Flavius Josephus's original name was Joseph son of Matthias. He was born in the first year of Caesar Caligula's reign in 37 A.D. His mother was a descendant of the Hasmonean king and priesthood clan. His father was a noble man with a great reputation in Jerusalem. His brother was named Matthias after their father.[a]

Josephus was appointed the governor of Galilee by the revolutionary community of Jerusalem,[b] who made war with the Romans around 66 A.D. The next year, Josephus was captured at Jotapata by Vespasian. He claimed that God had sent him to Vespasian, who was destined to become the Roman emperor.[c] Vespasian was in-

---

a "I am of the chief family of that first course also; nay, further, by my mother I am of the royal blood; for the children of Asamoneus, from whom that family was derived, had both the office of the high priesthood, and the dignity of a king, for a long time together… as was I born to Matthias in the first year of the reign of Caius [Caligula] Caesar… Now, my father Matthias was not only eminent on account of is nobility, but had a higher commendation on account of his righteousness, and was in great reputation in Jerusalem, the greatest city we have. I was myself brought up with my brother, whose name was Matthias" (Josephus, *Life*, 1–2).

b "For before ever I was appointed governor of Galilee by the community of Jerusalem, both thou and all the people of Tiberias had not only taken up arms, but had made war with Decapolis of Syria" (Josephus, *Life*, 65).

c "Thou, O Vespasian, thinkest no more than that thou hast taken Josephus himself captive; but I come to thee as a messenger of greater tidings; for had not I been sent by God to thee, I knew what was the law of the Jews in this case? And how it becomes generals to die. Dost thou send me to Nero? For why? Are Nero's successors till they come to thee still alive? Thou, O Vespasian, art Caesar and emperor, thou, and this thy son. Bind me now still faster, and keep me for thyself, for thou, O Caesar, are not only lord over me, but over the land and the sea, and all mankind; and certainly I deserve to be kept in closer custody than I now am in, in order to be punished, if I rashly affirm anything of God" (Josephus, *War*, 3.8.9).

trigued by his prediction and retained him as a hostage and an interpreter.

The Romans were operating in Galilee in preparation to capture Jerusalem. After Nero committed suicide in the summer of 68 A.D., subsequent leaders such as Galba and Otho were killed in civil wars in Rome.

Vespasian's legions proclaimed him emperor in the East in 69 A.D. When Vespasian was in Alexandria, Egypt, news of his son Domitian and general Antonius came to him reporting that they had defeated Vitellius's army and beheaded him. The people of Rome announced that Vespasian was the new emperor.[a] His eldest son Titus took command of the forces in Judea while Vespasian travelled to Rome to take the Roman Empire.

In 70 A.D., Josephus's parents and wife perished in the siege of Jerusalem by the Romans. He managed to save the lives of his brother Matthias and 50 other friends. In addition, he helped set free 190 captives on the temple mount who were his old acquaintances.[b]

Josephus left Judea and sailed with Titus to Rome after the Jewish war. Vespasian gave Josephus Roman citizenship and an annual pension. Furthermore, Vespasian provided Josephus with an apartment in his own house, where he lived before becoming emperor.[c] Likely, he also granted his family name, Flavius, to Josephus for his protection from Jews and Romans alike who might despise him.

Josephus completed *War of the Jews* in seven books sometime between 75 to 79 A.D.[271] Titus esteemed his books highly and ordered them to be published.[d]

---

a "But now within a day's time came Antonius, with his army, and were met by Vitellius and his army; and having had a battle in three several places, the last were all destroyed. Then did Vitellius come out of the palace, in his cups, and satiated with an extravagant and luxurious meal, as in the last extremity, and being drawn along through the multitude, and abused with all sorts of torments, had his head cut off in the midst of Rome, having retained the government eight months and five days and had he lived much longer, I cannot but think the empire would not have been sufficient for his lust… He then produced Domitian, and recommended him to the multitude, until his father should come himself; so the people being now freed from their fears, made acclamations of joy for Vespasian, as for their emperor, and kept festival days for his confirmation, and for the destruction of Vitellius" (Josephus, *War*, 4.11.4).

b "I had also the holy books by Titus's concession. Nor was it long after that I asked of him the life of my brother, and of fifty friends with him, and was not denied. When I also went once to the temple, by the permission of Titus, where there were a great multitude of captive women and children, I got all those that I remembered as among my own friends and acquaintances to be set free, being in number about one hundred and ninety" (Josephus, *Life*, 75).

c "I had great care taken of me by Vespasian; for he gave me an apartment in his own house, which he lived in before he came to the empire. He also honored me with the privilege of a Roman citizen, and gave me an annual pension" (Josephus, *Life*, 76).

d "Now the emperor Titus was so desirous that the knowledge of these affairs should be taken from these books alone, that he subscribed his own hand to them, and ordered that they should be pub-

Josephus then continued to expand his scope of Jewish history from creation all the way to his own era. He finished *Antiquities of the Jews* in 20 books in about 93 A.D.[272] He died around 100 A.D.

Josephus named all the months in *War of the Jews* using Syro-Macedonian designations, whereas in *Antiquities* he added some Hebrew equivalent names to educate the wider audience in Jewish culture. Evidently, he treated the Syro-Macedonian months as being fully compatible with the Jewish ones.[273] The Syro-Macedonian calendar—a.k.a. Seleucid calendar—is basically a Babylonian calendar with all the months relabeled under Greek names.[274] Josephus marked some major events using Greek Olympiads and Roman consular years.[a] In some cases, he also used the reigns of kings, ethnarchs, or Caesars to mark events.[b] Interestingly, Josephus never used the Roman AUC calendar in his books. Furthermore, he didn't use any Roman months in his own written text, except in direct quotes from Roman letters, decrees, and declarations.

Both the ancient Old Testament Hebrew and Macedonian calendars are lunisolar calendars with intercalations based on lunar and solar observations in addition to calculations, thus each Old Testament JHY in Josephus era was pretty much in synch with the seasons. For example, the Jewish festivals of the First Fruit and Shavuot (Pentecost) serve as temporal markers of the seasons in the Jewish calendar for harvesting barley and wheat, respectively.

Josephus's Old Testament chronology was obviously based on the Hebrew text of his era, and it is very similar to the Septuagint,[275] although with some minor numerical discrepancies. For example, the birth of Cainan when Arphaxad was 130 years old appears in the Septuagint but not in Josephus's text. Thus, we can only view Josephus's Hebrew creation calendar, as well as the others, as being approximate, since we don't know at the present time which

---

lished" (Josephus, *Life*, 65).

a Each Olympiad represents four Greek calendar years from about July 1 to June 30, whereas each Roman consular year after 153 B.C. spans the length of time from January 1 to December 31 (Finegan, *Handbook of Biblical Chronology*).

b For example, "This Matthias had a son called Matthias Curtus, and that in the first year of the government of Hyrcanus: his son's name was Joseph, born in the ninth year of the reign of Alexandra: his son Matthias was born in the tenth year of the reign of Archclaus; as was I born to Matthias in the first year of the reign of Caius [Caligula] Caesar. I have three sons: Hyrcanus, the eldest, was born in the fourth year of the reign of Vespasian, as was Justus born in the seventh, and Agrippa in the ninth" (Josephus, *Life*, 1).

The Timing of God's Visitations

list is correct.

From Josephus's *Antiquities of the Jews*, one can establish the age of the human race from Adam to Abraham.[a] In Table B.1, we have tabulated the age of individuals in the Bible who birthed a son, along with their corresponding birth years.

There are many other similar chronological accounts based on different sources, such as the Septuagint and Masoretic text.[276] They all somewhat differ from each other numerically, but the precise number of years marking the actual creation timeline is not the main concern here. An approximate relative timeline by Josephus would suffice for the present discussion. Based on the tally in Table B.1, creation occurred in 5415 B.C.

Table B.1. The birth year of biblical individuals from Adam to Abram according to Josephus.

Name	Age at Son's Birth	Birth Year (Actual)	Birth Year (B.C.)
Adam	230	1	5415
Seth	205	230	5185
Enos	190	435	4980
Cainan	170	625	4790
Malaleel (Mahalaleel)[a]	165	795	4620
Jared	162	960	4455
Enoch	165	1122	4293
Methuselah	187	1287	4128
Lamech	182	1474	3941
Noah	500	1656	3759
Shem	112	2156	3259
Arphaxad	135	2268	3147
Sala (Salah)	130	2403	3012
Heber (Eber)	134	2533	2882
Phaleg (Peleg)	130	2667	2748

a Josephus, *Antiquities*, 1.3.3, 1.3.4, 1.4.1, 1.6.5.

a Names in parentheses are found in the King James Bible. Otherwise they come from Josephus's text.

Ragau (Reu)	130	2797	2618
Serug	132	2927	2488
Nahor	120	3059	2356
Terah	70	3179	2236
Abram	-	3249	2166[a]

---

a A number of scholars have estimated the birth year of Abraham to be 2166 B.C. (Iain Provan, V. Philips Long, and Tremper Longman III, *A Biblical History of Israel* [Louisville, KY: John Knox Press, 2003]; Leon J. Wood, *A Survey of Israel's History* [Grand Rapids, MI: Zondervan, 1986]; *The Chronological Study Bible: Explore God's Word in Historical Order* [Nashville, TN: Thomas Nelson, 2008]; and Finegan, *Handbook of Biblical Chronology*).

Endnotes

1 *"Best-selling book,"* Guinness World Records. Date of access: July 6, 2022 (https://www.guinnessworldrecords.com/world-records/best-selling-book-of-non-fiction).

2 "How many different languages has the Bible been translated into?" *The International Bible Society*. Date of access: July 6. 2022 (https://www.biblica.com/resources/bible-faqs/how-many-different-languages-has-the-bible-been-translated-into).

3 Sharon R. Steadman, *Archaeology of Religion Cultures and Their Beliefs in Worldwide Context* (New York, NY: Taylor & Francis, 2016); and Joseph M. Holden and Norman Geisler, *The Popular Handbook of Archaeology and the Bible: Discoveries That Confirm the Reliability of Scripture* (Eugene, OR: Harvest House Publishers, 2013).

4 Emil Schürer, *A History of the Jewish People in the Time of Jesus Christ, Volume One*, tr. John MacPherson (New York, NY: Charles Scribner's Sons, 1891).

5 Flavius Josephus, *The Works of Flavius Josephus: Comprising the Antiquities of the Jews, A History of the Jewish War, and Life of Flavius Josephus, Written by Himself*, tr. William Whiston (Philadelphia, PA: Porter & Coates, 1870).

6 Tertullianus, *The Five Books of Quintus Septimus Floreus Tertullianus Against Marcion, Volume VII*, tr. Peter Holmes, eds. Alexander Roberts and James Donaldson (Edinburgh, UK: T&T Clark, 1868), 4.19.10.

7 Richard R. Racy, *Nativity: The Christmas Story Which You Have Never Heard Before* (Bloomington, IN: AuthorHouse, 2008); Jeff D. Huddleston, *God Logic, Observations: Christianity and the Jewish Roots of the Faith* (Morrisville, NC: Lulu Press, 2015); Alan Millard, *Discoveries from Bible Times: Archaeological Treasures Throw Light on the Bible* (Oxford, UK: Lion Publishing, 1997); and Alfred Plummer, *A Critical and Exegetical Commentary on the Gospel According to St. Luke* (New York, NY: Charles Scribner's Sons, 1896).

8 Ted Byfield and Calvin Demmon, eds., *The Christians, Their First Two Thousand Years: The Veil Is Torn, A.D. 30 to A.D. 70* (Edmonton, AB: Christian History Project, 2003); and Larry D. Edwards, *The Christian Holy Days: The Biblical Account of Christmas, Passion Week, Easter, Ascension, and Pentecost* (Maitland, FL: Xulon, 2010).

9 Cornelius Tacitus, *The Annals*, trs. Alfred J. Church and William J. Brodribb (New York, NY: MacMillan, 1879).

10 Victor Ehrenberg and A.H.M. Jones, *Documents Illustrating the Reigns of Augustus and Tiberius* (Kettering, UK: Oxford University Press, 1949).

11 John McRay, *Archaeology and the New Testament* (Grant Rapids, MI: Baker Academic, 1991); Josh McDowell and Sean McDowell, *Evidence That Demands a Verdict: Life-Changing Truth for a Skeptical World* (Nashville, TN: Thomas Nelson, 2017); and Willis C. Newman, *You Can Believe the Bible* (Tacoma WA: Newman International, 2010).

12 Jack Finegan, *Handbook of Biblical Chronology* (Peabody, MA: Hendrickson, 1998); and Dwight R. Hutchison, *The Lion Led the Way* (St. Paul-Trois-Chateaux, France: Editions Signes Célestes, 2015).

13 Alden A. Mosshammer, *The Easter Computus and the Origins of the Christian Era* (New York, NY: Oxford University Press, 2008); and C. Philipp E. Nothaft, *Dating the Passion: The Life of Jesus and the Emergence of Scientific Chronology (200–1600)* (Danvers, MA: Brill, 2012).

14 "Dionysius Exiguus," *Encyclopaedia Britannica*. Date of access: July 13, 2022 (https://www.britannica.com/biography/dionysius-exiguus).

15 Josephus, *The Works of Flavius Josephus*.

16 Josephus, *Antiquities* 14.16.4; and Appian of Alexandria, *Roman History IV*, tr. Horace White (London, UK: Harvard University Press, 2000), 5.8.75.

17 Nadav Sharon, *Judea under Roman Domination: The First Generation of Statelessness and Its Legacy* (Atlanta, GA: SBL Press, 2017); Louis H. Feldman, *Josephus and Modern Scholarship (1937–1980)* (Berlin, DE: Walter de Gruyter 1984); and Matthew B. O'Donnell, Stanley E. Porter, Wendy Porter, eds., *Journal of Greco-Roman Christianity and Judaism, Volume 14* (Eugene, OR: Wipf & Stock Publishers, 2019).

18 W.E. Filmer, "The Chronology of the Reign of Herod the Great." *Journal of Theological Studies*, 1966, volume 17, 283–298; James M. Scott, *Bacchius Iudaeus: A Denarius Commemorating Pompey's Victory Over Judea* (Bristol, CT: Vandenhoeck and Reprecht, 2015); Martin Goodman, *Rome and Jerusalem: The Clash of Ancient Civilizations* (New York, NY: Vintage Books, 2008); and Andrew E. Steinmann, "When Did Herod the Great Reign?" *Novum Testamentum*, 2009, volume 51, 1–29.

19 "Fast days," *Dictionary of Jewish Terms: A Guide to the Language of Judaism* (Rockville, MD: Schreiber Publishing, 2008).

20 Heinrich W. Guggenheimer, ed., tr., *The Jerusalem Talmu, First Order: Zeraim Tractate Berakhot* (Berlin DE: Walter De Gruyter, 2000).

21 Michael L. Rodkinson, tr., *The Babylonian Talmud, Volume VIII* (New York, NY: New Talmud Publishing, 1896).

22 R.H. Charles, ed., *The Apocrypha and Pseudepigrapha of the Old Testament, Volume II* (New York, NY: Oxford University Press, 1913).

23 "ModelE AR5 Simulations: Past Climate Change and Future Climate Predictions: Time and Date of Vernal Equinox." *National Aeronautics and Space Administration Goddard Institute for Space Studies*. Date of access: November 24, 2021 (https://data.giss.nasa.gov/modelE/ar5plots/srvernal.html); and "Phases of the Moon: -0099 To 0000 (0100 To 0001 BCE) Universal Time." *AstroPixels*.

com. Date of access: November 24, 2021 (http://astropixels.com/ephemeris/phasescat/phases-0099.html).

24 Filmer, "The Chronology of the Reign of Herod the Great"; Steinmann, "When Did Herod the Great Reign?"; Ernest L. Martin, *The Star that Astonished the World* (Portland, OR: Associates for Scriptural Knowledge, 1996); and Gerard Gertoux, *Herod the Great and Jesus: Chronological, Historical, and Archaeological Evidence* (Morrisville, NC: Lulu Press, 2015).

25 Henry Cotton, tr., *The Five Books of Maccabees in English with Notes and Illustrations* (London, UK: Oxford University Press, 1832); and Andrew E. Steinmann and Rodger C. Young, "Elapsed Times for Herod the Great in Josephus." *Bibliotheca Sacra*, 2020, volume 177, 308–328.

26 "Talmud, Mas. Rosh HaShana 2a," *The Entire English Babylonian Talmud*. Date of access: October 8, 2022 (https://halakhah.com/index.html).

27 "Talmud, Mas. Avodah Zarah 10a," *The Entire English Babylonian Talmud*. Date of access: October 8, 2022 (https://halakhah.com/index.html).

28 Ben Zion Wacholder, "The Calendar of Sabbatical Cycles during the Second Temple and the Early Rabbinic Period." *Hebrew Union College Annual*, 1973, volume 44, 153–196.

29 Jeffrey M. Cohen, *1,001 Questions and Answers on Rosh Hashanah and Yom Kippur* (Norhvale, NJ: Jason Aronson, 1997).

30 "Talmud and Midrash," *Encyclopaedia Britannica*. Date of access: July 22, 2022 (https://www.britannica.com/topic/Talmud/Early-compilations); and "Talmud," *New World Encyclopaedia*. Date of access: July 22, 2022 (https://www.newworldencyclopedia.org/entry/talmud).

31 Michael L. Rodkinson, tr., *The Babylonian Talmud, Volumes 1–10*. Date of access: March 20, 2022 (https://www.jewishvirtuallibrary.org/jsource/Judaism/FullTalmud.pdf); and Judith Z. Abrams, *The Talmud for Beginners Volume 1 Prayer* (Lanham, MD: Rowman & Littlefield, 1993).

32 Schürer, *A History of the Jewish People in the Time of Jesus Christ*.

33 Ibid., 465.

34 Ibid.

35 J.W.E. Pearce, *Elegiac Poems of Ovid, Volume II: The Roman Calendar Selection from the Fasti* (London, UK: Oxford University Press, 1914); and Nigel Wilson, ed., *Encyclopedia of Ancient Greece* (New York, NY: Routledge, 2010); and Lesley Adkins and Roy A. Adkins, *Handbook to Life in Ancient Rome* (New York, NY: Facts on File, 2004); and Jörg Rüpke, *The Roman Calendar from Numa to Constantine: Time, History, and the Fasti*, tr. David M.B. Richardson (West Sussex, UK: Wiley, 2011).

36 Filmer, "The Chronology of the Reign of Herod the Great"; and Steinmann, "When Did Herod the Great Reign?"

37 Gertoux, *Herod the Great and Jesus*; Evelyn S. Shuckburgh, *A History of Rome: To the Battle of Actium* (New York, NY: MacMillan, 1894); Hilary Swain and Mark E. Davies, *Aspects of Roman History, 82 B.C.–A.D. 14: A Source-Based Approach* (New York, NY: Routledge, 2010); and Timothy Venning, *A Chronology of the Roman Empire* (New York, NT: Continuum International, 2011).

38 James Evans, *The History and Practice of Ancient Astronomy* (New York, NY: Oxford University Press, 1998).

39 Matthew Bunson, *A Dictionary of the Roman Empire* (New York, NY: Oxford University Press, 1995).

40 Caissius Dio, *Roman History: Volume V*, tr. Earnest Cary (Cambridge, MA: Harvard University Press, 1917).

41 Plutarch, *Life of Antony*, ed. C.B.R. Pelling (Cambridge, UK: Cambridge University Press, 1988).

42 Matthew Bunson, *Encyclopedia of the Roman Empire* (New York, NY: Facts on File, 2002).

43 Carsten H. Lange, *Triumphs in the Age of Civil Water: The Late Republic and the Adaptability of Triumphal Tradition* (London, UK: Bloomsbury, 2016); John Rich, "The Triumph in the Roman Republic: Frequency, Fluctuation and Policy." *The Roman Republican Triumph Beyond the Spectacle*, eds. Carsten H. Lange and Frederik J. Vervaet (Rome, IT: Edizioni Quasar, 2014); Plutarch, *Life of Antony*, 34.4; and Pliny, *The Natural History, Volume One*, trs. John Bostock and H.T. Riley (London, UK: Henry G. Bohn, 1855), 7.44.1–2.

44 Filmer, "The Chronology of the Reign of Herod the Great"; Steinmann, "When Did Herod the Great Reign?"; and Andrew E. Steinmann and Rodger C. Young, "Consular and Sabbatical Years in Herod's Life." *Bibliotheca Sacra*, 2020, volume 177, 442–461.

45 Filmer, "The Chronology of the Reign of Herod the Great."

46 Edwin R. Thiele, *The Mysterious Numbers of the Hebrew Kings* (Grand Rapids, MI: Kregel, 1983).

47 Josephus, *Antiquities*, 15.7.5–6; Bunson, *A Dictionary of the Roman Empire*; and Matthew Sleater, *A Complete History of the Holy Bible* (Dublin, Ireland: James Charles, 1810).

48 Josephus, *Antiquities*, 15.7.7; *and* Samuel S. Kottek, *Medicine and Hygiene in the Works of Flavius Josephus* (Leiden, NL: E.J. Brill, 1994).

49 Archibald Alexander, *Annals of the Jewish Nation During the Period of the Second Temple* (New York, NY: Jonathan Leavitt, 1832); Larry R. Helyer, *Exploring Jewish Literature of the Second Temple Period: A Guide for New Testament Studies* (Downers Grove, IL: InterVarsity, 2002); and Dwight R. Hutchison, *A Sign Over Bethlehem: An Explanation of the Magi and the Messiah's Star* (St. Paul-Trois-Chateaux, France: Editions Signes Célestes, 2017).

50 Steinmann, "When Did Herod the Great Reign?"

51 Charles A.L. Totten, *The Facts of History, Sacred and Secular; Facts of Iron: The Times and Seasons of Rome, Part One* (New Haven, CT: Our Race Publishing, 1894).

52 Steinmann, "When Did Herod the Great Reign?"

53 Steinmann and Young, "Elapsed Times for Herod the Great in Josephus."

54 "Lunar Eclipses: Past and Future," *NASA*. Date of access: August 24, 2021 (https://eclipse.gsfc.nasa.gov/lunar.html).

55 Macrobius, *The Saturnalia*, tr. Percival V. Davis (New York, NY: Columbia University Press, 1969), 182.

56 Finegan, *Handbook of Biblical Chronology*.

57 Ibid.

Endnotes

58 Ibid.

59 Andrew Steinmann and Rodger Young, "Evidences that Herod the Great's Sons Antedated Their Reigns to a Time Before Herod's Death," *Rodger Young's Paper on Chronology*. Date of access: November 22, 2021 (http://www.rcyoung.org/articles/Antedating.html).

60 Ibid.; David Hendin, "A New Coin Type of Herod Antipas." *Israel Numismatic Journal*, 2003–2006, volume 15, 56–61; and Gregory C. Jenks, "'We Three Kings': Glimpses of the Herodian Succession in the Coins of Archelaus, Antipas, and Philip." *Paper for 2013 Session of the Bible Characters in the Three Traditions Seminar of the Society of Biblical Literature at St. Andrews, Scotland, 7–11 July, 2013*. Date of access: April 2, 2022 (https://www.academia.edu/4000855/_We_Three_Kings_Glimpses_of_the_Herodian_Succession_in_the_Coins_of_Archelaus_Antipas_and_Philip_).

61 Schürer, *A History of the Jewish People in the Time of Jesus Christ*, 465.

62 Filmer, "The Chronology of the Reign of Herod the Great"; Gertoux, *Herod the Great and Jesus*; Mel Wacks, *The Handbook of Biblical Numismatics, 45th Anniversary Edition* (Woodland Hills, CA: Mel Wacks, 2021); and Adam K. Marshak, "The Dated Coins of Herod the Great Towards a New Chronology." *Journal of the Study of Judaism*, volume 37, 212–240.

63 "A Biblical Calendar," *Mercer Dictionary of the Bible*, ed. Watson E. Mills (Macon, GA: Mercer University Press, 1991).

64 "3104. Yobel," *Bible Hub*. Date of access: October 7, 2022 (https://biblehub.com/hebrew/3104.htm).

65 Wacholder, "The Calendar of Sabbatical Cycles during the Second Temple and the Early Rabbinic Period."

66 Filmer, "Chronology of the Reign of Herod the Great."

67 Ibid.

68 Benedict Zuckermann, *A Treatise on the Sabbatical Cycle and the Jubilee, A Contribution to the Archaeology and Chronology of the Time Anterior and Subsequent to the Captivity: Accompanied by a Table of Sabbatical Years* (Bloomington, IN: Hermon Press, 1974); Donald W. Blosser, *Jesus and the Jubilee: Luke 4:16–30, The Year of Jubilee and its Significance in the Gospel of Luke* (Scotland, UK: University of St. Andrews, 1979); and Finegan, *Handbook of Biblical Chronology*.

69 Steinmann and Young, "Consular and Sabbatical Years in Herod's Life."

70 Filmer, "Chronology of the Reign of Herod the Great."

71 Herbert Danby, ed. tr., *The Mishnah* (London, UK: Oxford University Press, 1933), 200.

72 Heinrich W. Guggenheimer, tr., *Seder Olam: the Rabbinic View of Biblical Chronology* (Lanham, NY: Rowman & Littlefield Publishers, 1998), 264.

73 Chraetien E. Caspari, *A Chronological and Geographical Introduction to the Life of Christ*, tr. Maurice J. Evans (Edinburgh, SC: T&T Clark, 1876).

74 Michael L. Rodkinson, tr., *The Babylonian Talmud, Volume VIII* (New York, NY: New Talmud Publishing, 1896), 86.

75 Steinmann and Young, "Consular and Sabbatical Years in Herod's Life."

76 Caspari, *A Chronological and Geographical Introduction to the Life of Christ*.

77 Rodger C. Young and Andrew E. Steinmann, "Caligula's Statue for the Jerusalem Temple and Its Relation to the Chronology of Herod the Great." *Journal of the Evangelical Theological Society*, 2019, volume 62.4, 759–73.

78 Mel Wacks, *The Handbook of Biblical Numismatics*; David Hendin, "Jewish Coinage of Two Wars: Aims and Meaning" in David M. Jacobson and Nikos Kokkinos, ed., *Judaea and Rome in Coins 65 B.C.E.–135 CE: Papers Presented at the International Conference Hosted by Spink, 13th-14th September 2010* (London UK: Spink 2012); Stephen Pfann, "Dated Bronze Coinage of the Sabbatical Years of Release and the First Jewish City Coin." *Bulletin of the Anglo-Israel Archaeological Society*, 2006, volume 24, 101–113; and Michael O. Wise, *Language Literacy in Roman Judaea: A Study of the Bar Kokhba Documents* (London, UK: Yale University Press, 2015).

79 Finegan, *Handbook of Biblical Chronology*.

80 David Magie, tr., *Historia Augusta, Volume I* (Cambridge, MA: Harvard University Press, 1921).

81 Hendin, "Jewish Coinage of Two Wars: Aims and Meaning"; Pfann, "Dated Bronze Coinage of the Sabbatical Years of Release and the First Jewish City Coin"; and Michael O. Wise, *Language Literacy in Roman Judaea: A Study of the Bar Kokhba Documents*.

82 Jerome, *Commentary on Daniel*, tr. Gleason L. Archer (Grand Rapids, MI: Baker Book House, 1958).

83 Hannah M. Cotton, "The Impact of the Documentary Papyri from the Judaean Desert on the Study of Jewish History from 70 to 135 CE" in *Jüdische Geschichte in hellenistisch-römischer Zeit: Wege der Forschung: Vom alten zum neuen Schürer*, ed. Aharon Oppenheimer (München: Oldenbourg Wissenschaftsverlag, 2009). Date of access: April 4, 2022 (https://doi.org/10.1524/9783486596045–017).

84 Hendin, "Jewish Coinage of Two Wars: Aims and Meaning."

85 Eusebius, *The Ecclesiastical History, Volume I*, tr. Kirsopp Lake (London, UK: William Heinmann, 1926), 313.

86 Wacholder, "The Calendar of Sabbatical Cycles during the Second Temple and the Early Rabbinic Period," 177.

87 Hendin, "Jewish Coinage of Two Wars: Aims and Meaning."

88 Cecil Roth, "The Historical Implications of the Jewish Coinage of the First Revolt." *Israel Exploration Journal*, 1962, volume 12.1, 33–46.

89 Wacks, *The Handbook of Biblical Numismatics*.

90 Hendin, "Jewish Coinage of Two Wars: Aims and Meaning."

91 Wacholder, "The Calendar of Sabbatical Cycles During the Second Temple and the Early Rabbinic Period"; and Finegan, *Handbook of Biblical Chronology*.

92 Ben Zion Wacholder, "Chronomessianism: The Timing of Messianic Movements and the Calendar of Sabbatical Cycles." *Hebrew Union College Annual*, 1975, volume 46, 201–218.

93 Menahem Mor, *The Second Jewish Revolot: The Bar Kokhba War, 132–136 CE* (Boston, MA: Brill, 2016).

94 Rachel Hachlili, *The Menorah: Evolving into the Most Important Jewish Symbol* (Leiden, NL: E.J. Brill, 2018).

95 Yael Wilfand, "Aramaic Tombstones from Zoar and Jewish Conceptions of the Afterlike." *Journal for the Study of Judaism*, 2009, volume 40, 510–539.

96 Haggai Misgav, "Two Jewish Tombstones from Zoar." *IMSA*, 2006, volume 5, 36–46.

97 "Talud—Mas. Avodah Zarah 10a," *The Entire English Babylonian Talmud*. Date of access: October 8, 2022 (https://halakhah.com/index.html).

98 M. Margalioth, "A New Document on the Fast of the Earthquake." *Tarbitz*, 1960, volume 29, 339–344.

99 M. Margalioth, "The Date of an Earthquake in Tiberias." *Bulletin of Jewish Palestine Exploration Society*, 1941, volume 8, 97–104.

100 Yoram Tsafrir and Gideon Foerster, "The Dating of the Earthquake of Sabbatical year of 749 C.E. in Palestine." *Bulletin of the School of Oriental and African Studies*, 1922, volume 55 no. 2, 231–235; and Steinmann and Young, "Consular and Sabbatical Years in Herod's Life."

101 Schürer, *A History of the Jewish People in the Time of Jesus Christ*; Young and Steinmann, "Caligula's Statue for the Jerusalem Temple and Its Relation to the Chronology of Herod the Great"; and Steinmann and Young, "Consular and Sabbatical Years in Herod's Life."

102 Gaius Suetonius Tranquillus, *The Lives of the Caesars, Volume I*, tr. J.C. Rolfe (Cambridge, MA: Harvard University Press, 1914).

103 Philonis Alexandrini, *Legatio Ad Gaium*, ed., tr. E. Mary Smallwood (Leiden, NL: E.J. Brill, 1970).

104 Suetonius, *The Lives of the Caesars, Volume I*.

105 Filmer, "The Chronology of the Reign of Herod the Great."

106 Steinmann and Young, "Evidences that Herod the Great's Sons Antedated Their Reigns to a Time before Herod's Death."

107 Guggenheimer, *Seder Olam*, 264.

108 Rodkinson, *The Babylonian Talmud, Volume VIII*, 86.

109 Wilfand, "Aramaic Tombstones from Zoar and Jewish Conceptions of the Afterlike"; and Misgav, "Two Jewish Tombstones from Zoar."

110 Margalioth, "A New Document on the Fast of the Earthquake"; and Margalioth, "The date of an earthquake in Tiberias."

111 Lionel Casson, "Speed Under Sail of Ancient Ships." *Transactions of the American Philological Association*, 1951, volume 82, 136–148; and Edward N. Luttwak, *The Grand Strategy of the Roman Empire: From the First Century A.D. to the Third* (Baltimore, MD: John Hopkins University Press, 1976).

112 Adam J. Silverstein, *Postal Systems in the Pre-Modern Islamic World* (Cambridge, UK: Cambridge University Press, 2007).

113 Suetonius, *The Lives of the Twelve Caesars, Volume I*; and Cornelius van Tilburg, *Traffic and Congestion in the Roman Empire* (New York, NY: Routledge, 2007).

114 "Roads and Travel," *A Dictionary of the Bible*, ed. James Hastings (Edinburgh, UK: T&T Clark, 1909); A.M. Ramsay, "The Speed of the Roman Imperial Post." *Journal of Roman Studies*, 1925, volume 15, 60–74; and R.M. Sheldon, *Espionage in the Ancient World: An Annotated Bibliography of Books and Articles in Western Languages* (Jefferson, NC: McFarland and Co., 2008).

115 Charles W.J. Eliot, "New Evidence for the Speed of the Roman Imperial Post." *The Phoenix*, 1955, volume 9, 76–80; and Fredrick F. Bruce, "Herod Antipas, Tetrarch of Galilee and Peraea." *The Annual of Leeds University Oriental Society*, 1963, volume 5, 6–23.

116 Casson, "Speed Under Sail of Ancient Ships"; and Luttwak, *The Grand Strategy of the Roman Empire*.

117 Casson, "Speed Under Sail of Ancient Ships"; Reinhard Zimmermann, *The Law of Obligations – Roman Foundations of the Civilian Tradition* (New York, NY: Oxford University Press, 1996).

118 Casson, "Speed Under Sail of Ancient Ships"; and "Correspondence of Ancient Calendars, Seasons, and Mediterranean Transport," *Theos Sphragis*. Date of access: July 17, 2022 (http://theos-sphragis.info/calendar_seasons_transport.html).

119 Ibid.

120 Vered Noam, "Megillat Taanit: The Scroll of Fasting," *The Literature of the Sages, Second Part*, ed. Shmuel Safrai et al., 339–62. CRINT, Section 2: The Literature of the Jewish People in the Period of the Second Temple and the Talmud, 3a. Assen Gorcum (Minneapolis, MN: Fortress Press, 2006); Filmer, "The Chronology of the Reign of Herod the Great"; Martin, *The Star that Astonished the World*; and Gertoux, *Herod the Great and Jesus*.

121 Josephus, *War*, 2.2.2.

122 Ibid., *2.3.1–3*.

123 Noam, "Megillat Taanit: The Scroll of Fasting"; Filmer, "The Chronology of the Reign of Herod the Great"; Martin, *The Star that Astonished the World*; and Gertoux, *Herod the Great and Jesus*.

124 Josephus, *War*, 2.2.4.

125 Josephus, *Antiquities*, 17.10.10.

126 Ibid., 17.11.4.

127 Velleius Paterculus, *Compendium of Roman History: Res Gestae Divi Augusti*, tr. Frederick W. Shipley (Cambridge, MA: Harvard University Press, 1961).

128 Peter M. Swan, *The Augustan Succession: An Historical Commentary on Cassius Dio's Roman History books 55–56 (9 B.C.–A.D. 14)* (New York, NY: Oxford University Press, 2004).

129 Susan Raven, *Rome in Africa* (New York, NY: Routledge, 1993).

130 Christopher J. Simpson, "A Shrine of Mars Ultor Re-visited." *Revue belge de philologie et d'histoire*, 1993, volume 71, fasc. 1, 1993. Antiquité–Oudheid. 116–122.

Endnotes

131 Ovid, *Fasti*, eds. Anthony Boyle and Roger Woodard (New York, NY: Penguin Books, 2004).

132 Willy Liebenam, *Fasti Conslares Imperii Romani von 30 v. Chr. Bis 565 N. Chr. Mit Kaiserliste Und Anhang* (Hamburg, DE: Bonn, 1909).

133 L. Morawiecki, "Le monoptère sur les monnaies alexandriniennes de bronze du temps d'Auguste." *Eos*, 1976, volume 64, 59–82.

134 "Circus," *A Smaller Dictionary of Greek and Roman Antiquities*, ed. William Smith (London, UK: John Murray, 1865).

135 Swan, *The Augustan Succession*.

136 Atilius Degrassi, *Fasti Capitolini Recensuit Praefatus Est, Indicibus Instruxit* (Torino, IT: Paravia, 1954); and Liebenam, *Fasti Conslares Imperii Romani*.

137 Stefan G. Chrissanthos, *The Year of Julius and Caesar: 59 BC and the Transformation of the Roman Republic* (Baltimore, MD: John Hopkins University Press, 2019).

138 Ehrenberg and Jones, *Documents Illustrating the Reigns of Augustus and Tiberius*; Degrassi, *Fasti Capitolini Recensuit Praefatus Est, Indicibus Instruxit*; and Liebenam, *Fasti Conslares Imperii Romani*.

139 Ovid, *The Art of Love*, tr. Henry T. Riley, (Calgary, AB: Theophania Publishing, 1885).

140 Ehrenberg and Jones, *Documents Illustrating the Reigns of Augustus and Tiberius*.

141 Schürer, *A History of the Jewish People in the Time of Jesus Christ*.

142 Caesar Augustus, *Res Gestae Divi Augusti: The Achievements of the Divine Augustus*, tr. ed. Peter A. Brunt (London, UK: Oxford University Press, 1967).

143 Ehrenberg and Jones, *Documents Illustrating the Reigns of Augustus and Tiberius*; Degrassi, *Fasti Capitolini*; and Liebnam, *Fasti Consulares Imperii Romani*.

144 Ibid.

145 Tacitus, *The Annals*.

146 Schürer, *A History of the Jewish People in the Time of Christ*; and Velleius, *Compendium of Roman History: Res Gestae Divi Augusti*.

147 Tacitus, *The Annals*, 3.48.

148 "Quirinius," *The International Standard Bible Encyclopedia, Volume Four*, ed. Geffrey W. Bromiley (Grand Rapids, MI: Eerdman, 1979).

149 Cornelius Tacitus, *The Histories*, trs. Clifford H. Moore and John Jackson (London, UK: William Heinemann, 1962).

150 William M. Ramsay, *The Bearing of Recent Discovery on the Trustworthiness of the New Testament* (London, UK: Hodder and Stoughton, 1915).

151 Lucius Annaeus Florus, *Epitome of Roman History*, ed. Edward S. Forster (Cambridge, MA: Harvard University Press, 2005).

152 Strabo, *The Geography of Strabo in Eight Volumes, Volume V*, tr. Horace L. Jones (Cambridge, MA: Harvard University Press, 1961).

153 Suetonius, *The Lives of the Twelve Caesars, Volume I*.

154 Tacitus, *The Annals*, 3.48.

155 Pliny, *The Natural History*, 2.23.4.

156 Dio, *Roman History*, 54.28.

157 Ronald Syme, *The Roman Revolution* (London, UK: Oxford University Press, 1939), 399.

158 "Herod Archelaus," *Encyclopaedia Britannica*. Date of access: August 25, 2021 (https://www.britannica.com/biography/Herod-Archelaus).

159 Steinmann, "When Did Herod the Great Reign?" 5–6.

160 Steinmann and Young, "Evidences that Herod the Great's Sons Antedated Their Reigns to a Time before Herod's death."

161 Henry G. Liddell, *A History of Rome: From the Earliest Times to the Establishment of the Empire with Chapters on the History of Literature and Art* (New York, NY: Harper & Brothers, 1899).

162 "Calendar," *Encyclopedia of Ancient Greece*, ed. Nigel Wilson (New York, NY: Routledge, 2006.); and Sacha Stern, *Calendars in Antiquity: Empires, States, and Societies* (Oxford, UK: Oxford University Press, 2012).

163 Tim G. Parkin, *Old Age in the Roman World: A Culture and Social History* (Baltimore, MD: John Hopkins University Press, 2003).

164 Velleius, *Compendium of Roman History*.

165 Paulus Orosius, *Seven Books of History Against the Pagans*, tr. A.T. Fear (Liverpool, UK: Liverpool University Press, 2010).

166 *Orosius, Seven Books of History Against the Pagans, VI.18.1, VI.22.1, VI.22.6–7, VII.2.16*.

167 Ibid.

168 "Luke 2:2," *Bible Hub*. Date of access: August 24, 2021 (https://biblehub.com/interlinear/luke/2-2.htm).

169 "2230. hégemoneuó," *Bible Hub*. Date of access: August 24, 2021 (http://biblehub.com/greek/2230.htm).

170 "2232. hégemón," *Bible Hub*. Date of access: August 24, 2021 (http://biblehub.com/greek/2232.htm).

171 Martin, *The Star that Astonished the World*; and Paul J. Wigowsky, *Pilgrimage in the Holy Land: Israel* (Bloomington, IN: AuthorHouse, 2013).

172 Gertoux, *Herod the Great and Jesus*; and Helen K. Bond, *Pontius Pilate in History and Interpretation* (Cambridge, UK: Cambridge University Press, 2004).

173 Fiona Renoldson and David Taylor, *Living through History: The Roman Empire* (Oxford, UK: Heinemann Educational Publishers, 1997).

174 Bunson, *A Dictionary of the Roman Empire*.

175 "2012. epitrops," *Bible Hub*. Date of access: August 24, 2021 (http://biblehub.com/greek/2012.htm).

176 Justin Martyr, *The Apologies of Justin Martyr*, ed. Alfred W.F. Blunt (Cambridge, UK: Cambridge University Press, 1911), 1:34; and Renoldson and Taylor, *Living through History*.

177 Philo of Alexandria, *The Embassy to Gaius*, tr. F.H. Colson (Cambridge, MA: Harvard University Press, 1991).

178 Gertoux, *Herod the Great and Jesus*.

179 Nikos Kokkinos, "The Titulus Tiburtinus, Syme's Piso, Sentius Saturninus and the Province of Syria." *Scripta Judaica Cracoviensia*, 2012, volume 10, 37–69.

180 *Orosius, Seven Books of History Against the Pagans, VI.18.1, VI.22.1, VI.22.6–7, VII.2.16.*

181 Ramsey, *The Bearing of Recent Discovery on the Trustworthiness of the New Testament*.

182 Hutchison, *The Lion Led the Way*; and Guy de la Bédoyère, *Domina: The Women Who Made Imperial Rome* (London, UK: Yale University Press, 2018).

183 C. Velleius Paterculus, *The Roman History*, tr. Thomas Newcomb (Whitefish, MT: Kessiger Publishing, 2007); and Robert S. Sherk, *The Roman Empire: Augustus to Hadrian* (Cambridge, UK: Cambridge University Press, 1994).

184 Dio, *Roman History: Volume V*, 55.10; and Velleius, *The Roman History*, II:99–102.

185 Gertoux, *Herod the Great and Jesus*, 2.

186 William M. Ramsay, *Was Christ Born at Bethlehem? A Study on the Credibility of St. Luke* (London, UK: Hodder and Stoughton, 1898).

187 Ramsay, *The Bearing of Recent Discovery on the Trustworthiness of the New Testament*; Archibald T. Robertson, *Luke the Historian in the Light of Research* (Edinburgh, UK: T&T Clark, 1929); and John Argubright, *Bible Believer's Archaeology, Volume Two: The Search for Truth* (LaSalle, IL: John Argubright, 2013), 9.

188 "Duumvir," *Merriam-Webster*. Date of access: August 24, 2021 (http://www.merriam-webster.com/dictionary/duumvir); and William T. Arnold, *The Roman System of Provincial Administration to the Accession of Constantine the Great* (London, UK: MacMillan, 1879).

189 Ramsay, *The Bearing of Recent Discovery on the Trustworthiness of the New Testament*.

190 Alan Rodger, "The Jurisdiction of Local Magistrates: Chapter 84 of the Lex Irnitana." *Zeitschrift für Papyrologie und Epigraphik*, 1990, volume 84, 147–161; and Julián González and Michael H. Crawford, "A New Copy of the Flavian Municipal Law." *The Journal of Roman Studies*, 1986, volume 76, 147–243.

191 Ramsay, *The Bearing of Recent Discovery on the Trustworthiness of the New Testament*, 280.

192 Argubright, *Bible Believer's Archaeology, Volume Two*, 8.

193 Venning, *A Chronology of the Roman Empire*; and Argubright, *Bible Believer's Archaeology, Volume Two*; and Ehrenberg and Jones, *Documents Illustrating the Reigns of Augustus and Tiberius*.

194 Ibid; and Liebenam, *Fasti Conslares Imperii Romani*.

195 Florus, *Epitome of Roman History*, 2.31; and Syme, *The Roman Revolution*.

196 Velleius, *Compendium of Roman History*.

197 Tacitus, *The Annals*, 3.48; and Strabo, *Geography*, 12.6.5–7.

198 Raoul McLaughlin, *The Roman Empire and the Silk Routes: The Ancient World Economy and the Empires of Parthia, Central Asia, and Han China* (South Yorkshire, UK: Pen & Sword History, 2016).

199 Tacitus, *The Annals*, 16.4.

200 Josephus, *The Works of Flavius Josephus*.

201 Gertoux, *Herod the Great and Jesus*; and Orosius, *Seven Books of History Against the Pagans*.

202 Macrobius, *The Saturnalia*.

203 Noam, "Megillat Taanit: The Scroll of Fasting"; Filmer, "The Chronology of the Reign of Herod the Great"; Martin, *The Star that Astonished the World*; and Gertoux, *Herod the Great and Jesus*.

204 Hutchison, *The Lion Led the Way*; and Linda Jones Hall, *Roman Berytus: Beirut in Late Antiquity* (New York, NY: Routledge, 2016).

205 Suetonius, *The Lives of the Twelve Caesars, Volume I*; and Adrian Murdoch, *Rome's Greatest Defeat: Massacre in the Teutoburg Forest* (Gloucestershire, UK: The History Press, 2008).

206 Hall, *Roman Berytus*; and Murdoch, *Rome's Greatest Defeat*.

207 Thomas J. Craughwell, *How the Barbarian Invasions Shaped the Modern World: The Vikings, Vandals, Huns, Mongols, Goths, and Tartars Who Razed the Old World and Formed the New* (Beverly, MA: Fair Winds Press, 2008); and Thomas Cook, *Cook's Tourist's Handbook for Southern Italy* (London, UK: Thomas Cook and Sons, 1875).

208 Justin Martyr, *The Apologies of Justin Martyr*; and Renoldson and Taylor, *Living through History*.

209 Timothy D. Barnes, "The Date of Herod's Death." *Journal of Theological Studies*, 1968, volume 19, 204–209.

210 Gertoux, *Herod the Great and Jesus*.

211 Swan, *The Augustan Succession*, 112.

212 Barnes, "The Date of Herod's Death," 208.

213 Ibid., 204.

214 Jerry Vardaman and Edwin M. Yamauchi, eds., *Chronos, Kairos, Christos: Nativity and Chronological Studies Presented to Jack Finegan* (Winona Lake, IN: Eisenbrauns, 1989); and Feldman, *Josephus and Modern Scholarship (1937–1980)*; and Sharon, *Judea Under Roman Domination: The First Generation of Statelessness and Its Legacy*.

215 Ehrenberg and Jones, *Documents Illustrating the Reigns of Augustus and Tiberius*; Liebenam, *Fasti Conslares Imperii Romani*; and Degrassi, *Fasti Capitolini Recensuit Praefatus Est, Indicibus Instruxit*.

216 Barnes, "The Date of Herod's Death."

Endnotes

217 P.M. Bernegger, "Affirmation of Herod's Death in 4 B.C." *Journal of Theology Studies*, 1983, volume 34, 526–531.

218 Douglas Johnson, "And They Went Eight Stades towards Herodeion" in Jerry Vardaman and Edwin M. Yamauchi, eds., *Chronos, Kairos, Christos: Nativity and Chronological Studies Presented to Jack Finegan* (Winona Lake, IN: Eisenbrauns, 1989), 93.

219 Bernegger, "Affirmation of Herod's Death in 4 B.C.," 526.

220 Ibid., 528.

221 Ibid., 529.

222 Steinmann, "When Did Herod the Great Reign?" 5–6.

223 Bernegger, "Affirmation of Herod's Death in 4 B.C.," 529.

224 Steinmann, "When Did Herod the Great Reign?"; and James C. Vanderkam, *From Joshua to Caiaphas: High Priests after the Exile* (Minneapolis, MN: Fortress Press, 2004).

225 Epiphanius, *The Panarion of Epiphanius of Salamis, Book I (Sects 1–46)*, tr. Frank Williams (Leiden, NL: Brill, 2009).

226 Susan K. Roll, *Towards the Origin of Christmas* (Kampen, NL: Kok Pharos Publishing House, 1995).

227 Mosshammer, *The Easter Computus and the Origins of the Christian Era*.

228 "Tertullian Christian Theolofian," *Britannica*. Date of access: December 15, 2022 (https://www.britannica.com/biography/Tertullian).

229 "Climate and Average Weather Year Round in Bethlehem," *Weather Spark*. Date of access: January 8, 2023 (https://weatherspark.com/y/98811/Average-Weather-in-Bethlehem-Palestinian-Territories-Year-Round).

230 Alfred Edersheim, *The Life and Times of Jesus the Messiah, Volume 1* (New York, NY: E.R. Herrick & Company, 1886), 186–187.

231 Michael Rodkinson, *New Edition of the Babylonian Talmud, Volume II. (X): Section Jurisprudence (Damages) Tract Baba Kama (First Gate)* (Boston, MA: Talmud Society, 1918); and "The William Davidson Digital Edition of the Koren Noé Talmud," *Korenpub.com*. Date of access: January 14, 2023 (https://www.sefaria.org/Bava_Kamma.80a.1?lang=bi&with=About&lang2=en).

232 David I. Brewer, *Traditions of the Rabbis from the Era of the New Testament, Volume 2A, Feasts and Sabbaths: Passover and Atonement* (Grand Rapids, MI: Eerdmans Publishing, 2011); and "Joshua Kulp, English Explanation of Mishnah Skelaim 7:4" Sefaria. Date of access: February 2, 2023 (https://www.sefaria.org/English_Explanation_of_Mishnah_Shekalim.7.4.5?lang=bi).

233 George H. Trench, *The Birth and Boyhood of Jesus Christ* (London, UK: Sheffington & Son, 1911); Christine van Horn, *The Tower of the Flock: The Christmas Story* (Bloomington, IN: WestBow Press, 2017); Scott P. Mages, *A Place for Jesus: A Walking Tour of the Christmas Crèche* (Bloomington, IN: WestBow Press, 2020); Shirley A.B. Winders, *A Child, A Servant, A King* (Bloomington, IN: WestBow Press, 2020); and Harold W. Hoehner, "Chronological Aspects of the Life of Christ Part I: The Date of Christ's Birth." *Bibliotheca Sacra*, 1973, volume 130:520, 338–353.

234 Rodkinson, *New Edition of the Babylonian Talmud*; and "The William Davidson Digital Edition of the Koren Noé Talmud," Korenpub.com.

235 John Jennings, *Until Shiloh Comes: Reconciling the Chronology of Jesus of Nazareth* (Bloomington, IN: AuthorHouse, 2020); and D.A. Miller, *A Theological Study of the Book of Romans* (Roseville, MI: Showers of Blessings Ministries International Publishing, 2012).

236 "Hypothermia in Lambs," *Department of Natural Resources*. Date of access: January 15, 2023 (https://www.gov.nl.ca/ffa/files/publications-pdf-hypothermia-in-lambs.pdf); "Care of the Newborn Lamb," *Ministry of Agriculture, Food and Rural Affairs: Government of Ontario*. Date of access: January 15, 2023 (http://omafra.gov.on.ca/english/livestock/sheep/facts/98–087.htm); "Kid & Lamb Management," *Farmed Animal Antimicrobial Stewardship Initiative*. Date of access: January 15, 2023 (https://www.amstewardship.ca/about); and "Lambing Management and Neonatal Care," *National Library of Medicine*. Date of access: January 15, 2023 (https://www.ncbi.nlm.nih.gov/pmc/articles/PMC7149567/).

237 Marc M. Epstein, *The Medieval Haggadah: Art, Narrative, and Religious Imagination* (Bellevue, WA: Yale University Press, 2011).

238 Fred A. Stutman, *Walk to Win: The Easy 4-Day Diet and Fitness Plan* (Philadelphia, PA: Medical Manor Books, 1989).

239 "1096. ginomai." *Bible Hub*. Date of access: January 23, 2023 (https://biblehub.com/greek/1096.htm).

240 T. Lewis and H.P. Hollis, eds., *The Observatory: A Monthly Review of Astronomy Volume 31* (London, UK: Taylor and Francis, 1908).

241 Nehemia Gordon, "Aviv Barly in the Biblical Calendar." *Nehemia's Wall*. Date of access: November 22, 2022 (https://www.nehemiaswall.com/aviv-barley-in-the-biblical-calendar).

242 "24. abib." *Bible Hub*. Date of access: November 23, 2022 (https://biblehub.com/hebrew/24.htm).

243 "ModelE AR5 Simulations: Past Climate Change and Future Climate Predictions: Time and Date of Vernal Equinox," *National Aeronautics and Space Administration Goddard Institute for Space Studies*. Date of access: November 21, 2022 (https://data.giss.nasa.gov/modelE/ar5plots/srvernal.html); and "Phases of the Moon: -0099 To 0000 (0100 To 0001 BCE) Universal Time," *AstroPixels.com*. Date of access: November 21, 2022 (http://astropixels.com/ephemeris/phasescat/phases-0099.html).

244 Gertoux, *Herod the Great and Jesus*.

245 Holly M. Snead, *The Holy Days of God the Holidays of Man* (Bloomington, IN; iUniverse, 2012).

246 Colin Humphreys, "The Star of Bethlehem." *Science and Christian Belief*, 1995, volume 5, 83–101.

247 Robert Mimpriss, *Treasury Harmony of the Four Evangelists* (London, UK: Oxford University, 1849).

248 Finegan, *Handbook of Biblical Chronology*; and Lun, *Before the Beginning to Beyond the End*; Harold W. Hoehner, "The chronology of Jesus." In *Handbook for the Study of the Historical Jesus, Volume 1 How*

to *Study the Historical Jesus*, eds. Tom Holmén and Stanley E. Porter (Boston, MA: Brill, 2011); and Colin J. Humphreys, *The Mystery of the Last Super: Reconstructing the Final Days of Jesus* (New York, NY: Cambridge University Press, 2011).

249 "2022: A Year of Unprecedented Hunger," *World Food Programme*. Date of access: December 19, 2022 (https://www.wfp.org/global-hunger-crisis#:~:text=2022%3A%20a%20year%20of%20unprecedented%20hunger&text=As%20many%20as%20828%20million,on%20the%20edge%20of%20famine.).

250 "Search Earthquake Catalog," *United States Geological Survey*. Date of access: (https://earthquake.usgs.gov/earthquakes/search).

251 "Coronavirus Death Toll," *Worldometer*. Date of access: December 7, 2022 (https://www.worldometers.info/coronavirus/coronavirus-death-toll).

252 Finegan, *Handbook of Biblical Chronology*, 291.

253 Barbara Levick, *Augustus: Image and Substance* (New York, NY: Routledge, 2014); and Mosshammer, *The Easter Computus and the Origins of the Christian Era*.

254 Jerome W. Berryman, *Children and the Theologians: Clearing the Way of Grace* (New York, NY: Morehouse, 2009).

255 "Origen Christian Theologian," *Britannica*. Date of access: December 15, 2022 (https://www.britannica.com/biography/Origen).

256 Plutarch, *Life of Antony*, 86.4; and Alan K. Bowman, Edward Champoin, and Andrew Lintott, eds., *The Cambridge Ancient History Volume X: The Augustan Empire, 43 B.C.–A.D. 69* (Cambridge, UK: Cambridge University Press, 2004).

257 Epiphanius, *The Panarion of Epiphanius of Salamis, Books II and III, De Fide*, tr. Frank Williams (Boston, MA: Brill, 2013).

258 Irenaeus, *Five Books of S. Irenaeus: Against Heresies*, tr. John Keble (London, UK: James Parker, 1872).

259 Tertullianus, *Ante-Nicene Fathers, Volume 3*, eds. Philip Schaff and Allan Menzies (Grand Rapids, MI: Christian Classics Ethereal Library, 1885).

260 Clement of Alexandria, *Stromateis, Books 1–3* (Washington, DC: Catholic University Press, 2005).

261 Africanus, *Iulius Africanus: The Extant Fragments*, ed. Martin Wallraff, Umberto Roberto, Karl Pinggéra, tr. William Adler (Berlin, DE: Walter de Gruyter, 2007).

262 "Hippolytus, Some Exegetical Fragments of Hippolytus," *New Advent*. Date of access: December 15, 2022 (https://www.newadvent.org/fathers).

263 Origen, *Homilies on Luke: Fragments on Luke*, tr. Joseph T. Lienhard (Washington, DC: Catholic University Press, 1996).

264 Eusebius, *The Ecclesiastical History*, tr. Kirspp Lake (London, UK: William Heinemann, 1926).

265 "Sulpitius Severus, Sacred History (Book II), Chapter 27." *New Advent*. Date of access: December 15, 2022 (https://www.newadvent.org/fathers/35052.htm).

266 Orosius, *Seven Books of History Against the Pagan*.

267 Finegan, *Handbook of Biblical Chronology*.

268 Ibid.

269 Ibid.

270 Josephus, *The Works of Flavius Josephus: Comprising the Antiquities of the Jews, A History of the Jewish War, and Life of Flavius Josephus*.

271 Lois K.F. Dow, Craig A. Evans, and Andrew W. Pitts, eds., *The Language and Literature of the New Testament: Essays in Honor of Stanley E. Porter's 60th Birthday* (Boston, MA: Brill, 2016).

272 Ibid.

273 Finegan, *Handbook of Biblical Chronology*.

274 Bradley H. McLean, *An Introduction to Greek Epigraphy of the Hellenistic and Roman Periods from Alexander the Great Down to the Reign of Constantine (323 B.C.–A.D. 337)* (Ann Arbor, MI: University of Michigan Press, 2002).

275 *The Septuagint Version of the Old Testament, with an English Translation; and with Various Readings and Critical Notes* (London, UK: Samuel Bagster and Sons, 1879).

276 Finegan, *Handbook of Biblical Chronology*.

www.ingramcontent.com/pod-product-compliance
Lightning Source LLC
LaVergne TN
LVHW051554070426
835507LV00021B/2581